Anonymous

Hymns for the Reformed Church in the United States

Anonymous

Hymns for the Reformed Church in the United States

ISBN/EAN: 9783337297039

Printed in Europe, USA, Canada, Australia, Japan

Cover: Foto ©Lupo / pixelio.de

More available books at **www.hansebooks.com**

HYMNS

FOR THE

REFORMED CHURCH

IN THE

UNITED STATES.

PHILADELPHIA:
REFORMED CHURCH PUBLICATION BOARD,
No. 907 ARCH STREET.

HYMNS.

FIRST SUNDAY IN ADVENT.

"Jesus, the Hope of Israel, the Desire of all Nations."

1 L. M.

HAIL, Jesus! Israel's Hope and Light!
    Prophets and Priests prepared Thy way,
Thy people, through the breaking night,
    With waiting joy foresaw Thy day.

2 By Jacob's Star the Gentiles found
    Light on their mystic longings poured;
Wise men from dismal regions round,
    Bowed at Thy manger and adored.

3 Thy Advent, Lord, revives the world;
    Thy life shall waiting nations know;
The banner of Thy truth unfurled,
    Shall glorious on the mountains glow.

4 The vales, where darkness lingers last,
    Now kindle in prophetic light;
The morning breaks! for ever past
    The fearful reign of ancient night.

5 Hail, glorious Advent! heavenly birth!
    Shout, saints, in triumph Christ appears;
Good will to men, and peace on earth,
    Shall reign throughout the golden years.

"Hosanna to the Son of David."

2 8s, 8s, 8s, 8s, 11s.

HOSANNA to the living Lord!
    Hosanna to th' Incarnate Word!
To Christ, Creator, Saviour, King,
Let earth, let heaven, hosanna sing.
    Hosanna! Lord! Hosanna in the highest!

FIRST SUNDAY IN ADVENT.

2 "Hosanna," Lord, Thine angels cry;
"Hosanna," Lord, Thy saints reply:
Above, beneath us, and around,
The dead and living swell the sound.
  Hosanna! Lord! Hosanna in the highest!

3 O Saviour, with protecting care
Return to this, Thy house of prayer,
Assembled in Thy sacred name,
Where we Thy parting promise claim.
  Hosanna! Lord! Hosanna in the highest!

4 But, chiefest, in our cleansèd breast,
Eternal, bid Thy Spirit rest;
And make our secret soul to be
A temple pure, and worthy Thee.
  Hosanna! Lord! Hosanna in the highest!

5 So, in the last and dreadful day,
When earth and heaven shall melt away,
Thy flock, redeem'd from sinful stain,
Shall swell the sound of praise again.
  Hosanna! Lord! Hosanna in the highest!
                    Reginald Heber, 1811.

"Blessed is He that cometh in the name of the Lord."

3   L. M. 6 *lines.*

O COME, O come, Emanuel,
   And ransom captive Israel;
That mourns in lowly exile here,
Until the Son of God appear.
  Rejoice! Rejoice! Emanuel
  Shall come to thee, O Israel!

2 O come, Thou Rod of Jesse, free
Thine own from Satan's tyranny;
From depths of hell Thy people save,
And give them victory o'er the grave.
  Rejoice! Rejoice! Emanuel
  Shall come to thee, O Israel!

3 O come, Thou Day-Spring, come and cheer
Our spirits by Thine Advent here;
Disperse the gloomy clouds of night,
And death's dark shadows put to flight.
  Rejoice! Rejoice! Emanuel
  Shall come to thee, O Israel!

4 O come, Thou Key of David, come
And open wide our heavenly home;
Make safe the way that leads on high
And close the path to misery.
   Rejoice! Rejoice! Emanuel
   Shall come to thee, O Israel!

5 O come, O come, Thou Lord of Might!
Who to Thy tribes, on Sinai's height
In ancient times dids't give the law,
In cloud, and majesty, and awe.
   Rejoice! Rejoice! Emanuel
   Shall come to thee, O Israel!
               Latin Hymn, 12th Century.
               Altered from J. M. Neale.

"*The night is far spent, the day is at hand.*"

4   8s, 7s, 4s.

O'ER the distant mountains breaking,
   Comes the red'ning dawn of day:
Rise, my soul, from sleep awaking,
   Rise and sing, and watch and pray:
      'Tis thy Saviour,
   On His bright returning way.

2 O Thou long-expected, weary
   Waits my anxious soul for Thee:
Life is dark, and earth is dreary,
   Where Thy light I do not see:
      O my Saviour,
   When wilt Thou return to me?

3 Long, too long in sin and sadness,
   Far away from Thee I pine,
When, O when, shall I the gladness
   Of Thy Spirit feel in mine?
      O my Saviour,
   When shall I be wholly Thine?

4 Nearer is my soul's salvation,
   Spent the night, the day at hand;
Keep me in my lonely station,
   Watching for Thee, till I stand,
      O my Saviour,
   In Thy bright and promised land.

5 With my lamp well-trimmed and burning
   Swift to hear, and slow to roam,

FIRST SUNDAY IN ADVENT.

> Watching for Thy glad returning
> To restore me to my home:
> Come, my Saviour,
> O my Saviour, quickly come!
>
> J. S. B. Monsell.

"Watchman! what of the night?"

5   7s, 8 lines.

WATCHMAN! tell us of the night,
  What its signs of promise are;
Traveler! o'er yon mountain's height,
  See that glory-beaming star!
Watchman! does its beauteous ray
  Aught of joy or hope foretell?
Traveler! yes; it brings the day,
  Promised day of Israel:

2 Watchman! tell us of the night;
  Higher yet that star ascends;
Traveler! blessedness and light,
  Peace and truth, its course portends;
Watchman! will its beams alone
  Gild the spot that gave them birth?
Traveler! ages are its own;
  See, it bursts o'er all the earth!

3 Watchman! tell us of the night,
  For the morning seems to dawn;
Traveler! darkness takes its flight,
  Doubt and terror are withdrawn;
Watchman! let thy wanderings cease;
  Hie thee to thy quiet home!
Traveler! lo! the Prince of peace,
  Lo! the Son of God, is come!

John Bowring, 1825.

"For now is our salvation nearer than when we believed."

6   L. M. 8 lines.

GOD bless the calm and holy cheer
  That ushers in the Christian year;
And, whatsoe'er of gloom or shade
Season or sorrow may have made,
Lifts us, with its mysterious power,
Out of the dark and dying hour,
Into the lights which ever play
Round children of th' Eternal Day.

SECOND SUNDAY IN ADVENT.

2 Blest Advent of our ling'ring Lord!
How high the hope, how sure the word,
That thus, with every year's return,
Makes our dull hearts within us burn
For that long-sought and promised day,
When "heaven and earth shall pass away,"
And Christ from highest heav'ns shall come
To take His waiting people home.

3 Since childhood's early hours, our eyes
Have watch'd the East for red'ning skies!
Year after year has Advent brought
Nearer to us the Prize we sought;
But still it lingers—O that we
Were more prepared to welcome Thee!
Thine Advent, with its angel throng,
Would not be tarrying, Lord, so long.

J. S. B. Monsell, 1857.

SECOND SUNDAY IN ADVENT.

"And there shall be signs in the sun, and in the moon, and in the stars."

7 C. M. 8 *lines.*

ONCE more, O Lord, Thy sign shall be
  Upon the heavens displayed,
And earth and its inhabitants
  Be terribly afraid:
For, not in weakness clad, Thou com'st,
  Our woes, our sins to bear,
But girt with all Thy Father's might,
  His judgment to declare.

2 The terrors of that awful day,
  O who can understand?
Or who abide, when Thou in wrath
  Shalt lift Thy holy hand?
The earth shall quake, the sea shall roar,
  The sun in heaven grow pale;
But Thou hast sworn, and wilt not change,
  Thy faithful shall not fail.

3 Then grant us, Saviour, so to pass
  Our time in trembling here,

That when upon the clouds of heaven
  Thy glory shall appear,
Uplifting high our joyful heads
  In triumph we may rise,
And enter, with Thine angel train,
  Thy palace in the skies.

George W. Doane.

"And then shall they see the Son of Man coming in a cloud with power and great glory."

8 8s, 7s, 4s.

LO! He comes, with clouds descending,
  Once for favored sinners slain!
Thousand thousand saints attending
  Swell the triumph of His train:
    Hallelujah!
  God appears, on earth to reign!

2 Every eye shall now behold Him,
    Robed in dreadful majesty;
  Those who set at naught and sold Him,
    Pierced, and nailed Him to the tree,
      Deeply wailing,
    Shall the true Messiah see.

3 Every island, sea, and mountain,
    Heaven and earth shall flee away;
  All who hate Him must, confounded,
    Hear the trump proclaim the day;
      Come to judgment!
    Come to judgment, come away!

4 Now Redemption, long expected,
    See in solemn pomp appear!
  All His saints, by man rejected,
    Now shall meet Him in the air:
      Hallelujah!
    See the day of God appear!

5 Answer Thine own Bride and Spirit!
    Hasten, Lord, the general doom;
  The new heav'n and earth t' inherit
    Take Thy pining exiles home;
      All creation
    Travails, groans, and bids Thee come!

6 Yea, Amen! let all adore Thee,
    High on Thine eternal throne:

Saviour, take the power and glory;
  Claim the kingdom for Thine own;
    O come quickly,
  Everlasting God, come down.
Charles Wesley and John Cennick.
Altered by M. Madan.

9

"A light to lighten the Gentiles."
          8s, 7s.

LIGHT of those whose dreary dwelling
    Borders on the shades of death!
Come, and, by Thy love's revealing,
  Dissipate the clouds beneath.

2 Still we wait for Thine appearing;
    Life and joy Thy beams impart,
  Chasing all our fears, and cheering
    Every poor benighted heart.

3 Save us in Thy great compassion,
    O Thou mild, pacific Prince!
  Give the knowledge of salvation,
    Give the pardon of our sins;

4 By Thine all-sufficient merit,
    Every burdened soul release;
  Every weary, wandering spirit
    Guide into Thy perfect peace.
Charles Wesley, 1744.

10

"Praise the Lord, all ye Gentiles."
          8s, 7s.

HAIL, Thou source of every blessing,
    Sovereign Father of mankind,
  Gentiles now, Thy grace possessing,
    In Thy courts admission find.

2 Gratefully we bend before Thee,
    In Thy Church obtain a place,
  Now, by faith, behold Thy glory,
    Praise Thy truth and sing Thy grace.

3 Hail, Thou ever-blessed Saviour;
    Gentiles now their offerings bring,
  In Thy temple seek Thy favor,
    Worship Thee their Lord and King.

4 May we all, sincere in spirit,
    Live devoted to Thy praise,

    Glorious realms of bliss inherit,
        Grateful anthems ever raise.

"And I saw the dead, small and great stand before God."
11   *German Choral.*

GREAT God, what do I see and hear?
    The end of things created:
The Judge of all men doth appear
    On clouds of glory seated:
The trumpet sounds, the graves restore
The dead which they contained before;
    Prepare, my soul, to meet Him.

2 The dead in Christ are first to rise
    At that last trumpet's sounding;
Caught up to meet Him in the skies,
    With joy their Lord surrounding;
No gloomy fears their souls dismay;
His presence sheds eternal day
    On those prepared to meet Him.

3 The ungodly, filled with guilty fears,
    Behold His wrath prevailing;
In woe they rise, but all their tears
    And sighs are unavailing.
The day of grace is past and gone;
Trembling they stand before His Throne,
    All unprepared to meet Him.

4 Great Judge, to Thee our prayers we pour,
    In deep abasement bending!
O shield us through that last dread hour,
    Thy wondrous love extending;
May we, in this our trial day,
With faithful hearts Thy word obey,
    And thus prepare to meet Thee.

                    Bartholomew Ringwaldt, 1585.
            Trans. W. B. Collyer (1812) *and others.*

THIRD SUNDAY IN ADVENT.

"Behold, I send my messenger before thy face."
12   L. M.

ON Jordan's bank the Baptist's cry
    Announces that the Lord is nigh:
Awake, and hearken, for he brings
Glad tidings of the King of kings.

2 Earth, air and sea, with joy elate,
  For their Creator's Advent wait;
  The very elements rejoice,
  And welcome Him with cheerful voice.

3 We, too, will greet our coming God;
  And cleanse our hearts, and smooth the road;
  And make within a place of rest,
  Meet home for such a royal Guest.

4 For Thou art our salvation, Lord,
  Our refuge, and our great reward:
  Without Thy aid, like withering grass,
  Man into nothingness must pass.

5 To heal the sick stretch forth Thine hand,
  And bid the fallen sinner stand;
  Reveal Thy face, and joy restore,
  And make earth paradise once more.

Latin Hymn.
Translated by J. Chandler.

"*The blind receive their sight, and the lame walk.*"

13   C. M.

HARK the glad sound! the Saviour comes!
  The Saviour promised long!
Let every heart prepare a throne,
  And every voice a song.

2 On Him the Spirit largely poured,
    Exerts His sacred fire;
  Wisdom and might, and zeal and love,
    His holy breast inspire.

3 He comes, the prisoners to release,
    In Satan's bondage held;
  The gates of brass before Him burst,
    The iron fetters yield.

4 He comes, from thickest films of vice
    To clear the mental ray,
  And on the eye-balls of the blind
    To pour celestial day.

5 He comes, the broken heart to bind,
    The bleeding soul to cure;
  And with the treasures of His grace
    T'enrich the humble poor.

THIRD SUNDAY IN ADVENT.

6 Our glad hosannas, Prince of Peace,
    Thy welcome shall proclaim;
  And heav'n's eternal arches ring
    With Thy beloved name.

                                Philip Doddridge.

"O let the nations be glad and sing for joy."

14   C. M.

JOY to the world, the Lord is come!
    Let earth receive her King;
  Let every heart prepare Him room,
    And heav'n and nature sing.

2 Joy to the earth, the Saviour reigns;
    Let men their songs employ;
  While fields and floods, rocks, hills, and plains,
    Repeat the sounding joy.

3 No more let sins and sorrows grow,
    Nor thorns infest the ground:
  He comes to make His blessings flow
    Far as the curse is found.

4 He rules the world with truth and grace,
    And makes the nations prove
  The glories of His righteousness,
    And wonders of His love.

                                Isaac Watts, 1709.

"All the ends of the earth shall see the salvation of our God."

15   S. M.

COME, Kingdom of our God,
    Sweet reign of life and love,
  Shed peace, and hope, and joy abroad
    And wisdom from above.

2 Over our spirits first
    Extend Thy healing reign;
  Then raise and quench the sacred thirst
    That never pains again.

3 Come, Kingdom of our God,
    And make the broad earth Thine,
  Stretch o'er her land and isles the rod
    That flow'rs with grace divine.

4 Soon may all tribes be blest
    With fruit from life's glad tree:

  And in its shade like brothers rest,
   Sons of one family.

5 Come, Kingdom of our God,
  And raise Thy glorious throne
In worlds by the undying trod,
  When God shall bless His own.
Johns (*Lyr. Amer.* 1865).

"Therefore, judge nothing before the time, until the Lord come."

16
C. M.

GOD moves in a mysterious way
 His wonders to perform;
He plants His footsteps in the sea,
 And rides upon the storm.

2 Deep in unfathomable mines
  Of never-failing skill,
He treasures up His bright designs,
  And works His sov'reign will.

3 Ye fearful saints, fresh courage take;
  The clouds ye so much dread,
Are big with mercy, and shall break
  In blessings on your head.

4 Judge not the Lord by feeble sense,
  But trust Him for His grace;
Behind a frowning providence
  He hides a smiling face.

5 His purposes will ripen fast,
  Unfolding every hour;
The bud may have a bitter taste,
  But sweet will be the flower.

6 Blind unbelief is sure to err,
  And scan His work in vain;
God is His own interpreter,
  And He will make it plain.
William Cowper, 1772.

FOURTH SUNDAY IN ADVENT.

"I am the voice of one crying in the wilderness."

17
8s, 7s.

HARK! a thrilling voice proclaiming,
 Sounds aloud the coming light.

From the heav'ns, brightly gleaming,
  Christ shall chase away the night.

2 Souls, immersed in sin, and torpid,
    Wounded by its venom'd stings,
  Now shall rise: for lo! the Day-Star
    Comes with healing in His wings.

3 From on high, the Lamb, commissioned
    To remove our guilt, appears:
  Let us all, to gain His pardon
    Pray with penitential tears—

4 That, when at His second Advent,
    Clouds of glory mark His path,
  And the world in fiery deluge
    Sinks beneath His dreadful wrath;—

5 We may not for sins be driven
    Exiles into endless doom,
  But, beneath His strong protection
    Sheltered, reach eternal Home.

Ambrose.
Translated by E. E. Higbee.

"Repent ye, for the kingdom of heaven is at hand."

18   H. M.

LO! from the desert homes
    Where He hath hid so long,
  The new Elias comes
    In sternest wisdom strong;
  The voice that cries—of Christ from high
  And judgment nigh, from opening skies.

2 Your God e'en now doth stand
    At heaven's opening door,
  His fan is in His hand,
    And He will purge His floor;
  The wheat He claims, and with Him stows,
  The chaff He throws, to quenchless flames.

3 Ye haughty mountains, bow
    Your sky-aspiring heads;
  Ye valleys, hiding low,
    Lift up your gentle meads;
  Make His way plain, your King before,
  For evermore—He comes to reign.

4 May Thy dread voice around,
    Thou harbinger of Light,

FOURTH SUNDAY IN ADVENT.

On our dull ears still sound,
   Lest here we sleep in night,
Till judgment come, and on our path
Shall burst the wrath, and deathless doom.

5 O God, with love's sweet might
   Who dost anoint and arm
Thy soldiers for the fight
   With grace that shields from harm,
Thrice blessed Three, heav'n's endless days
Shall sing Thy praise eternally.
Latin Hymn.
Translated by Isaac Williams.

"The Lord is at hand."

19 L. M. 6 *lines.*

COME, quickly come, dread Judge of all;
   For, awful though Thine Advent be,
All shadows from the truth will fall,
   And falsehood die, in sight of Thee:
Come, quickly come: for doubt and fear
Like clouds dissolve when Thou art near.

2 Come, quickly come, great King of all;
   Reign all around us, and within;
Let sin no more our souls enthral,
   Let pain and sorrow die with sin:
Come, quickly come: for Thou alone
Canst make Thy scattered people one.

3 Come, quickly come, true Life of all;
   The curse of death is on the ground;
On every home his shadows fall,
   On every heart his mark is found:
Come, quickly come: for grief and pain
Can never cloud Thy glorious reign.

4 Come, quickly come, sure Light of all,
   For gloomy night broods o'er our way;
And fainting souls begin to fall
   With weary watching for the day:
Come, quickly come: for round Thy throne
No eye is blind, no night is known.
Lawrence Tuttiett.

"To give light to them that sit in darkness, and in the shadow of death."

20 C. M.

O VERY God of very God,
   And very Light of Light,
Whose feet this earth's dark valley trod,
   That so it might be bright;

2 Our hopes are weak, our fears are strong,
   Thick darkness blinds our eyes;
Cold is the night, and oh! we long
   That Thou, our Sun, would'st rise.

3 And even now, though dull and grey,
   The east is bright'ning fast,
And kindling to the perfect day,
   That never shall be past.

4 Oh, guide us till our path is done,
   And we have reached the shore
Where Thou, our Everlasting Sun,
   Art shining evermore.

5 We wait in faith, and turn our face
   To where the daylight springs,
Till Thou shalt come our gloom to chase,
   With healing on Thy wings.

J. M. Neale.

"We have waited for Him, and He will save us."

21 L. M.

WHEN shades of night around us close,
   And weary limbs in sleep repose,
The faithful soul awake may be,
And longing sigh, O Lord, to Thee.

2 Thou true Desire of nations, hear;
Thou Word of God, Thou Saviour dear,
In pity heed our humble cries,
And bid at length the fallen rise.

3 O come, Redeemer, come and free
Thine own from guilt and misery;
The gates of heaven again unfold,
Which Adam's sin had closed of old.

Latin Hymn.
Hymns A. & M.

"When the fullness of time was come, God sent forth His Son, made of a woman."

22
L. M.

COME, Thou Redeemer of the earth,
Come, testify Thy Virgin-birth:
All lands admire, all times applaud;
Thy wondrous birth proclaims Thee God.

2 The Word made flesh His race began,
Begotten of no mortal man,
But of the Holy Spirit's might,
A Babe yet waiting for the light.

3 Forth from the Father's bosom sent,
Down to the realms of death He went,
To Him returned — He claimed His own,
And rose to share th' eternal throne.

4 And there with God the Father One,
He wears forever on the throne
The Flesh in which He fought, to be
The trophy of His victory.

5 O,hear our prayer, Eternal Son,
Made flesh to be our Champion!
The weakness of our mortal state
With deathless might invigorate.

6 Thy cradle here shall glitter bright,
And darkness breathe a newer light,
Where endless faith shall shine serene,
And twilight never intervene.

Latin Hymn, 6th Century.
Translation Compiled.

"Even so, Come, Lord Jesus."

23
L. M.

JESUS, Thy Church with longing eyes
For Thine expected coming waits.
When will the promised light arise,
And glory beam from Zion's gates?

2 O come and reign o'er every land;
Let Satan from his throne be hurled,
All nations bow to Thy command,
And grace revive a dying world.

3 Teach us, in watchfulness and prayer,
To wait for the appointed hour;
And fit us, by Thy grace, to share
The triumphs of Thy conq'ring power.
Wm. H. Bathurst.

CHRISTMAS-DAY.

"Glory to God in the highest, and on earth, peace, good-will toward men."

24 7s.

HARK! the herald-angels sing
Glory to the new-born King:
Peace on earth, and mercy mild,
God and sinners reconciled.

2 Joyful, all ye nations, rise,
Join the triumph of the skies;
With th' angelic host proclaim
Christ is born in Bethlehem.

3 Christ, by highest heav'n adored,
Christ, the everlasting Lord,
Late in time behold Him come,
Offspring of a Virgin's womb.

4 Veiled in flesh the Godhead see!
Hail, th' incarnate Deity!
Pleased as Man with man to dwell,
Jesus, our Immanuel.

5 Hail, the heaven-born Prince of Peace!
Hail, the Sun of Righteousness!
Light and life to all He brings,
Ris'n with healing in His wings.

6 Mild He lays His glory by,
Born that man no more may die,
Born to raise the sons of earth,
Born to give them second birth.
Charles Wesley.

"Unto you is born this day, in the city of David, a Saviour, which is Christ the Lord."

25 C. M.

WHILE shepherds watched their flocks by night,
All seated on the ground,

The angel of the Lord came down,
  And glory shone around.
2 "Fear not," said he; (for mighty dread
    Had seized their troubled mind;)
  "Glad tidings of great joy I bring
    To you and all mankind.
3 "To you, in David's town, this day
    Is born of David's line
  The Saviour, who is Christ the Lord;
    And this shall be the sign.
4 "The heav'nly Babe you there shall find
    To human view displayed,
  All meanly wrapt in swathing bands,
    And in a manger laid."
5 Thus spake the Seraph; and forthwith
    Appeared a shining throng
  Of angels, praising God, and thus
    Address'd their joyful song.
6 "All glory be to God on high,
    And to the earth be peace;
  Good-will henceforth from heav'n to men
    Begin, and never cease!"
                            Nahum Tate, 1696.

"And suddenly there was with the Angel a multitude of the heavenly host praising God."

26 8s, 7s.

HARK! what mean those holy voices,
    Sweetly sounding through the skies?
  Lo! th' angelic host rejoices,
    Heav'nly hallelujahs rise.
2 Listen to the wondrous story,
    Which they chant in hymns of joy;
  "Glory in the highest, glory!
    Glory be to God most high!
3 "Peace on earth, good will from heaven,
    Reaching far as man is found;
  Souls redeemed, and sins forgiven,
    Loud our golden harps shall sound.
4 "Christ is born, the great Anointed;
    Heav'n and earth His praises sing!

O receive whom God appointed
For your Prophet, Priest, and King.

5 "Hasten, mortals, to adore Him;
Learn His name, and taste His joy
Till in heaven ye sing before Him,
Glory be to God most high!"

John Cawood, 1825.

"And let all the angels of God worship Him."

27   L. M.

WHEN Jordan hushed his waters still,
    And silence slept on Zion's hill;
When Bethlehem's shepherds through the night
Watched o'er their flocks by starry light;

2 Hark! from the midnight hills around
A voice of more than mortal sound,
In distant Alleluias stole,
Wild murm'ring o'er the raptured soul.

3 Then swift to every startled eye,
New streams of glory light the sky,
Heav'n bursts her azure gates, to pour
Her Spirits to the midnight hour.

4 On wheels of light, on wings of flame,
The glorious hosts of Zion came;
High heav'n with songs of triumph rang,
While loud they struck their harps and sang.

5 O Zion! lift thy raptured eye,
The long-expected hour is nigh,
The joys of nature rise again,
The Prince of Salem comes to reign.

6 He comes! to cheer the trembling heart;
Bid Satan and his wiles depart:
Again the day-star gilds the gloom,
Again the bowers of Eden bloom!

7 O Zion! lift Thy raptured eye,
The long-expected hour is nigh.
Sing praises, with the angel host,
To Father, Son, and Holy Ghost.

Thomas Campbell, 1820.

"Break forth into joy, sing together, ye waste places of Jerusalem."

28   11s, 11s, 12s, 11s, 10s, 10s.

ZION! the marvellous story be telling;
    The Son of the Highest, how lowly His birth!
The brightest archangel in glory excelling,
    He stoops to redeem thee, He reigns upon earth.
Shout the glad tidings, exultingly sing,
Jerusalem triumphs, Messiah is King.

2 Tell how He cometh: from nation to nation,
    The heart-cheering news let the earth echo round;
How free to the faithful He offers salvation,
    His people with joy everlasting are crown'd.
Shout the glad tidings, exultingly sing,
Jerusalem triumphs, Messiah is King.

3 Mortals, your homage be gratefully bringing,
    And sweet let the gladsome hosanna arise;
Ye angels, the full hallelujah be singing,
    One chorus resound through the earth and the skies.
Shout the glad tidings, exultingly sing,
Jerusalem triumphs, Messiah is King.

                        Wm. A. Muhlenberg.

"Let us go now even unto Bethlehem and see this thing which has come to pass."

29   12s, 11s, 11s, 7s, 7s, 10s.

DRAW nigh, all ye faithful, joyous and triumphant,
    And greet ye at Bethlehem the Babe, the Word!
In lowly manger lies the King of angels!
    O come let us adore Him,
    O come let us adore Him,
O come let us adore Him, Christ the Lord!

2 God of God Almighty, Light of Light Eternal,
    Thou hast not, O Christ, The Virgin's womb abhorred:
Very God of Very God, begotten not created:
    O come let us adore Him, &c.

3 Shout Alleluia, all ye choirs of angels,
    Rejoice, heav'nly citizens, with glad accord.
Glory to God! to God on high be glory,
    O come let us adore Him, &c.

4 Here, Lord! we would greet Thee, born this happy morning,
 O Jesus! for ever be Thy Name adored,
Word of the Father, now for us Incarnate!
 O come let us adore Him, &c.

Latin Hymn.
XV. Century. Trans.?

"The Word was made flesh, and dwelt among us."

30   L. M.

O CHRIST, Redeemer of our race,
 Thou Brightness of the Father's face,
Of Him and with Him ever One,
Ere times and seasons had begun;

2 Thou that art very Light of Light,
Unfailing Hope in sin's dark night,
Hear Thou the prayers Thy people pray
The wide world o'er, this blessed day.

3 Remember, Thou, who all didst make,
How, for Thy fallen creatures' sake,
Thou, in the Holy Virgin's womb,
Didst our humanity assume.

4 To-day, as year by year its light
Sheds o'er the world a radiance bright,
One precious truth is echoed on,
"'Tis Thou hast saved us, Thou alone."

5 Thou from the Father's throne didst come
To call His banished children home;
And heav'n and earth, and sea and shore
His love who sent Thee here adore.

6 And gladsome too are we to-day,
Whose guilt Thy blood has washed away;
Redeemed, the new-made song we sing;
It is the birthday of our King.

Latin Hymn, 6th Century.
H. W. Baker, & E. Caswall.

*"In the Lord shall all the seed of Israel be justified,
and shall glory."*

31   C. M.

HIGH let us swell our tuneful notes,
 And join th' angelic throng;
The angels no such love have known
As we, to wake their song.

2 Good will to sinful man is shown,
    And peace on earth is given;
  For, lo! th' incarnate Saviour comes
    With messages from heav'n.

3 Justice and grace, with sweet accord,
    His rising beams adorn:
  Let heaven and earth in concert join,
    "The promis'd Child is born."

4 Glory to God in highest strains
    By highest worlds is paid;
  Be glory then by us proclaimed,
    And by our lives displayed.

5 When shall we reach those blissful realms,
    Where Christ exalted reigns,
  And learn of the celestial choir
    Their own immortal strains? *Doddridge*, 1740.

"The redeemed of the Lord shall return, and come with singing unto Zion."

32   8s, 7s, 8 *lines.*

NO more sadness now, nor fasting:
    Now we put our grief away:
God came down, the Everlasting,
    Taking human flesh, to-day.
God came down on earth a Stranger,
    Working out His mighty plan;
God was cradled in a manger,
    Very God, and very Man.

2 There were shepherds once abiding
    In the field to watch by night,
  And they saw the clouds dividing,
    And the sky above was bright;
  And a glory shone around them
    On the grass as they were laid;
  And a holy angel found them,
    And their hearts were sore afraid.

3 "Fear ye not," he said; "for cheerful
    Are the tidings that I bring.
  Unto you, so weak and fearful,
    Christ is born, the Lord and King."
  As the angel told the story
    Of the Saviour's lowly birth,
  Multitudes were singing "Glory
    Be to God, and peace on earth!"

ST. STEPHEN'S DAY.

4 Since Thy love for our salvation,
   Saviour, covered Thee with shame,
Let Thy Church, in every nation,
   Sing the glory of Thy Name;
Let Thy Holy Spirit make us
   Full of humbleness and love,
Like Thyself, until Thou take us
   To our Father's house above. *Jno. M. Neale.*

"And the light shineth in darkness."

33 L. M. 8 *lines.*

WHEN marshaled on the nightly plain
   The glittering host bestud the sky,
One star alone, of all the train,
   Can fix the sinner's wandering eye:
Hark! hark! to God the chorus breaks,
   From every host, from every gem;
But one alone the Saviour speaks;
   It is the Star of Bethlehem.

2 Once on the raging seas I rode;
   The storm was loud, the night was dark;
The ocean yawned, and rudely blowed
   The wind, that tossed my foundering bark:
Deep horror then my vitals froze;
   Death-struck, I ceased the tide to stem;
When suddenly a star arose;
   It was the Star of Bethlehem.

3 It was my guide, my light, my all;
   It bade my dark forebodings cease;
And, thro' the storm, and danger's thrall,
   It led me to the port of peace:
Now, safely moored, my perils o'er,
   I'll sing, first in night's diadem,
For ever and for ever more,
   The Star—the Star of Bethlehem.
                    Henry Kirke White, 1804.

ST. STEPHEN'S DAY.

"The noble army of martyrs praise Thee."

34 7s, 6s, 8 *lines.*

FROM all Thy saints in warfare,
   For all Thy saints at rest,

ST. STEPHEN'S DAY.

To Thee, O blessed Jesus,
  All praises be address'd.
Thou, Lord, didst win the battle,
  That they might conqu'rors be;
Their crowns of living glory
  Are lit with rays from Thee.

2 Praise for the first of martyrs,
  Who saw Thee ready stand
To aid in midst of torments,
  To plead at God's right hand.
Share we with Him, if summon'd
  By death our Lord to own,
On earth the faithful witness,
  In heaven the martyr crown.

3 Apostles, prophets, martyrs,
  And all the sacred throng,
Who wear the spotless raiments,
  Who raise the ceaseless song;
For these, pass'd on before us,
  Saviour, we Thee adore,
And, walking in their footsteps,
  Would serve Thee evermore.

4 Then praise we God, the Father,
  And praise we God, the Son,
And God the Holy Spirit,
  Eternal Three in One;
Till all the ransom'd number
  Fall down before the throne,
And honor, power, and glory
  Ascribe to God alone.   *Earl Nelson.*

"*We rejoice before Thee in the blessed communion of all Thy saints.*"

35
S. M.

FOR Thy true servants, Lord,
  Who strove in Thee to live,
Who follow'd Thee, obeyed, adored,
  Our grateful hymn receive.

2 For Thy true servants, Lord,
  Who strove in Thee to die,
And found in Thee a full reward,
  Accept our thankful cry.

3 Thine earthly members fit
   To join Thy saints above,
 In one communion ever knit,
   One fellowship of love.

4 Jesus, Thy name we bless,
   And humbly pray that we
 May follow them in holiness
   Who lived and died for Thee.

Altered from Richard Mant, 1849.

"Be thou faithful unto death, and I will give thee a crown of life."

36   8s, 7s, 8 lines.

PRAISE to Thee, O Lord most Holy,
   King of earth, and sea, and sky;
 Be Thy name adorèd solely
   For each martyr's victory.
 Let the voice of praise and blessing
   Evermore to Thee ascend,
 For Thy glories everlasting,
   For Thy mercies without end.

2 For the saints of every nation,
   Who with joy their blood outpoured;
 Gave themselves a pure oblation
   In the service of their Lord;
 Who, in life and death undaunted,
   By their faith the world o'ercame;
 Scorned alike its pleasures vaunted,
   And its doom of sword and flame.

3 Fearless, though by foes surrounded,
   Threats and bribes unmoved they heard;
 And the hearts of kings confounded
   By the Truth's soul-piercing word.
 Therefore heav'n's bright crown of laurel
   Decks each calm and sainted brow;
 Therefore clothed in white apparel
   With the Lamb they triumph now.

4 In His sacred footsteps treading
   They His glorious throne will share;
 And with anthems never ending
   Praise Him in heav'n's mansions fair.

In our joyful celebration
  Of the martyr host above,
May our hearts' deep adoration
  Mingle with their songs of love.
H. M. C. in Hymnary.

ST. JOHN the EVANGELIST'S DAY.

"I, John, was in the isle called Patmos, for the word of God, and for the testimony of Jesus Christ."

37 S. M.

A N exile for the faith
  Of his Incarnate Lord,
Beyond the stars, beyond all space
  The loved disciple soared:

2 There saw in glory Him
    Who liveth and was dead;
  There Judah's Lion and the Lamb
    That for our ransom bled;

3 There of the kingdom learnt
    The mysteries sublime;
  How, sown in martyrs' blood, the faith
    Should spread from clime to clime.

4 Lord, give us grace, like him,
    In Thee to live and die;
  To spurn the fleeting things of earth,
    And seek for joys on high.
Latin Hymn.
Altered from E. Caswall's Trans.

"The disciple whom Jesus loved."

38 L. M.

O THOU, who gav'st Thy servant grace
  On Thee the living rock to rest,
To look on Thine unveilèd face,
  And lean on Thy protecting breast;

2 Grant us, O King of mercy, still
    To feel Thy presence from above,
  And in Thy word and in Thy will
    To hear Thy voice and know Thy love;

ST. JOHN THE EVANGELIST'S DAY.

3 And when the toils of life are done,
   And nature waits Thy just decree,
     To find our rest beneath Thy throne,
   And look in certain hope to Thee.
Reginald Heber.

"The love of Christ, which passeth knowledge."

39   C. P. M.

O LOVE divine, how sweet thou art!
   When shall I find my willing heart
     All taken up by thee?
I thirst, I faint, I die to prove
The greatness of redeeming love,
     The love of Christ to me!

2 O that I could, with favor'd John,
   Recline my weary head upon
     The dear Redeemer's breast!
From care, and sin, and sorrow free,
Give me, O Lord, to find in Thee
     My everlasting rest!

3 Only Thy love do I require,
   Nothing on earth below desire,
     But this in heav'n above;
Let earth, and heav'n, and all things go,
Give me Thy only love to know,
     Impart to me Thy love.
Charles Wesley.

"Who is he that overcometh the world, but he that believeth that Jesus is the Son of God."

40   L. M.

NOT by the martyr's death alone
   The martyr's crown in heav'n is won:
There is a triumph set on high
For bloodless fields of victory.

2 What though he was not called to feel
The cross, or flame, or torturing wheel,
Yet daily to the world he died,
His flesh, through grace, he crucified.

3 What though nor chains, nor scourges sore,
Nor cruel beasts his members tore,
Enough if perfect love arise
To Christ a grateful sacrifice.

4 When self-control the flesh subdues,
　And faith the wayward soul imbues,
　Love, with her torch-light from the skies,
　Shall fire the holy sacrifice.

5 Lord, grant us so to Thee to turn,
　That we to die through life may learn;
　And when this fleeting life is o'er
　May live with Thee for evermore.

Latin Hymn.
Translation Compiled.

THE INNOCENTS' DAY.

"These were redeemed from among men, being the first fruits unto God, and to the Lamb."

41　　　　　　S. M.

GLORY to Thee, O Lord,
　Who from this world of sin,
By cruel Herod's ruthless sword
　Those precious ones didst win.

2 Baptized in their own blood,
　　Earth's untried perils o'er,
They passed unconsciously the flood,
　　And safely gained the shore.

3 Glory to Thee for all
　　The ransomed infant band,
Who since that hour have heard Thy call,
　　And reached the quiet land.

4 Oh that our hearts within,
　　Like theirs, were pure and bright!
Oh that as free from deeds of sin
　　We shrank not from Thy sight!

5 Lord, help us every hour
　　Thy cleansing grace to claim;
In life to glorify Thy power,
　　In death to praise Thy name.

Emma Toke.

FIRST SUNDAY AFTER CHRISTMAS.

"Conceived by the Holy Ghost, born of the Virgin Mary."

42 L. M. 6 *lines.*

O COME, loud anthems let us sing;
  Come, praise the birth of Christ our King:
Let all the hosts of heav'n rejoice,
And praise Him both with heart and voice:
Sing ye, from greatest unto least,
Our blest Redeemer's marriage feast.

2 See, o'er the earth new light is shed,
  And all the ancient gloom is fled;
  God's grace descending open throws
  The courts that sin of old did close;
  For Mary, Virgin undefiled,
  Folds in her arms the new-born Child.

3 'Twas hers upon her breast to rear
  Him, who alone man's guilt may bear,
  To whom, o'er all in earth and heaven,
  The rod of might and power is given,
  To whom from earth's remotest ends
  The voice of prayer and praise ascends.

4 So we, in lowly homage bent,
  Our tribute due of love present;
  Beseeching Him with pitying eye
  To look on us His family,
  To fill our hearts with plenteous peace,
  And bid all wars and tumults cease.

5 And then when all our course is run,
  And sorrows ended, task-work done,
  Then may He lead us there, where sin
  And sorrow never enter in;
  Where He at God's right hand is throned,
  As Lord and King for ever owned.

6 There, as in His surpassing might,
  Things far and near He orders right;
  He on the just their portion blest
  Bestows, the chiefest and the best,
  Where shines the light on that blest shore,
  Our joy, our peace for evermore.   *E. H. Plumptre.*

"Blessed be the Lord God of Israel: for He hath visited and redeemed His people."

43 8s, 7s.

HAIL! Thou long-expected Jesus,
    Born to set Thy people free;
From our fears and sins release us;
    Let us find our rest in Thee.

2 Israel's strength and consolation,
    Hope of all the earth Thou art;
Long-desired of every nation,
    Joy of every waiting heart.

3 Born Thy people to deliver,
    Born a Child, yet God our King,
Born to reign in us for ever,
    Now Thy gracious kingdom bring.

4 By Thine own eternal Spirit,
    Rule in all our hearts alone;
By Thine all-sufficient merit,
    Raise us to Thy glorious throne.

Charles Wesley, 1744.

"Behold, a Virgin shall be with child, and shall bring forth a Son."

44 S. M.

BEHOLD! the grace appears,
    The promise is fulfilled;
Mary, the wondrous virgin, bears,
    And Jesus is the Child.

2 The Lord, the highest God,
    Calls Him His only Son;
He bids Him rule the lands abroad,
    And gives Him David's throne.

3 O'er Jacob shall He reign
    With a peculiar sway;
The nations shall His grace obtain,
    His kingdom ne'er decay.

4 To bring the glorious news,
    A heavenly form appears;
He tells the shepherds of their joys,
    And banishes their fears:

5 "Glory to God on high!
    And heavenly peace on earth,
  Good will to men, to angels joy,
    At the Redeemer's birth."

6 In worship so divine
    Let saints employ their tongues;
  With the celestial hosts we join,
    And loud repeat their songs.
                    Isaac Watts, 1707.

45
"The Prince of peace."
S. M.

FATHER! our hearts we lift
  Up to Thy gracious throne,
And thank Thee for the precious gift
  Of Thine incarnate Son.

2 Jesus, the holy Child,
    Doth, by His birth, declare,
  That God and man are reconciled,
    And one in Him we are.

3 A peace on earth He brings,
    Which never more shall end;
  The Lord of hosts, the King of kings,
    Declares Himself our Friend.

4 Oh! may we all receive
    The new-born Prince of peace;
  And meekly in His spirit live,
    And in His love increase.
                    Charles Wesley, 1745.

SECOND SUNDAY AFTER CHRISTMAS.

46
"And in His temple doth every one speak of His glory."
8s, 7s, 6 *lines.*

IN His temple now behold Him,
  See the long-expected Lord;
Ancient prophets had foretold Him,
  God has now fulfilled His word.
Now to praise Him His redeemèd
  Shall break forth with one accord.

2 In the arms of her who bore Him,
      Virgin pure, behold Him lie,
While His aged saints adore Him
      Ere in perfect faith they die.
Hallelujah! Hallelujah!
      Lo! th' Incarnate God most high.

3 Jesus, by Thy presentation,
      Thou who cam'st in lowly mien,
Make us see our great salvation,
      Make our hearts all pure within.
O present us in Thy glory
      To Thy Father pure and clean.
Johann Scheffler.
(Angelus Silesius.)

"Blessed are the pure in heart, for they shall see God."

47   S. M.

BLEST are the pure in heart,
      For they shall see our God:
The secret of the Lord is theirs,
      Their soul is Christ's abode.

2 The Lord, who left the heav'ns
      Our life and peace to bring,
To dwell in lowliness with men,
      Their Pattern and their King:

3 He to the lowly soul
      Doth still Himself impart,
And for His dwelling and His throne
      Chooseth the pure in heart.

4 Lord, we Thy presence seek!
      May ours this blessing be:
Give us a pure and lowly heart,
      A temple meet for Thee.
John Keble, 1819

"Verily He took not on Him the nature of angels: but He took on Him the seed of Abraham."

48   S. M.

YE saints, proclaim abroad
      The honors of your King;
To Jesus, your Incarnate God,
      Your songs of praises sing.

2 Not angels round the throne
   Of majesty above,
Are half so much obliged as we,
   To our Immanuel's love.

3 They never sank so low,
   They are not raised so high;
They never knew such depths of wo,
   Such heights of majesty:

4 The Saviour did not join
   Their nature to His own;
For them He shed no blood divine,
   Nor breathed a single groan.

5 May we with angels vie,
   The Saviour to adore;
Our debts are greater far than theirs,
   O be our praises more!   *Jno. Ryland.*

"How amiable are Thy tabernacles, O Lord of hosts."

49   H. M.

LORD of the worlds above!
   How pleasant and how fair,
The dwellings of Thy love,
   Thine earthly temples are!
To Thine abode my heart aspires,
With warm desires, to see my God.

2 O happy souls that pray
   Where God appoints to hear!
O happy men that pay
   Their constant service there!
They praise Thee still; and happy they
That love the way to Zion's hill.

3 They go from strength to strength,
   Through this dark vale of tears,
Till each arrives at length,
   Till each in heaven appears;
O glorious seat, when God our King,
Shall thither bring our willing feet!

4 God is our sun and shield,
   Our light and our defence;
With gifts His hands are filled,
   We draw our blessings thence:
He shall bestow on Jacob's race
Peculiar grace and glory too.

5 The Lord His people loves;
   His hand no good withholds
 From those His heart approves, —
   From pure and pious souls.
 Thrice happy He, O God of hosts,
   Whose spirit trusts alone in Thee!

                        Isaac Watts, 1719.

"Lord, now lettest Thou Thy servant depart in peace, for mine eyes have seen Thy salvation."

50   C. M.

JESUS! I love Thy charming name,
   'Tis music to mine ear;
 Fain would I sound it out so loud,
   That earth and heaven might hear.

2 Yes, Thou art precious to my soul,
   My Transport and my Trust;
 Jewels to Thee, are gaudy toys,
   And gold is sordid dust.

3 All my capacious powers can wish,
   In Thee doth richly meet;
 Not to mine eyes is life so dear,
   Nor friendship half so sweet.

4 Thy grace still dwells upon my heart,
   And sheds its fragrance there;
 The noblest balm of all its wounds,
   The cordial of its care.

5 I'll speak the honors of Thy name,
   With my last laboring breath;
 Then, speechless, clasp Thee in mine arms,
   The antidote of death.   *Philip Doddridge,* 1740.

THE CIRCUMCISION OF CHRIST.

"Without shedding of blood is no remission."

51   C. M.

THY blood, O Christ, hath made our peace:
   Not only that, whereby
 The ground of Calvary was stained,
   When Thou wert hung on high;

2 Not only that, which in Thine hour
    Of fear and agony,
  Distilled upon Thy trembling frame
    In dark Gethsemane:

3 But that shed from Thee, when at first
    In childhood Thou didst deign
  Thus to endure for sinful man
    The legal rite of pain.

4 And as with suffering and with Thee
    Our yearly course begins;
  So teach us to renounce the flesh
    And put away our sins;

5 That in the Israel of Thy Church
    We may not lose our part:
  In spirit and in body pure,
    And circumcised in heart. *Henry Alford*, 1845.

"And when eight days were accomplished for the circumcising of the Child, His name was called Jesus."

52
S. M.

THE ancient law departs
  And all its terrors cease;
For Jesus makes with faithful hearts
  A covenant of peace.

2 The Light of Light divine,
    True Brightness undefiled,
  He bears for us the shame of sin,
    A holy, spotless Child.

3 To-day the Name is Thine,
    At which we bend the knee;
  They call Thee Jesus, Child Divine!
    Our Jesus deign to be.

Latin Hymn.
Hymns A. & M.

"Thy name is an ointment poured out."

53
C. M.

HOW sweet the name of Jesus sounds
  In a believer's ear!
It soothes his sorrows, heals his wounds,
  And drives away his fear.

2 It makes the wounded spirit whole,
    And calms the troubled breast;
'Tis manna to the hungry soul,
    And to the weary rest.

3 Dear name! the rock on which I build,
    My shield and hiding-place;
My never-failing treas'ry, filled
    With boundless stores of grace.

4 Jesus! my Shepherd, Husband, Friend!
    My Prophet, Priest, and King!
My Lord, my Life, my Way, my End!
    Accept the praise I bring.

5 Weak is the effort of my heart,
    And cold my warmest thought;
But when I see Thee as Thou art,
    I'll praise Thee as I ought.

6 Till then I would Thy love proclaim
    With every fleeting breath;
And may the music of Thy name
    Refresh my soul in death.

John Newton, 1779.

"For there is none other name under heaven given among men, whereby we must be saved."

54   8s, 7s, 6 lines.

TO the Name of our salvation
    Honor, worship, thanks, we pay;
Which, for many a generation
    Hid in God's foreknowledge lay,
But with holy exultation
    We may sing aloud to-day.

2 Jesus is the Name we treasure,
    Name beyond what words can tell;
Name of gladness, Name of pleasure,
    Ear and heart delighting well;
Name of sweetness, passing measure,
    Saving us from sin and hell.

3 'Tis the Name for adoration;
    'Tis the Name of Victory;
'Tis the Name for meditation
    In this vale of misery;
'Tis the Name for veneration
    By the citizens on high.

4 Jesus is the Name exalted
   Over every other name;
 In this Name, whene'er assaulted,
   We can put our foes to shame;
 Strength to them who else had halted,
   Eyes to blind, and feet to lame.

5 Jesus, we Thy Name adoring,
   Long to see Thee as Thou art;
 Of Thy clemency imploring
   So to write it in our heart,
 That hereafter, upwards soaring,
   We with angels may have part.

Latin Hymn, 15th Century.
Altered from & translated by J. M. Neale.

"For in Him dwelleth all the fulness of the Godhead bodily; and ye are complete in Him."

55
10*s.*

ETERNAL Word! God's true and only Son,
   Maker, and Lord, and Heir, and Judge of all;
 First-born of every creature; Holy One!
   We praise Thy name, and on Thy name we call.

2 Jehovah dwells from everlasting years
   In silence and in solitude concealed:
 And yet from everlasting He appears
   In Thee to all His universe revealed.

3 And life and love and truth and joy and might,
   And all the creature lieth incomplete,
 Some darkness lingering in their purest light—
   Only in Thee doth all their fulness meet.

4 True Son of God, our Sonship is in Thee;
   True Light of God, our Wisdom too Thou art;
 O Lamb from earth's foundation slain for me,
   Thou bringest life and peace into my heart.

5 Ever in Thee the Father is revealed,
   Ever in Thee all things are reconciled,
 Ever in Thee our sins and wounds are healed,
   Glory to Thee, the Pure and Undefiled.

Orwell.

THE EPIPHANY.

"My times are in Thy hand."

56   7s.

FOR Thy mercy and Thy grace,
  Faithful through another year,
Hear our song of thankfulness,
  Father, and Redeemer, hear!

2 In our weakness and distress,
  Rock of strength! be Thou our stay!
In the pathless wilderness
  Be our true and living way!

3 Who of us death's awful road
  In the coming year shall tread?
With Thy rod and staff, O God,
  Comfort Thou his dying head!

4 Keep us faithful, keep us pure,
  Keep us evermore Thine own!
Help, O help us to endure!
  Fit us for Thy promised crown!

5 So within Thy palace gate
  We shall praise, on golden strings,
Thee, the only Potentate,
  Lord of lords, and King of kings!

Henry Downton, 1843.

THE EPIPHANY.

"There shall come a star out of Jacob, and a sceptre shall rise out of Israel."

57   L. M.

WHAT star is this, with beams so bright,
  More beauteous than the noonday light?
It shines to herald forth the King,
And Gentiles to His cradle bring.

2 And lo! the eastern sages stand
To read in heaven the Lord's command:
Children of faith they come; they find
The Prince and Saviour of mankind.

3 They bless the meek and holy Child,
An infant Lord, and Monarch mild:
Their riches at His feet they pour
And with the heart their King adore.

4 O heavenly Lord, O holy Light,
That shines through Nature's wondering night,
What marvels in Thy love we trace,
What power divine, what glorious grace.

5 And now, thou bright and morning star,
Arise again, and shine afar
From sea to sea, from shore to shore,
Till utmost tribes their King adore.

Latin Hymn.
Translation compiled.

"Great is the mystery of godliness: God was manifest in the flesh."

58   7s, 8 *lines.*

SONGS of thankfulness and praise,
Jesus, Lord, to Thee we raise.
Manifested by the star
To the sages from afar;
Branch of royal David's stem
In Thy birth at Bethlehem;
Anthems be to Thee addrest,
God in Man made manifest.

2 Manifest at Jordan's stream,
Prophet, Priest, and King supreme;
And at Cana wedding-guest
In Thy Godhead manifest;
Manifest in power divine,
Changing water into wine;
Anthems be to Thee addrest,
God in Man made manifest.

3 Manifest in making whole
Palsied limbs and fainting soul;
Manifest in valiant fight,
Quelling all the devil's might;
Manifest in gracious will,
Ever bringing good from ill;
Anthems be to Thee addrest,
God in Man made manifest.

4 Sun and moon shall darkened be,
Stars shall fall, the heaven shall flee:
Christ will then like lightning shine,
All will see His glorious sign;

All will then the trumpet hear,
All will see the Judge appear:
Thou by all wilt be confest,
God in Man made manifest.

5 Grant us grace to see Thee, Lord,
Mirrored in Thy holy Word;
May we imitate Thee now,
And be pure, as pure art Thou;
That we like to Thee may be,
At Thy great Epiphany;
And may praise Thee, ever blest,
God in Man made manifest. *C. Wordsworth.*

"*They presented unto Him gifts: gold, frankincense, and myrrh.*"
11s, & 10s.

59

BRIGHTEST and best of the sons of the morning,
  Dawn on our darkness, and lend us Thine aid;
Star of the East, the horizon adorning,
  Guide where our infant Redeemer is laid.

2 Cold on His cradle the dew-drops are shining,
    Low lies His head with the beasts of the stall;
  Angels adore Him, in slumber reclining,
    Maker and Monarch and Saviour of all!

3 Say, shall we yield Him, in costly devotion,
    Odors of Edom, and offerings divine,
  Gems of the mountain and pearls of the ocean,
    Myrrh from the forest or gold from the mine?

4 Vainly we offer each ample oblation,
    Vainly with gifts would His favor secure;
  Richer by far is the heart's adoration,
    Dearer to God are the prayers of the poor.

5 Brightest and best of the sons of the morning,
    Dawn on our darkness, and lend us Thine aid;
  Star of the East, the horizon adorning,
    Guide where our infant Redeemer is laid.
                                Reginald Heber, 1811.

"*The star went before them, till it came and stood over where the young child was.*"
L. M.

60

SEE now fulfilled what God decreed,
  "From Jacob shall a Star proceed;"
And eastern sages with amaze
Upon the wondrous vision gaze.

2 The guiding Star above is bright,
　Within them shines a clearer Light,
　Which leads them on with power benign
　To seek the Giver of the sign.

3 True love can brook no dull delay;
　Nor toil nor dangers stop their way:
　Home, kindred, father-land, and all
　They leave at their Creator's call.

4 O Jesus! while the Star of Grace
　Allures us now to seek Thy face,
　Let not our slothful hearts refuse
　The guidance of that Light to use.

Latin Hymn.
Altered from J. Chandler.

"*The Gentiles shall come to Thy light, and kings to the brightness of Thy rising.*"

61 7s & 6s.

HAIL to the Lord's Anointed,
　　Great David's greater Son!
See in the time appointed
　　His reign on earth begun!

2 He comes to break oppression,
　　To set the captive free,
　To take away transgression,
　　To rule in equity.

3 Before Him on the mountains
　　Shall peace, the herald, go;
　And from a thousand fountains
　　Shall grace unceasing flow.

4 Kings shall fall down before Him,
　　And gold and incense bring;
　All nations shall adore Him,
　　His praise all people sing;

5 To Him shall prayer unceasing
　　And daily vows ascend;
　His kingdom still increasing,
　　A kingdom without end.

6 O'er every foe victorious,
　　He on His throne shall rest;
　From age to age more glorious,
　　All blessing and all blest;

7 The tide of time shall never
   His covenant remove;
   His name shall stand for ever,
   Jesus, sweet name of love.
                James Montgomery, 1822.

"*When they saw the star they rejoiced with exceeding great joy.*"

62   7s, 6 *lines.*

AS with gladness men of old
   Did the guiding star behold;
As with joy they hailed its light,
Leading onward, beaming bright;
So, most gracious Lord, may we
Evermore be led to Thee.

2 As with joyful steps they sped
   To that lowly manger-bed;
   There to bend the knee before
   Him whom heaven and earth adore;
   So may we with willing feet
   Ever seek Thy mercy-seat.

3 As they offered gifts most rare
   At that manger rude and bare;
   So may we with holy joy,
   Pure and free from sin's alloy,
   All our costliest treasures bring,
   Christ! to Thee our heavenly King.

4 Holy Jesus! every day
   Keep us in the narrow way;
   And when earthly things are past,
   Bring our ransomed souls at last,
   Where they need no star to guide,
   Where no clouds Thy glory hide.

5 In the heavenly country bright
   Need they no created light;
   Thou its Light, its Joy, its Crown,
   Thou its Sun which goes not down;
   There for ever may we sing
   Alleluias to our King.
                Wm. Chatterton Dix, 1860.

"*We have seen His star in the East.*"

63   L. M. 8 *lines.*

WELCOME! that star in Judah's sky,
   That voice o'er Bethlehem's palmy glen,

The lamp far sages hailed on high,
  The tones that thrilled the shepherd-men:
Glory to God in loftiest heaven—
  Thus angels smote the echoing chord—
Glad tidings unto man forgiven;
  Peace from the presence of the Lord.

2 The shepherds sought that birth divine;
  The wise-men traced their guided way;
There, by strange light and mystic sign,
  The God they came to worship lay:
A human Babe in beauty smiled,
  Where lowing oxen round Him trod;
A Virgin clasped her awful Child,
  Pure Offspring of the Breath of God.

3 Those voices from on high are mute;
  The star the wise-men saw is dim;
But hope still guides the wand'rer's foot,
  And faith renews the angel-hymn:
Glory to God in loftiest heaven—
  Touch with glad hand the ancient chord—
Good tidings unto man forgiven:
  Peace from the presence of the Lord.
                                            R. S. Hawker.

64 *"The unsearchable riches of Christ."*
            7s & 4s.

THOU that art the Father's Word,
  Thou that art the Lamb of God,
Thou that art the Virgin's Son,
Thou that savest souls undone,
Sacred Sacrifice for sin,
Fount of piety within,
    Hail, Lord Jesus.

2 Thou to whom Thine angels raise
Choiring songs of sweetest praise,
Thou that art the flower and fruit,
Virgin-born from Jesse's root,
Shedding holy peace abroad,
Perfect Man and perfect God,
    Hail, Lord Jesus.

3 Thou that art the Door of heaven,
Living Bread in mercy given,
Brightness of the Father's face,
Everlasting Prince of Peace,

THE EPIPHANY.

  Precious Pearl beyond all price,
  Brightest Star in all the skies,
   Hail, Lord Jesus.

4 King and Spouse of holy hearts,
 Fount of love that ne'er departs,
 Sweetest Life, and brightest Day,
 Truest Truth, and surest Way
 Leading onward to the blest
 Sabbath of eternal rest,
  Hail, Lord Jesus.
Henry Alford, 1832.

"All the ends of the earth shall see the salvation of our God."

65   L. M.

JESUS shall reign where'er the sun
 Does his successive journeys run;
 His kingdom stretch from shore to shore,
Till moons shall wax and wane no more.

2 For Him shall endless prayer be made,
 And endless praises crown His head;
 His name like sweet perfume shall rise
 With every morning sacrifice.

3 People and realms of every tongue
 Dwell on His love with sweetest song;
 And infant voices shall proclaim
 Their early blessings on His name.

4 Blessings abound where'er He reigns;
 The joyful pris'ner bursts his chains;
 The weary find eternal rest,
 And all the sons of want are blest.

5 Where He displays His healing power,
 Death and the curse are known no more;
 In Him the tribes of Adam boast
 More blessings than their father lost.

6 Let every creature rise and bring
 Peculiar honors to our King:
 Angels descend with songs again,
 And earth repeat the loud Amen!
Isaac Watts, 1719.

THE EPIPHANY.

"I am the bright and morning star."

66 7s, 6 *lines.*

CHRIST, whose glory fills the skies,
   Christ, the true, the only Light;
Sun of righteousness, arise,
   Triumph o'er the shades of night:
Day-spring from on high, draw near;
Day-star in our hearts appear.

2 Dark and cheerless is the morn,
   Unaccompanied by Thee;
Joyless is the day's return,
   Till Thy mercy's beams we see:
Lord, Thy inward light impart,
Cheering each benighted heart.

3 Visit every soul of Thine,
   Pierce the gloom of sin and grief;
Fill with radiancy divine,
   Scatter all our unbelief:
More and more Thyself display,
Shining to the perfect day.
                     Charles Wesley, 1740.

"By the mystery of Thy holy incarnation: by Thy holy nativity and circumcision: good Lord deliver us."

67 7s, 8 *lines.*

BY the Angel's word of love,
   That announced Thee from above;
By Thine Infant Form so fair
Trembling on the midnight air;
   Babe of Bethlehem, hear our cry:
      Thou wert helpless once as we;
   Hear the loving litany
      We Thy children sing to Thee.

2 By Thy poor and lowly lot;
By the manger in the grot;
By Thy tender feet and hands
Folded fast in swaddling bands;
   Babe of Bethlehem, hear our cry: &c.

3 By the Name which Thou didst take,
Suffering sorely for our sake;
Name of grace and majesty,
Name adored on bended knee;
   Word Incarnate, hear our cry: &c.

4 By the joy of Simeon blest,
   When he clasped Thee to his breast;
   By the widow'd Anna's song,
   Poured amid the wondering throng;
      Word Incarnate, hear our cry: &c.

5 By the worship shepherds paid;
   By the gifts that sages made,
   Gold and myrrh and incense sweet,
   Laid in homage at Thy feet;
      Word Incarnate, hear our cry: &c.

6 By Thine angel-bidden flight
   Into Egypt in the night;
   By Thy home at Herod's death
   In despisèd Nazareth;
      Word Incarnate, hear our cry: &c.
                           Frederick W. Faber.

FIRST SUNDAY AFTER THE EPIPHANY.

"They found Him in the temple, sitting in the midst of the doctors."

68 S. M.

WITHIN the Father's house
   The Son hath found His home;
And to His temple suddenly
   The Lord of Life hath come.

2 The doctors of the law
   Gaze on the wondrous Child,
And marvel at His gracious words
   Of wisdom undefiled.

3 Yet not to them is given
   The mighty truth to know,
To lift the fleshly veil which hides
   Incarnate God below.

4 The secret of the Lord
   Escapes each human eye,
And faithful pondering hearts await
   The full Epiphany.

5 Lord, visit Thou our souls,
   And teach us by Thy grace
Each dim revealing of Thyself
   With loving awe to trace;

6 Till from our darkened sight
      The cloud shall pass away,
    And on the cleansèd soul shall burst
      The everlasting day.
                          James R. Woodford.

"I am the root and the offspring of David."

69   C. M.

HOSANNA to the royal Son
    Of David's ancient line!
His natures two, His person one,
    Mysterious and divine.

  2 The root of David, here we find,
      And offspring is the same;
    Eternity and time are joined
      In our Immanuel's name.

  3 Blest He that comes to wretched men,
      With peaceful news from heaven;
    Hosannas of the highest strain,
      To Christ the Lord be given!

  4 Let mortals ne'er refuse to take
      The hosanna on their tongues,
    Lest rocks and stones should rise, and break
      Their silence into songs.
                              Isaac Watts.

"The Lord loveth the gates of Zion more than all the dwellings of Jacob."

70   L. M.

GOD in His earthly temples lays
    Foundations for His heavenly praise:
He likes the tents of Jacob well;
But still in Zion loves to dwell.

  2 His mercy visits every house,
    That pays its night and morning vows;
    But makes a more delightful stay,
    Where churches meet to praise and pray.

  3 What glories were described of old!
    What wonders are of Zion told!
    Thou city of our God below!
    Thy fame shall Tyre and Egypt know.

4 Egypt and Tyre, and Greek and Jew,
　Shall there begin their lives anew;
　Angels and men shall join to sing
　The hill where living waters spring.

5 When God makes up His last account
　Of natives in His holy mount,
　'Twill be an honor to appear
　As one new-born and nourished there.
　　　　　　　　　　Isaac Watts, 1719.

"Bestow upon Thy people plenteously the aid of Thy heavenly grace."

71 S. M.

O JESUS, God and Man,
　On this Thy holy day,
To Thee for precious gifts of grace
　Thy ransomed people pray.

2 We pray for childlike hearts,
　　For gentle, holy love,
　For strength to do Thy will below,
　　As angels do above.

3 We pray for simple faith,
　　For hope that never faints,
　For true communion evermore
　　With all Thy blessèd saints.

4 On friends around us here
　　O let Thy blessing fall;
　We pray for grace to love them well,
　　But Thee beyond them all.

5 O joy to live for Thee!
　　O joy in Thee to die!
　O very joy of joys to see
　　Thy Face eternally.
　　　　　　　　Henry W. Baker, 1852.

"No man cometh unto the Father but by Me."

72 C. M.

THOU art the way; to Thee alone
　From sin and death we flee;
And he who would the Father seek,
　Must seek Him, Lord, by Thee.

2 Thou art the Truth; Thy word alone
 True wisdom can impart;
Thou only canst inform the mind
 And purify the heart.

3 Thou art the Life; the rending tomb
 Proclaims Thy conquering arm;
And those who put their trust in Thee
 Nor death nor hell shall harm.

4 Thou art the Way, the Truth, the Life;
 Grant us that Way to know;
That Truth to keep, that Life to win,
 Whose joys eternal flow.

George W. Doane.

SECOND SUNDAY AFTER THE EPIPHANY.

"This beginning of miracles did Jesus in Cana of Galilee, and manifested forth His glory."

73   S. M.

ALL praise to Thee, O Lord
 Who by Thy mighty power
Didst manifest Thy glory forth
 In Cana's marriage hour.

2 Thou speakest: it is done:
 Obedient to Thy word,
The water redd'ning into wine
 Proclaims the present Lord.

3 Blest were the eyes which saw
 That wondrous mystery,
The great beginning of Thy works,
 That kindled faith in Thee.

4 And blessèd they who know
 Thine unseen Presence true,
When in the Kingdom of Thy grace
 Thou makest all things new.

5 For by Thy loving hand
 Thy people still are fed;
Thou art the Cup of blessing, Lord,
 And Thou the heavenly Bread.

6 Oh, may that grace be ours,
   In Thee for aye to live,
And drink of those refreshing streams
   Which Thou alone canst give.

7 So, led from strength to strength,
   Grant us, O Lord, to see
The marriage Supper of the Lamb,
   Thy great Epiphany.

Hyde W. Beadon.

"Who hast called us out of darkness into marvelous light."

74   L. M. 8 *lines.*

THY glory Thou didst manifest,
   O Christ, by miracle divine,
When, at Thy word, for ev'ry guest
   The water sparkled into wine;
And *now*, in all the sons of men
   Who feel Thy Spirit's quick'ning breath,
That miracle is wrought again,
   As life is kindled out of death.

2 What festal raptures fill our hearts
   When heaven and earth are married there!
What hope, what love, the Lord imparts!
   What tenderness and strength of prayer!
For then *within*, His glory glows;
   And gifts and graces all divine
Again that miracle disclose
   Of water glorified in wine.

3 O Christ, unfold Thy quick'ning might
   From day to day, that all may see
Within each Saint, still beaming bright,
   Thy glorious Epiphany:
And find that best of wine at last,
   That sweetest gift of grace outpour'd,
Richer than Cana's humble feast,
   The marriage Supper of the Lord.

E. E. Higbee.

" Let the children of Zion be joyful in their King."

75   C. M.

O JESUS, King most wonderful,
   Thou Conqueror renowned;
Spirit of grace ineffable,
   In whom all joys are found!

2 When once Thou visitest the heart,
  Then truth begins to shine;
  Then earthly vanities depart;
  Then wakens love divine.

3 O Jesus, Light of all below!
  Thou Fount of living fire,
  Surpassing all the joys we know
  And all we can desire.

4 May every heart confess Thy name,
  And ever Thee adore;
  And seeking Thee, itself inflame
  To seek Thee more and more.

5 Thee may our tongues forever bless;
  Thee may we love alone;
  And ever in our lives express
  The image of Thine Own.

Bernard of Clairvaux.
Translated by Edward Caswall.

"*He that abideth in Me, and I in him, the same bringeth forth much fruit.*"

76 C. M.

ABIDE among us with Thy grace,
  Lord Jesus evermore;
Nor let us e'er to sin give place,
  Nor grieve Him we adore.

2 Abide among us with Thy word,
  Redeemer whom we love:
  Thy help and mercy here afford,
  And life with Thee above.

3 Abide among us with Thy ray,
  O Light that lighten'st all;
  And let Thy truth preserve our way,
  Nor suffer us to fall.

4 Abide with us to bless us still,
  O bounteous Lord of peace;
  With grace and power our souls fulfill,
  Our faith and love increase.

5 Abide among us as our Shield,
  O Captain of Thy host;
  That to the world we may not yield,
  Nor e'er forsake our post.

6 Abide with us in faithful love,
   Our God and Saviour be!
Thy help at need, oh! let us prove,
   And keep us true to Thee.
                       J. Stegmann.
         Translated by Catherine Winkworth.

"*Jesus of Nazareth, a man approved of God among you by miracles, and wonders, and signs.*"

77   L. M.

THROUGH Israel's coasts, in times of old,
   When Thou didst dwell with men below,
By signs and wonders manifold
   Thou didst, O Lord, Thy glory show.

2 But not alone Thy mighty power
   Shone forth from every wondrous sign:
Day unto day, and hour to hour,
   Spoke forth Thy love and grace divine.

3 And now Thou reignest, Lord, above,
   We none the less Thy wonders trace:
Unwearied are Thy calls of love,
   Unspent Thy miracles of grace.

4 Thou who didst make the water wine,
   Our earthly with Thy heavenly fill:
Our scant obedience change to Thine,
   Our passions to Thy blessed will.
                          Henry Alford.

THIRD SUNDAY AFTER THE EPIPHANY.

"*Is there no balm in Gilead; is there no physician there?*"

78   C. M.

DOWN from the mountain Jesus came,
   And stretching forth his hand,
"Be clean," he said: the Leper then
   Was cleansed at His command.

2 Our nature was defiled by sin,
   But God from heaven came down;
Stretched forth His hand, our nature touched,
   And joined it to His own.

5*

3 O God, made manifest in flesh,
   We render thanks to Thee;
 O great Physician, Thou hast cleansed
   A world from leprosy.

4 The Gentile Captain comes in faith;
   Thou blessest his appeal;
 Far off as Man, but near as God,
   Thou dost his servant heal.

5 Fever and plague serve in Thy camp,
   They are Thy soldiers, Lord,
 And when to Health Thou sayest, "Come,"
   It cometh at Thy word.

6 Stretch forth Thy hand, and heal us, Lord,
   In body and in soul;
 From sickness and from taint of sin
   Cleanse us, and make us whole.

C. Wordsworth.

"*If Thou wilt, Thou canst make me clean.*"

79   10s.

O LORD of health and life, what tongue can tell
  How at Thy word were loosed the bands of hell;
How Thy pure touch removed the leprous stain,
And the polluted flesh grew clean again?

2 O! wash our hearts, restore the contrite soul,
 Stretch forth Thy healing hand, and make us whole;
 O! bend our stubborn knees to kneel to Thee;
 Speak but the word, and we once more are free.

3 Yea, Lord, we claim the promise of Thy love,
 Thy love, which can all guilt, all pain remove;
 Nigh to our souls Thy great salvation bring,
 Then sickness hath no pang, and death no sting.

4 We hail this pledge in all Thy deeds of grace;
 As once disease and sorrow fled Thy face,
 So, when that face again unveiled we see,
 Sickness and tears and death no more shall be.

5 Then grant us strength to pray "Thy kingdom come,"
 When we shall know Thee in Thy Father's home,
 And at Thy great Epiphany adore
 The co-eternal Godhead evermore.

Greville Phillimore.

"He that believeth in Me, though he were dead, yet shall he live."

80 C. M.

O FOR a thousand tongues to sing
   My great Redeemer's praise !
The glories of my God and King,
   The triumphs of His grace !

2 My gracious Master, and my God,
   Assist me to proclaim,
To spread through all the earth abroad
   The honors of Thy Name.

3 Jesus ! the Name that charms our fears,
   That bids our sorrows cease ;
'Tis music in the sinner's ears,
   'Tis life, and health, and peace.

4 He breaks the power of cancelled sin,
   He sets the prisoner free ;
His blood can make the foulest clean,
   His blood availed for me.

5 He speaks,—and listening to His voice,
   New life the dead receive ;
The mournful, broken hearts rejoice ;
   The humble poor believe.

6 Look unto Him, ye nations ; own
   Your God, ye fallen race :
Look, and be saved through faith alone,
   Be justified by grace.

Charles Wesley.

" The Lord is my rock, and my fortress, and my deliverer."

81 L. M. 6 *lines.*

THOU hidden Source of calm repose !
   Thou all-sufficient Love divine !
My help and refuge from my foes,
   Secure I am, for Thou art mine.
Thou art my fortress, strength, and tower,
My trust and portion evermore.

2 Jesus, my All in all Thou art,
   My rest in toil, my ease in pain ;
The medicine of my broken heart ;
   In storms my peace ; in loss, my gain ;
My strength beneath the tyrant's frown ;
In shame my glory and my crown.

 3 In want, my plentiful supply ;
  In weakness, my almighty power ;
  In bonds, my perfect liberty ;
   My refuge in temptation's hour ;
   My comfort 'midst all grief and thrall ;
   My life in death, my All in all.

Charles Wesley.

" Look mercifully upon our weakness, and stretch forth the right hand of Thy majesty for our protection and help."

82   L. M. 6 *lines.*

FORTH from the dark and stormy sky,
 Lord ! to Thy altar's shade we fly ;
Forth from the world, its hope and fear,
Saviour ! we seek Thy shelter here :
Weary and weak, Thy grace we pray ;
Turn not, O Lord ! Thy guests away.

 2 Long have we roamed in want and pain ;
 Long have we sought Thy rest in vain ;
 Wildered in doubt, in darkness lost,
 Long have our souls been tempest-tost :
 Low at Thy feet our sins we lay,
 Turn not, O Lord ! Thy guests away.

Reginald Heber.

"I will also give Thee for a light to the Gentiles, that Thou mayest be my salvation unto the end of the earth."

83   C. M.

SALVATION ! O the joyful sound !
 'Tis pleasure to our ears ;
A sov'reign balm for every wound,
 A cordial for our fears.

 2 Buried in sorrow and in sin,
  At hell's dark door we lay ;
 But we arise by grace divine,
  To see a heavenly day.

 3 Salvation ! let the echo fly
  The spacious earth around,
 While all the armies of the sky
  Conspire to raise the sound.

Isaac Watts, 1707.

FOURTH SUNDAY AFTER THE EPIPHANY.

"Then he arose and rebuked the wind and the sea : and there was a great calm."

84 S. M.

FIERCE raged the storm of wind,
 The surging waves ran high,
Failed Thy disciples' hearts with fear,
 Though Thou, their Lord, wast nigh.

2 But at the stern rebuke
 Of Thy Almighty word,
The wind was hushed, the billows ceased,
 And owned Thee God and Lord.

3 So, now, when depths of sin
 Our souls with terror fill,
Arise, and be our helper, Lord,
 And speak Thy "Peace, be still."

4 When death's dark sea we cross,
 Be with us in Thy power,
Nor let the water-floods prevail
 In that dread trial hour.

5 And, when amid the signs,
 Which speak Thine Advent near,
The roaring of the sea and waves
 Fills faithless hearts with fear;

6 May we all undismayed
 Thy raging tempest see,
Lift up our heads and hail with joy
 Thy great Epiphany.

7 All praise to Thee, of old
 By sign and wonder known;
All praise to Thee, to be revealed
 Upon the judgment throne.
 Hyde W. Beadon.

"Lord, save us: we perish."

85 8s, 8s, 8s, 3s.

FIERCE raged the tempest o'er the deep,
 Watch did Thine anxious servants keep,
But Thou wast wrapt in guileless sleep,
 Calm and still.

2 "Save, Lord, we perish,"—was their cry,
 "O save us in our agony!"
 Thy word above the storm rose high,
 "Peace, be still."

3 The wild winds hushed; the angry deep
 Sank, like a little child, to sleep;
 The sullen billows cease to leap
 At Thy will.

4 So, when our life is clouded o'er,
 And storm-winds drift us from the shore,
 Say (lest we sink to rise no more)
 "Peace, be still."

Godfrey Thring.

"*Why are ye fearful, O ye of little faith?*"

86   12s & 11s.

WHILE Thou, O my God, art my Help and Defender,
 No cares can o'erwhelm me, no terrors appall;
The wiles and the snares of this world will but render
 More lively my hope in my God and my All.

2 Yes; Thou art my Refuge in sorrow and danger;
 My Strength, when I suffer; my hope when I fall;
My comfort and joy in this land of the stranger;
 My Treasure, my Glory, my God and my All.

3 To Thee, dearest Lord, will I turn without ceasing;
 Though grief may oppress me, or sorrow befall;
And love Thee, till death, my blest spirit releasing,
 Secures to me Jesus, my God and my All.

4 And when Thou demandest the life Thou hast given,
 With joy will I answer Thy merciful call;
And quit Thee on earth, but to find Thee in heaven,
 My portion forever, my God and my All.

W. Young.

"*The powers that be are ordained of God.*"

87   C. M.

SHINE on our land, Jehovah, shine,
 With beams of heavenly grace!
Reveal Thy power through all our coasts,
 And show Thy smiling face.

2 Here fix Thy throne exalted high,
    And here our glory stand;
And like a wall of guardian fire
    Surround Thy favorite land.

3 When shall Thy name from shore to shore
    Sound all the earth abroad,
And distant nations know and love
    Their Saviour and their God?

4 Sing to the Lord, ye distant lands,
    Sing loud, with solemn voice;
Let thankful tongues exalt His praise,
    And thankful hearts rejoice.

5 He, the great Lord, the sov'reign Judge,
    That sits enthroned above,
Wisely commands the worlds He made
    In justice and in love.

6 Earth shall confess her Maker's hand,
    And yield a full increase;
Our God will crown His chosen land
    With fruitfulness and peace.

7 God, the Redeemer, scatters round
    His choicest favors here,
While the creation's utmost bound
    Shall see, adore, and fear.

Isaac Watts.

"Grant unto us grace to look beyond the things which are seen and temporal."

88
L. M.

'TIS by the faith of joys to come,
    We walk through deserts dark as night;
Till we arrive at heaven, our home,
    Faith is our guide, and faith our light.

2 The want of sight she well supplies;
    She makes the pearly gates appear;
Far into distant worlds she pries,
    And brings eternal glories near.

3 Cheerful we tread the desert through,
    While faith inspires a heavenly ray;
Though lions roar and tempests blow,
    And rocks and dangers fill the way.

4 So Abr'am, by divine command,
  Left his own house to walk with God;
His faith beheld the promised land,
  And fired his zeal along the road.

Isaac Watts, 1709.

FIFTH SUNDAY AFTER THE EPIPHANY.

"The kingdom of heaven is likened unto a man which sowed good seed in his field."

89 S. M.

NOT by Thy mighty Hand,
  Thy wondrous works alone,
But by the marvels of Thy word,
  Thy glory, Lord, is known.

2 Forth from the eternal gates,
  Thine everlasting home,
To sow the seed of truth below,
  Thou didst vouchsafe to come.

3 And still from age to age
  Thou, gracious Lord, hast been
The Bearer forth of goodly seed,
  The Sower still unseen.

4 And Thou wilt come again,
  And heaven beneath Thee bow,
To reap the harvest Thou hast sown,
  Sower and Reaper Thou.

5 Watch, Lord, Thy harvest-field
  With Thine unsleeping eye;
The children of the Kingdom keep
  To Thine Epiphany.

6 That when in Thy great day
  The tares shall severed be,
We may be gathered by Thy grace
  With all Thy saints to Thee.

J. R. Woodford.

"Keep Thy church and household continually in Thy true religion."

90 7s, 6 lines.

GOD of mercy, God of grace,
  Show the brightness of Thy face.

Shine upon us, Saviour, shine,
Fill Thy Church with light divine;
And Thy saving health extend
Unto earth's remotest end.

2 Let the people praise Thee, Lord!
Let Thy love on all be poured;
Let the nations shout and sing
Glory to their Saviour King;
At Thy feet their tribute pay,
And Thy holy will obey.

3 Let the people praise Thee, Lord!
Earth shall then her fruits afford;
God to man His blessings give,
Man to God devoted live;
All below, and all above,
One in joy, and light, and love.

H. F. Lyte.

"*Let the children of Zion be joyful in their King.*"

L. M.

SHOUT, for the blessed Jesus reigns,
　Thro' distant lands His triumphs spread,
And sinners, freed from endless pains,
　Own Him their Saviour and their Head.

2 He calls His chosen from afar,
　They all at Zion's gates arrive;
Those who were dead in sin before,
　By sov'reign grace are made alive.

3 Gentiles and Jews His laws obey,
　Nations remote their off'rings bring,
And unconstrain'd their homage pay
　To their exalted God and King.

4 O may His holy Church increase,
　His Word and Spirit still prevail,
While angels celebrate His praise,
　And saints His growing glories hail!

5 Loud hallelujahs to the Lamb,
　From all below, and all above!
In lofty songs exalt His name,—
　In songs as lasting as His love.

Benj. Beddome.

"*Forbearing one another, and forgiving one another.*"

92 L. M.

O LORD, how joyful 'tis to see
The brethren join in love to Thee:
On Thee alone their heart relies,
Their only strength Thy grace supplies.

2 How sweet, within Thy holy place,
With one accord to sing Thy grace,
Besieging Thine attentive ear
With all the force of fervent prayer.

3 O may we love the House of God,
Of peace and joy the blest abode;
O may no angry strife destroy
That sacred peace, that holy joy.

4 The world without may rage, but we
Will only cling more close to Thee,
With hearts to Thee more wholly given,
More weaned from earth, more fixed on heaven.

5 Lord, shower upon us from above
The sacred gift of mutual love;
Each other's wants may we supply,
And reign together in the sky.

Latin Hymn,
Trans. by J. Chandler.

"*And whatsoever ye do in word or deed, do all in the name of the Lord Jesus.*"

93 S. M.

TEACH me, my God and King,
Thy will in all to see;
And what I do in any thing,
To do it as for Thee:

2 To scorn the senses' sway,
While still to Thee I tend;
In all I do, be Thou the Way,
In all, be Thou the End.

3 All may of Thee partake;
Nothing so small can be,
But draws, when acted for Thy sake,
Greatness and worth from Thee.

4 If done beneath Thy laws,
  E'en servile labors shine :
  Hallowed is toil, if this the cause ;
  The meanest work, divine.
George Herbert.

SIXTH SUNDAY AFTER THE EPIPHANY.

" He bringeth them up into a high mountain, and was transfigured before them."

94 L. M.

O THOU, who once on Tabor's hill
  Didst shine before the favored three,
The souls which love Thee favor still
  Thy nearer glory, Lord, to see.

2 E'en now let faith's far-gazing eye
  The brightness of Thy Godhead scan,
And view Thee, throned in heaven on high,
  The almighty Lord, the Son of Man.

3 There Moses, and Elias there,
  With thousand thousand saints beside,
Thy glittering rays reflected wear,
  And spread through heaven Thy glories wide :

4 And while each knee amid the crowd
  Before Thy throne in worship bends,
They are like Tabor's saints, allowed
  To talk with Thee, their God, as friends.

5 Delightful converse ! It is good
  To see Thee thus at distance now,
To join in spirit those who stood
  In wondering love on Tabor's brow.

6 Earth drags us from the mount awhile ;
  But we ere long shall break the spell,
And gaze on Thine unclouded smile,
  And in Thine endless glory dwell.
Hymn. Christ.

"Lord, it is good for us to be here."

95 L. M. double.

O MASTER, it is good to be
  High on the mountain here with Thee :
Where stand revealed to mortal gaze
Those glorious saints of other days ;

Who once received on Horeb's height
The eternal laws of truth and right;
Or caught the still small whisper, higher
Than storm, than earthquake, or than fire.

2 O Master, it is good to be
With Thee, and with Thy faithful three:
Here, where the apostle's heart of rock
Is nerved against temptation's shock;
Here, where the son of thunder learns
The thought that breathes, and word that burns;
Here, where on eagle's wings we move
With him whose last best creed is love.

3 O Master, it is good to be
Entranced, enwrapt, alone with Thee;
And watch Thy glistering raiment glow,
Whiter than Hermon's whitest snow;
The human lineaments that shine
Irradiant with a light divine:
Till we too change from grace to grace,
Gazing on that transfigured Face.

4 O Master, it is good to be
Here on the holy Mount with Thee:
When darkling in the depths of night,
When dazzled with excess of light,
We bow before the heavenly Voice
That bids bewildered souls rejoice,
Though love wax cold, and faith be dim—
"This is My Son—O hear ye Him." *A. P. Stanley.*

"And the voice which came from heaven we heard when we were with Him in the holy mount."

96   10*s* & 4*s*.

UPON the solitary mountain's height,
   In radiant beauty, but with power concealed,
The Son of Man, unveiled to mortal sight,
   Once stands revealed.

2 Yet not alone—the witnesses are there,
   The deathless and the dead are at His side,
Their lips the end predestinate declare,
   Nor seek to hide!

3 But why this world from thy mysterious grave,
   Lawgiver of God's people, hast thou trod—
Why come thy steeds of fire o'er Jordan's wave,
   Prophet of God?

4 Do ye revisit earth to testify
   That Law and Voice Prophetic, shadows dim,
 Are swallowed up in Christ's last victory,
   Finished in Him?

5 Yet on the passing brightness of that hour
   The shadow of the cross still darkly fell,
 As if alone the hiding of His power
   Ye dared to tell.

6 Come, O my soul! in holy rapture hear
   Tabor and Hermon in His name rejoice,
 How good for us to be forever near,
   Listening His voice.

7 Lord, pour Thy Spirit all our souls to fill,
   Transfigured to the image of Thine own,
 Until we rest upon Thy holy hill,
   Before the Throne.
                       Edward A. Dayman, 1866.

"The love of God, which is in Christ Jesus our Lord."

97   8s & 7s, double.

LOVE divine, all loves excelling,
   Joy of heaven, to earth come down!
Fix in us Thy humble dwelling;
   All Thy faithful mercies crown:
Jesus! Thou art all compassion,
   Pure unbounded love Thou art;
Visit us, with Thy salvation;
   Enter every trembling heart.

2 Breathe, Oh! breathe Thy loving Spirit
   Into every troubled breast;
 Let us all in Thee inherit,
   Let us find the promised rest:
 Take away our power of sinning;
   Alpha and Omega be;
 End of faith, as its beginning!
   Set our hearts at liberty.

3 Come, almighty to deliver,
   Let us all Thy life receive;
 Suddenly return, and never,
   Never more Thy temples leave:
 Thee we would be always blessing,
   Serve Thee as Thy hosts above,
 Pray, and praise Thee without ceasing,
   Glory in Thy perfect love.

4 Finish then Thy new creation;
   Pure and sinless let us be;
 Let us see Thy great salvation,
   Perfectly restored in Thee.
 Changed from glory into glory,
   Till in heaven we take our place;
 Till we cast our crowns before Thee,
   Lost in wonder, love, and praise.
                          Charles Wesley, 1746.

"Behold what manner of love the Father hath bestowed upon us."

98 S. M.

BEHOLD! what wondrous grace
   The Father hath bestowed
 On sinners of a mortal race
   To call them sons of God!

2 'Tis no surprising thing,
   That we should be unknown;
 The Jewish world knew not their King,
   God's everlasting Son.

3 Nor doth it yet appear
   How great we must be made;
 But, when we see our Saviour here,
   We shall be like our Head.

4 A hope so much divine
   May trials well endure,
 May purge our souls from sense and sin,
   As Christ, the Lord, is pure.

5 If, in my Father's love,
   I share a filial part,
 Send down Thy Spirit like a dove,
   To rest upon my heart.

6 We would no longer lie
   Like slaves beneath the throne;
 My faith shall—"Abba, Father!"—cry
   And Thou the kindred own.
                          Isaac Watts, 1707.

"I heard a great voice of much people in heaven, saying, Alleluia."

99 8*s* & 7*s*, 6 *lines.*

ALLELUIA, song of sweetness,
   Voice of joy that cannot die,

SEPTUAGESIMA.

Alleluia is the anthem
  Ever dear to choirs on high;
In the house of God abiding,
  Thus they sing eternally.

2 Alleluia thou resoundest
  True Jerusalem and free;
Alleluia, joyful Mother,
  All thy children sing with thee:
But by Babylon's sad waters
  Mourning exiles now are we.

3 Alleluia cannot always
  Be our song while here below;
Alleluia our transgressions
  Make us for a while forego;
For the solemn time is coming
  When our tears for sin must flow.

4 Therefore in our hymns we pray Thee,
  Grant us, blessed Trinity,
At the last to keep Thine Easter
  In our home beyond the sky;
There to Thee forever singing
  Alleluia joyfully.

Adam St. Victor.
Trans. by J. M. Neale. Altered.

SEPTUAGESIMA.

"Why stand ye here all the day idle?"
L. M.

100

THE God of mercy warns us all
  From day to day, from year to year;
And each must hear His awful call,
  "No longer stand ye idle here."

2 Ye, whose young cheeks with health are bright,
  Whose hands are strong, whose hearts are clear,
Why will ye waste the morning light?
  Alas, why stand ye idle here?

3 And ye, whose scanty locks of gray
  Foretell your latest travail near,
How swiftly fades your closing day,
  And yet ye stand thus idle here.

 4 O Thou, in heaven and earth adored,
  Who makest erring souls Thy care,
  Now call us to Thy vineyard, Lord,
  And give us grace to serve Thee there.
Hymn. Christ.

"Know ye not, that they which run, run all, but one receiveth the prize?"

101
C. M.

AWAKE, my soul, stretch every nerve,
 And press with vigor on!
A heavenly race demands thy zeal,
 And an immortal crown.

2 A cloud of witnesses around
 Holds thee in full survey;
Forget the steps already trod,
 And onward urge thy way.

3 'Tis God's all-animating voice,
 That calls thee from on high;
Tis His own hand presents the prize
 To thine aspiring eye.

4 Then wake, my soul, stretch every nerve,
 And press with vigor on;
A heavenly race demands thy zeal,
 And an immortal crown.
Philip Doddridge, 1740.

"So run that ye may obtain."

102
8s & 7s.

NOW the Church's songs of gladness
 Change their key to heart and ear—
Now steals on with sober sadness
 The dim twilight of her year.

2 Late, her Saviour Lord's appearing
 Filled each heart and swelled each strain.
Now the solemn time is nearing
 When He passes into pain.

3 Late, tho' round a lowly manger,
 Angels sang and glory shone.
Now He passes into danger,
 In the wilderness alone.

4 Lord, our souls and bodies render
    Meet to watch, and kneel, and pray,
By Thy love, so true and tender,
    All thro' that long battle-day.

5 Grant us that instinctive yearning
    Which the Christian's soul doth move,
To be near Thee, ever learning
    The deep secrets of Thy love.

6 Keep us near Thee, in Thy fasting,
    In Thy peril and Thy pain;
That, our garland everlasting,
    Running so, we may obtain.
J. S. B. Monsell, 1857.

"*There is forgiveness with Thee, that Thou mayest be feared.*"

103   C. M.

HOW oft, alas! this wretched heart
    Has wandered from the Lord!
How oft my roving thoughts depart
    Forgetful of His word!

2 Yet sovereign mercy calls—"Return!"
    Dear Lord! and may I come?
My vile ingratitude I mourn;
    Oh! take the wanderer home.

3 And canst Thou—wilt Thou yet forgive,
    And bid my crimes remove?
And shall a pardoned rebel live
    To speak Thy wondrous love?

4 Almighty grace! Thy healing power,
    How glorious, how divine!
That can to life and bliss restore
    A heart so vile as mine!

5 Thy pard'ning love, so free, so sweet,
    Dear Saviour! I adore;
Oh! keep me at Thy sacred feet,
    And let me rove no more.
Anne Steele, 1760.

"*For when we were yet without strength, in due time Christ died for the ungodly.*"

104   C. M.

ALAS! and did my Saviour bleed?
    And did my Sovereign die?
Would He devote that sacred head
    For such a worm as I?

2 Was it for crimes that I had done
    He groaned upon the tree?
  Amazing pity! grace unknown!
    And love beyond degree!

3 Well might the sun in darkness hide,
    And shut his glories in,
  When God, the mighty Maker, died
    For man the creature's sin.

4 Thus might I hide my blushing face
    While His dear cross appears;
  Dissolve my heart in thankfulness,
    And melt mine eyes to tears.

5 But drops of grief can ne'er repay
    The debt of love I owe;
  Here, Lord, I give myself away;
    'Tis all that I can do.
                        Isaac Watts, 1707.

"*For ye have need of patience, that after ye have done the will of God, ye might receive the promise.*"

105   6s, 6s, 8s, 6s, 6s, 6s, 8s, 6s, 6s.

THE Church has waited long
    Her absent Lord to see;
  And still in loneliness she waits;—
    A friendless stranger she.
    Age after age has gone,
    Sun after sun has set,
  And still in weeds of widowhood
    She weeps a mourner yet;
      Come, then, Lord Jesus, come!

2 Saint after saint on earth
    Has lived, and loved, and died;
  And as they left us one by one,
    We laid them side by side;
    We laid them down to sleep,
    But not in hope forlorn;
  We laid them but to ripen there,
    Until the glorious morn;
      Come, then, Lord Jesus, come!

3 We long to hear Thy Voice,
    To see Thee face to face,
  To share Thy crown and glory there,
    As now we share Thy grace.

Should not the loving Bride
The absent Bridegroom mourn?
Should she not wear the weeds of grief
Until her Lord's return?
   Come, then, Lord Jesus, come!

4 The whole creation groans,
And waits to hear that Voice,
That shall restore her comeliness
And make her wastes rejoice.
Come, Lord, and wipe away
The curse, the sin, the stain,
And make this blighted world of ours
Thine own fair world again;
   Come, then, Lord Jesus, come!
               Horatius Bonar, 1856.

SEXAGESIMA.

" A sower went forth to sow his seed."
        L. M.

106

O THOU at whose divine command
  Good seed is sown in every land,
Thy Holy Ghost to us impart,
And for Thy Word prepare each heart.

2 Not among thorns of worldly thought,
Nor soon by passing plunderers caught,
Nor lacking depth the root to feed,
May we receive Thy Spirit's seed.

3 But may it, while Thy sowers toil,
Fall in a good and honest soil;
And springing up from firmest root,
With patience bear abundant fruit.
                  Hy. Alford, 1845.

" The seed is the word of God."
        C. M.

107

ALMIGHTY God, Thy word is cast
  Like seed into the ground;
Now let the dews of heaven descend,
  And righteous growth abound.

2 Let not the foe of Christ and man
    This holy seed remove;
  But give it root in every heart,
    To bring forth fruits of love.

3 Let not the world's deceitful cares
    The rising plant destroy;
  But let it yield an hundred fold
    Returns of peace and joy:

4 Nor let Thy Word, so kindly sent
    To raise us to Thy throne,
  Go back to Thee, and sadly tell
    That we reject Thy Son.

5 Oft as the precious seed is sown,
    Thy quickening grace bestow,
  That all, whose souls the truth receive,
    Its saving power may know.

Jno. Cawood, 1825, *altered.*

" Not unto us, O Lord, not unto us, but unto Thy name give glory."

108 7s, 6 *lines.*

NOT in any thing we do,
  Thought that's pure, or word that's true,
Saviour, would we put our trust,
Frail as vapor, vile as dust.
All that flatters we disown:
Righteousness is Thine alone.

2 Though we underwent for Thee
  Perils of the land and sea,—
  Though we cast our lives away,
  Dying for Thee day by day,
  Boast we never of our own:
  Grace and strength are Thine alone.

3 Native cumberers of the ground,
  All our fruit from Thee is found,
  Grafted in Thine olive, Lord,
  New-begotten by Thy word,
  All we have is Thine alone:
  Life and power are not our own.

4 And when Thy returning voice
  Calls Thy faithful to rejoice,

When the countless throng to Thee
Cast their crown of victory,
We will sing before the Throne,
"Thine the glory, not our own!"
Henry Alford, 1866.

" Look mercifully on our low estate, and cause Thy grace to triumph in our weakness."

109
8s, 7s, & 4s.

GUIDE me, O Thou great Jehovah,
  Pilgrim through this barren land;
I am weak, but Thou art mighty,
  Hold me with Thy powerful hand;
    Bread of heaven!
  Feed me now and evermore.

2 Open now the crystal fountain,
  Whence the healing streams do flow;
Let the fiery, cloudy pillar
  Lead me all my journey through;
    Strong Deliverer!
  Be Thou still my Strength and Shield.

3 When I tread the verge of Jordan,
  Bid my anxious fears subside;
Death of death, and hell's Destruction!
  Land me safe on Canaan's side;
    Songs of praises,
  I will ever give to Thee.
William Williams, 1774.

" By grace are ye saved, through faith; and that not of yourselves: it is the gift of God."

110
L. M.

I THIRST, Thou wounded Lamb of God,
To wash me in Thy cleansing blood,
To dwell within Thy wounds; then pain
Is sweet, and life or death is gain.

2 Take my poor heart, and let it be
Forever closed to all but Thee!
Seal Thou my breast, and let me wear
That pledge of love forever there.

3 How blest are they who still abide
Close shelter'd in Thy bleeding side!
Who thence their life and strength derive,
And by Thee move, and in Thee live.

4 What are our works but sin and death,
   Till Thou Thy quick'ning Spirit breathe?
   Thou giv'st the power, the grace to move:
   Oh, wondrous grace! Oh, boundless love!
                                        J. Wesley.

"Thou art my hiding-place."

111   S. M.

TO Christ, the Prince of Peace,
   And Son of God, we sing;
To Him who saved us by His love,
   Let holy anthems ring.

2 Deep in His heart for us
   The wound of love He bore;
That love, which still He kindles in
   The hearts that Him adore.

3 O Jesus! Victim blest!
   What else but love divine,
Could Thee constrain to open thus
   That sacred heart of Thine?

4 O Fount of endless life!
   O Spring of water clear!
O Flame celestial, cleansing all
   Who unto Thee draw near!

5 Hide me in Thy dear heart,
   For thither do I fly;
There seek Thy grace through life, in death
   Thine immortality.
                                        Latin Hymn.
                                Translated by E. Caswall.

"For I am not ashamed of the gospel of Christ."

112   L. M.

JESUS! and shall it ever be,
   A mortal man ashamed of Thee?
   Ashamed of Thee! whom angels praise,
Whose glories shine through endless days?

2 Ashamed of Jesus! sooner far
   Let evening blush to own a star;
   He sheds the beams of light divine,
   O'er this benighted soul of mine.

3 Ashamed of Jesus! just as soon
   Let midnight be ashamed of noon:
   'Tis midnight with my soul, till He,
   Bright Morning-Star, bid darkness flee.

4 Ashamed of Jesus! that dear Friend,
  On whom my hopes of heaven depend!
  No; when I blush, be this my shame,
  That I no more revere His name.

5 Ashamed of Jesus! yes, I may,
  When I've no guilt to wash away,
  No tear to wipe, no good to crave,
  No fears to quell, no soul to save.

6 Till then—nor is my boasting vain—
  Till then, I boast a Saviour slain:
  And, Oh! may this my glory be,
  That Christ is not ashamed of me.
                    Joseph Grigg, 1774.
                    Altered by Benj. Francis.

QUINQUAGESIMA.

"*Send Thy Holy Ghost, and pour into our hearts that most excellent gift of charity.*"

113   8s, 5s, 8s, 5s.

THOU, who on that wondrous journey
    Sett'st Thy face to die,
By Thy holy meek example
    Teach us Charity!

2 Thou, who that dread cup of suffering
    Didst not put from Thee,
  O most loving of the loving,
    Give us Charity!

3 Thou, who reignest, bright in glory,
    On God's throne on high,
  O, that we may share Thy triumph,
    Grant us Charity!

4 Send us Faith, that trusts Thy promise,
    Hope, with upward eye,
  But more blest than both, and greater,
    Send us Charity!   *Henry Alford*, 1866.

"*Greater love hath no man than this, that a man lay down his life for his friends.*"

114   L. M.

JESUS, Thy boundless love to me
  No thought can reach, no tongue declare;
  Unite my thankful heart to Thee,
  And reign without a rival there.

2 Thy love, how cheering is its ray!
   All pain before its presence flies:
   Care, anguish, sorrow, melt away,
   Where'er its healing beams arise.

3 O, let Thy love my soul inflame,
   And to Thy service sweetly bind;
   Transfuse it through my inmost frame,
   And mould me wholly to Thy mind.

4 Thy love, in sufferings, be my peace;
   Thy love, in weakness, make me strong;
   And when the storms of life shall cease,
   Thy love shall be, in heaven, my song.

Paul Gerhardt, 1659.
Trans. by John Wesley, 1739. Altered.

"Charity, the very bond of perfectness, and of all virtues."

115 8s & 7s.

LORD of life, whose words have taught us
   How to serve Thee and obey:
Lord of love, whose deeds have brought us
   Wondering at Thy feet to pray:

2 Fill our hearts with ample measure
   Of the Christian graces three;
   Most of all with Thy dear treasure,
   Never-failing charity:

3 Charity that ever bindeth
   Mortal men with cords of love;
   Charity that still remindeth
   Earthly souls of heaven above:

4 Charity, the Spirit's token
   Sinners have received of Thee:
   He whom Jesus loved hath spoken
   "God Himself is Charity."

Hymn. Christ.

"And now abideth faith, hope, charity, these three: but the greatest of these is charity."

116 S. M.

LORD of the hearts of men!
   Thou hast vouchsafed to bless,
From age to age, Thy chosen saints
   With fruits of holiness.

2 Here faith, and hope, and love
  Reign in sweet bond allied;
 There, when this little day is o'er,
  Shall love alone abide.

3 O love, O truth, O light!
  Light never to decay!
 O rest from thousand labors past!
  O endless Sabbath-day!

4 Here amid cares and tears,
  Bearing the seed we come;
 There with rejoicing hearts we bring
  Our harvest-burdens home.

5 Give, mighty Lord divine,
  The fruits Thyself dost love;
 Soon shalt Thou from Thy judgment seat,
  Crown Thine own gifts above.
                    Latin Hymn.
              Trans. Jas. R. Woodford.

"For with Thee is the fountain of life."

117   8s & 7s, double.

JESUS, Refuge of the weary,
  Object of the spirit's love,
 Fountain in life's desert dreary,
  Saviour from the world above:
 O how oft Thine eyes, offended,
  Gaze upon the sinner's fall!
 Yet upon the cross extended,
  Thou didst bear the pain of all.

2 Do we pass that cross unheeding,
   Breathing no repentant vow,
  Though we see Thee wounded, bleeding,
   See Thy thorn-encircled brow!
  Yet Thy sinless death hast brought us
   Life eternal, peace and rest;
  Only what Thy grace has taught us
   Calms the sinner's stormy breast.

3 Jesus, may our hearts be burning
   With more fervent love for Thee!
  May our eyes be ever turning
   To Thy cross of agony;

ASH WEDNESDAY.

Till in glory, parted never
From the blessed Saviour's side,
Graven in our hearts for ever,
Dwell the cross, the Crucified.

Jerome Savonarola, 1498.
Trans. Anon.

"All mercy will I keep for him forevermore, and my covenant shall stand fast with him."

118 8s & 7s.

FAR beyond all comprehension
    Is Jehovah's cov'nant love:
Who can fathom its dimension,
    Or its unknown limits prove?

2 Ere the earth upon its basis,
    By creating power was built,
His designs were wise and gracious,
    For removing human guilt.

3 He displayed His grand intention,
    On the mount of Calvary;
When He died for our redemption,
    Lifted high upon the tree.

4 O! how sweet to view the flowing
    Of His soul-redeeming blood,
With divine assurance knowing
    That it made my peace with God!

5 Freely Thou wilt bring to heaven
    All Thy chosen ransomed race,
Who to Thee, their Head were given,
    In the covenant of grace.

ASH WEDNESDAY.

"Jesus, Master, have mercy upon us."

119 7s, double.

SAVIOUR, when in dust to Thee,
    Low we bend th' adoring knee;
When, repentant, to the skies,
Scarce we lift our weeping eyes;
Oh! by all Thy pains and woe,
Suffered once for man below,
Bending from Thy throne on high,
Hear our solemn Litany!

2 By Thy helpless infant years;
By Thy life of want and tears;
By Thy days of sore distress,
In the savage wilderness;
By the dread, mysterious hour
Of th' insulting Tempter's power,
Turn, O turn, a favoring eye;
Hear our solemn Litany.

3 By the sacred griefs that wept
O'er the grave where Lazarus slept;
By the boding tears that flowed
Over Salem's loved abode;
By the anguished eye that told
Treach'ry lurk'd within the fold:
From Thy seat above the sky
Hear our solemn Litany.

4 By Thine hour of dire despair;
By Thine agony of prayer;
By the cross, the nail, the thorn,
Piercing spear and torturing scorn;
By the gloom that veiled the skies
O'er the dreadful sacrifice:
Listen to our humble cry,
Hear our solemn Litany.

5 By Thy deep expiring groan;
By the sad sepulchral stone;
By the vault whose dark abode
Held in vain the rising God!
Oh! from earth to heaven restor'd,
Mighty, re-ascended Lord:
Listen, listen to the cry
Of our solemn Litany. *Robert Grant*, 1815.

"Turn ye even to me with all your hearts, and with fasting, and with weeping, and with mourning."

120 C. M.

THE solemn season calls us now
  A holy fast to keep;
To crowd within the temple walls,
  Lament, and pray, and weep.

2 And yet, O God, no plaintive sobs
  From Thee can pardon win,
Unless the heart be moved with grief,
  And penitent for sin.

3 With Thee avail not smitten breast,
   Sad face, and garments rent,
Unless the contrite soul be sad,
   And all its guilt lament.

4 With tears that speak a mourning heart,
   We Thee entreat, O God,
From us Thine anger turn away,
   And stay th' avenging rod.

5 Thou art a righteous Judge; O deign
   To spare the bruisèd reed:
We pray for time to turn again,
   For grace to turn indeed.

6 Blest Trinity in Unity,
   Vouchsafe us, in Thy love,
To gather from these fasts below
   Immortal fruit above.   *Latin Hymn.*
               Translated by J. Chandler, altered.

"*Turn unto the Lord, your God: for He is gracious and merciful.*"

121   L. M.

THOU loving Saviour of mankind,
   Before Thy throne we pray and weep;
O strengthen us, with grace divine,
   This sacred fast aright to keep.

2 Searcher of hearts! Thou dost our ills
   Discern and all our weakness know:
Again to Thee in tears we turn;
   Again to us Thy mercy show.

3 Much have we sinn'd, but we confess
   Our guilt and all our faults deplore:
O, for the praise of Thy great name,
   These fainting souls to health restore!

4 And grant us, while by fasts we strive
   This mortal body to control,
To fast from all the food of sin,
   And so to purify the soul.   *Gregory the Great.*
               Translated by E. Caswall, altered.

"*My sin is ever before me.*"

122   7s, 6s, double.

MY sins, my sins, my Saviour!
   They take such hold on me,
I am not able to look up,
   Save only, Christ, to Thee:

In Thee is all forgiveness,
 In Thee abundant grace,
My shadow and my sunshine
 The brightness of Thy face.

2 My sins, my sins, my Saviour!
 How sad on Thee they fall!
Seen through Thy gentle patience,
 I tenfold feel them all.
I know they are forgiven;
 But still, their pain to me
Is all the grief and anguish
 They laid, my Lord, on Thee.

3 My sins, my sins, my Saviour!
 Their guilt I never knew,
Till, with Thee, in the desert
 I near Thy passion drew,
Till, with Thee, in the garden
 I heard Thy pleading prayer,
And saw the sweat-drops bloody
 That told Thy sorrow there.

4 Therefore my songs, my Saviour!
 E'en in this time of woe,
Shall tell of all Thy goodness
 To suffering man below,
Thy goodness and Thy favor,
 Whose presence from above,
Rejoice those hearts, my Saviour,
 That live in Thee, and love.
Jno. S. B. Monsell, 1863.

"For we have not a High Priest, which cannot be touched with a feeling of our infirmities."

123 11s, 10s, 11s, 10s, 10s, 10s.

THOU knowest, Lord, the weariness and sorrow
 Of the sad heart that comes to Thee for rest;
Cares of to-day, and burdens for to-morrow,
 Blessings implored, and sins to be confessed;
We come before Thee at Thy gracious word,
And lay them at Thy feet: Thou knowest, Lord.

2 Thou knowest all the past: how long and blindly
 On the dark mountains the lost wand'rer strayed;
How the good Shepherd followed, and how kindly
 He bore it home, upon His shoulders laid;

And healed the bleeding wounds, and soothed the pain,
And brought back life, and hope, and strength again.

3 Thou knowest, not alone as God, all-knowing;
  As Man, our mortal weakness Thou hast proved:
On earth, with purest sympathies o'erflowing,
  O Saviour, Thou hast wept, and Thou hast loved;
And love and sorrow still to Thee may come,
And find a hiding-place, a rest, a home.

4 Therefore we come, Thy gentle call obeying,
  And lay our sins and sorrows at Thy feet;
On everlasting strength our weakness staying,
  Clothed in Thy robe of righteousness complete:
Then rising and refreshed, we leave Thy throne,
Then follow on to know as we are known.
                                   Jane Borthwick.

FIRST SUNDAY IN LENT.

"Then was Jesus led up of the Spirit into the wilderness to be tempted of the Devil."

124   C. M.

JESUS our Lord, who tempted wast
  In all points like as we,
And didst achieve in that dread fight
  Undoubted victory;

2 Behold Thy spouse, a season laid
    Beneath the Tempter's power,
  Led up into the wilderness
    To wait her trying hour.

3 May she her forces ready make,
    And gird her weapons fast,
  And in the armor of her God
    Stand fearless to the last.

4 Teach us, when angered at our lot
    Our faithless souls repine,
  Man liveth not by bread alone,
    But by each word divine.

5 When we would rush on danger's point,
    And dare the lifted sword,
  Speak in our ears the warning voice,
    "Thou shalt not tempt the Lord."

6 And when, deceived by pride or power,
    Earth's idols we espouse,
  Teach us that Thou art God alone,
    And on us are Thy vows.

7 Thus more than conq'rors we shall be
    In this our deadly strife,
  Till angels come and minister
    To the glad heirs of life.
              Henry Alford, 1845.

"And when He had fasted forty days and forty nights."

125   7s.

FORTY days and forty nights
    Thou wast fasting in the wild:
Forty days and forty nights
    Tempted and yet undefiled.

2 Sunbeams scorching all the day:
    Chilly dew-drops nightly shed:
  Prowling beasts about Thy way,
    Stones Thy pillow, earth Thy bed.

3 Shall we not Thy sorrow share,
    And from earthly joys abstain,
  Fasting with unceasing prayer,
    Glad with Thee to suffer pain?

4 And if Satan vexing sore
    Flesh or spirit should assail,
  Thou, his Vanquisher before,
    Grant we may not faint nor fail.

5 So shall we have peace divine,
    Holier gladness ours shall be:
  Round us too shall angels shine
    Such as ministered to Thee.
              Geo. H. Smyttan, altered.

"If we confess our sins, He is faithful and just to forgive us our sins."

126   L. M.

SHOW pity, Lord, O Lord, forgive,
  Let a repenting rebel live,
Are not Thy mercies large and free?
May not a sinner trust in Thee?

2 My crimes are great, but ne'er surpass
   The power and glory of Thy grace;
   Great God, Thy nature hath no bound,
   So let Thy pard'ning love be found.

3 O wash my soul from every sin,
   And make my guilty conscience clean;
   Here on my heart the burden lies,
   And past offences pain mine eyes.

4 My lips with shame my sins confess
   Against Thy law, against Thy grace;
   Lord, should Thy judgments grow severe,
   I am condemned, but Thou art clear.

5 Yet save a trembling sinner, Lord!
   Whose hope, still hov'ring round Thy word,
   Would light on some sweet promise there,
   Some sure support against despair.   *Isaac Watts*, 1719.

"Lord, remember me."

127   C. M.

O THOU from whom all goodness flows,
    I lift my heart to Thee;
In all my sorrows, conflicts, woes,
    O Lord, remember me.

2 When with a broken, contrite heart,
    I lift mine eyes to Thee;
  Thy name proclaim, Thyself impart,
    In love remember me.

3 In sore temptations, when no way
    To shun the ill I see,
  My strength proportion to my day,
    And then remember me.

4 And when I tread the vale of death
    And bow at Thy decree,
  Then, Saviour, with my latest breath,
    I'll cry, Remember me.   *Thos. Hawcis*, 1792.

*" Whom have I in heaven but Thee, and there is none upon earth
that I desire in comparison of Thee."*

128   6s & 4s.

NEARER, my God to Thee,
    Nearer to Thee!
E'en though it be a cross
    That raiseth me;

Still all my song shall be,
Nearer, my God, to Thee,
Nearer to Thee!

2 Though like a wanderer,
   The sun gone down,
Darkness be over me,
   My rest a stone;
Yet in my dreams I'd be
Nearer, my God, to Thee,
Nearer to Thee!

3 There let the world appear
   Steps unto heaven;
All that Thou sendest me
   In mercy given;
Angels to beckon me
Nearer, my God, to Thee;
Nearer to Thee!

4 Then with my waking thoughts
   Bright with Thy praise,
Out of my stony griefs
   Bethel I'll raise;
So by my woes to be
Nearer, my God, to Thee,
Nearer to Thee!

5 Or if on joyful wing
   Cleaving the sky,
Sun, moon, and stars forgot,
   Upward I fly,
Still all my song shall be,
Nearer, my God, to Thee,
Nearer to Thee.

Sarah F. Adams, 1841.

"Have mercy upon me, O God, according to Thy loving-kindness."

129 S. M.

THOU Lord of all above,
   And all below the sky!
Prostrate before Thy feet I fall,
   And for Thy mercy cry.

2 Forgive my follies past,
   The crimes which I have done;
Bid a repenting sinner live,
   Through Thine incarnate Son.

3 Guilt, like a heavy load,
  Upon my conscience lies;
To Thee I make my sorrows known,
  And lift my weeping eyes.

4 The burden which I feel,
  Thou canst alone remove;
Do Thou display Thy pard'ning grace,
  And Thine unbounded love.

Benjamin Beddome, 1790.

SECOND SUNDAY IN LENT.

"Lord, help me."

130   C. M.

O HELP us, Lord! each hour of need
  Thy heavenly succor give;
Help us in thought, and word, and deed,
  Each hour on earth we live!

2 O help us when our spirits bleed
  With contrite anguish sore;
And when our hearts are cold and dead,
  O help us, Lord, the more!

3 O help us, through the prayer of faith,
  More firmly to believe;
For still, the more the servant hath,
  The more shall he receive.

4 O help us, Jesus, from on high!
  We know no help but Thee:
O help us so to live and die
  As Thine in heaven to be!

Henry H. Milman.

"Vouchsafe unto us both the outward and inward defence of Thy guardian care."

131   C. M.

THE burden of my sins, O Lord,
  Is more than I can bear—
To Thee I bring the guilty load,
  To Thee address my prayer.

2 For naught of good that I have done,
   On Thy dear name I call,
Alone upon the cross I lean,
   My Saviour and my All.

3 Teach me to feel how weak I am
   Without Thy strength'ning power,
And fresh supplies of grace renew
   For every passing hour.

4 Dangers unseen on every side
   Crowd thick life's troubled way,
O guard me through the shadowy night,
   And guide my steps by day.

5 If sorrow shade, if grief oppress,
   Whatever be Thy will,
O, may I bow to Thy behest,
   And own Thy mercy still.

6 And when the chilling shades of death
   Obscure life's fading ray,
Through all may I descry the dawn
   Of an eternal day.

C. C. Cox, 1859.

"*The rock of our salvation.*"

132
7s, 6 lines.

ROCK of Ages, cleft for me!
   Let me hide myself in Thee;
Let the water and the blood,
From Thy riven side which flowed,
Be of sin the double cure;
Cleanse me from its guilt and power.

2 Not the labors of my hands
   Can fulfil Thy law's demands;
Could my zeal no respite know,
Could my tears forever flow,
All for sin could not atone;
Thou must save, and Thou alone!

3 Nothing in my hand I bring;
   Simply to Thy cross I cling;
Naked, come to Thee for dress,
Helpless, look to Thee for grace;
Foul, I to the fountain fly,
Wash me, Saviour, or I die.

4 While I draw this fleeting breath,
When my eyelids close in death,
When I soar through tracts unknown,
See Thee on Thy judgment throne,
Rock of ages cleft for me!
Let me hide myself in Thee.

Augustus M. Toplady, 1776.

"Death passed upon all men, for that all have sinned."

133 L. M.

LORD, I am vile, conceiv'd in sin,
And born unholy and unclean;
Sprung from the man whose guilty fall
Corrupts the race and taints us all.

2 Soon as we draw our infant breath,
The seeds of sin grow up for death;
Thy law demands a perfect heart;
But we're defiled in every part.

3 Great God, create my heart anew,
And form my spirit pure and true;
O make me wise betimes to see
My danger and my remedy.

4 Behold, I fall before Thy face;
My only refuge is Thy grace;
No outward forms can make me clean;
The leprosy lies deep within.

5 No bleeding bird, nor bleeding beast,
Nor hyssop branch, nor sprinkling priest,
Nor running brook, nor flood, nor sea,
Can wash the dismal stain away.

6 Jesus, my God, Thy blood alone
Hath power sufficient to atone;
Thy blood can make me white as snow
No Jewish types could cleanse me so.

7 While guilt disturbs and breaks my peace,
Nor flesh nor soul hath rest or ease;
Lord, let me hear Thy pard'ning voice,
And make my broken bones rejoice.

Isaac Watts, 1719.

SECOND SUNDAY IN LENT.

"In the world ye shall have tribulation, but be of good cheer: I have overcome the world."

134
L. M.

ETERNAL Beam of Light divine,
    Thou Fount of unexhausted love;
In whom the Father's glories shine
    Through earth beneath and heaven above:

2 Jesus, the weary wanderer's Rest,
    Give us Thy easy yoke to bear;
With steadfast patience arm each breast,
    With spotless love, and lowly fear.

3 In faith we take the cup from Thee,
    Prepared and mingled by Thy skill:
Though bitter to the taste it be,
    'Tis strong the wounded soul to heal.

4 Be Thou, O Rock of Ages, nigh;
    So shall each murmuring thought be gone;
And grief, and fear, and care shall fly,
    As clouds before the mid-day sun.

5 Oh! speak our warring passions peace;
    And bid our trembling hearts, Be still:
Thy power our strength and fortress is,
    For all things serve Thy sovereign will.

6 Thou, Lord, the dreadful fight hast won;
    Alone, Thou hast the wine-press trod:
In us Thy strength'ning grace be shown,
    And make us conquer in Thy Blood.
John Wesley.

"O, that I knew where I might find Him."

135
8s & 7s, 6 lines.

BEHOLD me here, in grief draw near,
    Pleading at Thy throne, O King;
To Thee each tear, each trembling fear,
    Jesus, Son of Man! I bring.
Let me find Thee—let me find Thee,
    Me, a vile and worthless thing!

2 Look down in love, and from above,
    With Thy Spirit satisfy;
Thou hast sought me, Thou hast bought me,
    And Thy purchase, Lord am I.
Let me find Thee—let me find Thee,
    Here on earth, and there on high!

8*

3 No other prayer to Thee I bear,
   O my Lord, but only this,
To share Thy grace, to see Thy face,
   And know Thy people's bliss.
Let me find Thee—let me find Thee,
   Thee to find is blessedness.

4 Hear the broken, scarcely spoken
   Utt'rance of my heart to Thee;
All the crying, all the sighing
   Of Thy child accepted be.
Let me find Thee—let me find Thee,
   Thus my soul longs ardently.

5 Worldly pleasures, earthly treasures,
   Joys and honors will not stay;
They often pain, and, oh! how vain,
   Looking to eternity!
Let me find Thee—let me find Thee,
   Find Thee, O my God, this day!

           Joachim Neander, 1679.
        Trans. (Hymns from Land of Luther.)

"The Lord shall preserve thee: He shall preserve thy soul."

136   C. M.

DEAR Father! to Thy mercy-seat
   My soul for shelter flies;
'Tis here I find a safe retreat
   When storms and tempests rise.

2 My cheerful hope can never die,
   If Thou, my God, art near;
Thy grace can raise my comforts high,
   And banish every fear.

3 My great Protector, and my Lord,
   Thy constant aid impart;
Oh, let Thy kind, Thy gracious word
   Sustain my trembling heart!

4 Oh, never let my soul remove
   From this divine retreat!
Still let me trust Thy power and love,
   And dwell beneath Thy feet.

                    Anne Steele.

THIRD SUNDAY IN LENT.

"He taketh from him all his armor wherein he trusted, and divideth the spoil."

137 *German Choral.*

A STRONG tower is the Lord our God,
  To shelter and defend us:
Our shield His arm, our sword His rod,
  Against our foes befriend us:
    That ancient Enemy,
    His gathering power we see,
    His terrors and his toils,
    Yet victory with its spoils,
  Not earth, but Heaven shall send us.

2. Though wrestling with the wrath of hell,
  No might of man avail us:
Our Captain is Immanuel,
  And angel comrades hail us!
    Still challenge ye His name
    "Christ in the flesh who came,"
    "The Lord, the Lord of hosts!"
    Our cause His succor boasts,
  And God shall never fail us.

3 Though earth by peopling fiends be trod,
  Embattled all, yet hidden;
And though their proud usurping gods
  O'er thrones and shrines have stridden;
    Nay, let them stand reveal'd,
    And darken all the field;
    We fear not: fall they must!
    The Word, wherein we trust,
  Their triumph hath forbidden.

4 While mighty truth with us remains,
  Hell's arts shall move us never;
Nor parting friendships, honors, gains,
  Our love from Jesus sever:
    They leave us, when they part,
    With Him a peaceful heart;
    And when from death we rise,
    Death yields us, as he dies,
  The crown of life forever.

Martin Luther.
Trans. W. M. Bunting.

"Lord, to whom shall we go?"

138 C. M.

DEAR Refuge of my weary soul!
  On Thee, when sorrows rise;
On Thee, when waves of trouble roll,
  My fainting hope relies.

2 To Thee, I tell each rising grief,
    For Thou alone canst heal;
  Thy word can bring a sweet relief
    For every pain I feel.

3 But, Oh! when gloomy doubts prevail,
    I fear to call Thee mine;
  The springs of comfort seem to fail,
    And all my hopes decline.

4 Hast Thou not bid me seek Thy face?
    And shall I seek in vain?
  And can the ear of sovereign grace
    Be deaf, when I complain?

5 No; still the ear of sovereign grace
    Attends the mourner's prayer;
  Oh! may I ever find access
    To breathe my sorrows there!

6 Thy mercy-seat is open still,
    Here let my soul retreat;
  With humble hope attend Thy will,
    And wait beneath Thy feet.

                          Anne Steele, 1760.

"Behold the Lamb of God, which taketh away the sin of the world."

139 L. M.

JUST as I am, without one plea,
  But that Thy blood was shed for me,
  And that Thou bid'st me come to Thee,
    O Lamb of God! I come—I come!

2 Just as I am, and waiting not
    To rid my soul of one dark blot,
  To Thee, whose blood can cleanse each spot,
    O Lamb of God! I come—I come!

3 Just as I am, though tossed about
With many a conflict, many a doubt,
Fightings and fears within, without,
    O Lamb of God! I come—I come!

4 Just as I am, poor, wretched, blind!
Sight, riches, healing of the mind,
Yea, all I need, in Thee to find,
    O Lamb of God! I come—I come!

5 Just as I am; Thou wilt receive,
Wilt welcome, pardon, cleanse, relieve;
Because Thy promise I believe,
    O Lamb of God! I come—I come!

6 Just as I am; Thy love unknown
Has broken every barrier down;
Now, to be Thine, yea, Thine alone,
    O Lamb of God! I come—I come!
Charlotte Elliott, 1836.

"If any man sin, we have an advocate with the Father, Jesus Christ the righteous."

140
7s, 6s, 8 lines.

O JESUS, our salvation,
  Low at Thy cross we lie;
Lord, in Thy great compassion,
  Hear our bewailing cry.
We come to Thee with mourning,
  We come to Thee in woe;
With contrite hearts returning,
  And tears that overflow.

2 O gracious Intercessor,
  O Priest within the Veil,
Plead, for each lost transgressor,
  The blood that cannot fail.
We spread our sins before Thee,
  We tell them one by one;
O for Thy name's great glory,
  Forgive all we have done.

3 O by Thy cross and passion,
  Thy tears and agony,
And crown of cruel fashion,
  And death on Calvary;
By all that untold suff'ring
  Endured by Thee alone;
O Priest, O spotless Off'ring,
  Plead for us, and atone.

4 And in these hearts now broken
 Re-enter Thou and reign:
And say, by that dear token,
 We are absolved again.
And build us up, and guide us,
 And guard us day by day;
And in Thy presence hide us,
 And take our sins away.

J. Hamilton.

"In all time of our tribulation: in all time of our wealth: in the hour of death, and in the day of judgment, good Lord, deliver us."

141   8s, 7s, 4s.

JESUS, Lord, we kneel before Thee;
 Bend from heaven Thy gracious ear;
While our waiting souls adore Thee,
 Friend of helpless sinners, hear;
  By Thy mercy,
 O deliver us, Good Lord!

2 From the death of nature's blindness,
 From the hardening power of sin,
From all malice and unkindness,
 From the pride that lurks within,
  By Thy mercy,
 O deliver us, Good Lord!

3 When temptation sorely presses,
 In the day of Satan's power,
In our times of deep distresses,
 In each dark and trying hour,
  By Thy mercy,
 O deliver us, Good Lord!

4 In the weary night of sickness,
 In the throes of grief and pain,
When we feel our mortal weakness,
 When all human help is vain,
  By Thy mercy,
 O deliver us, Good Lord!

5 In the solemn hour of dying,
 In the awful judgment-day,
May our souls on Thee relying
 Find Thee still our Hope and Stay;
  By Thy mercy,
 O deliver us, Good Lord!

FOURTH SUNDAY IN LENT.

6 Jesus, may Thy promis'd blessing
  Comfort to our souls afford;
May we now Thy love possessing
  Find at last the great reward;
    By Thy mercy,
  O deliver us, Good Lord!

James J. Cummins, 1849.

" Thou art my hiding-place; Thou shalt preserve me from trouble."

142   8s, 7s, 4s.

JESUS, to Thy cross I hasten,
  In all weariness my home;
Let Thy dying love come o'er me—
  Light and covert in the gloom:
    Saviour, hide me,
  Till the hour of gloom is o'er.

2 Where life's tempests dark are rolling
    Fearful shadows o'er my way;
  Let firm faith in Thee sustain me,
    Every rising fear allay:
      Hide, oh! hide me,
    Hide me till the storm is o'er.

3 When stern death at last shall lead me
    Through the dark and lonely vale;
  Let Thy hope uphold and cheer me,
    Though my flesh and heart should fail.
      Safely hide me
    With Thyself forevermore.

FOURTH SUNDAY IN LENT.

"Whence shall we buy bread, that these may eat?"

143   C. M.

O BLESSED Lord! The earth is Thine.
    By Thy creative hand
  The golden harvests crown the year,
    And deck the fertile land.

2 O blessed Lord! Thou Bread of life
    That cometh down from heaven!
  Supplies of everlasting food
    By Thee to man are given.

3 Thy Godhead is the well-spring, Lord,
   The pure, exhaustless source,
 From which they flow, through age to age,
   In never-ending course.

4 In channels form'd by Thee they flow,
   In rivulets of grace,
 Refreshing all who wander here
   In this world's desert place.

5 O feed us, weary pilgrims, Lord,
   And to Thy Zion bring,
 To keep a heavenly feast with Thee
   Our Prophet, Priest, and King. *C. Wordsworth.*

"In that day there shall be a fountain opened to the house of David."

144 C. M.

THERE is a fountain filled with blood
   Drawn from Immanuel's veins;
 And sinners plunged beneath that flood
   Lose all their guilty stains.

2 The dying thief rejoiced to see
   That fountain in his day;
 And there have I, as vile as he,
   Washed all my sins away.

3 Dear, dying Lamb! Thy precious blood
   Shall never lose its power,
 Till all the ransomed Church of God
   Be saved to sin no more.

4 E'er since by faith, I saw the stream
   Thy flowing wounds supply,
 Redeeming love has been my theme,
   And shall be, till I die.

5 Then, in a nobler, sweeter song,
   I'll sing Thy power to save,
 When this poor, lisping, stamm'ring tongue
   Lies silent in the grave.
             William Cowper, 1779.

"We love Him, because He first loved us."

145 L. M.

I LOVE Thee, O most gracious Lord,
   Not that Thou sav'st me by Thy Word;
 Nor yet because Thy wrath shall doom
 Those loving not to endless gloom.

2 Thou, Thou, my Jesus, full of grace,
　Didst me upon the cross embrace;
　Didst bear the nails, the bloody spear,
　The great disgrace, the rabble's jeer.

3 Innumerable griefs were Thine,
　Great sweats and anguish, Lord of mine!
　The pangs of death, and all for me,
　That I, poor wretch, might come to Thee!

4 Then why not love with all my heart?
　O Jesus, most beloved Thou art!
　Not that Thou sav'st my soul above,
　Nor me condemn'st, do I Thee love.

5 Not for the hope of sure reward,
　But for Thy love, O blessed Lord!
　My love is Thine, and e'er shall be,
　Because, my King, Thou reign'st o'er me!
　　　　　　　　　　Francis Xavier.
　　　　　　　　　Trans. C. C. Cox.

"The rock of my strength, and my refuge is in God."

146　　　　　C. M.

GOD, my Supporter and my Hope,
　My Help forever near!
Thine arm of mercy held me up,
　When sinking in despair.

2 Thy counsels, Lord! shall guide my feet,
　　Through this dark wilderness:
　Thy hand conduct me near Thy seat,
　　To dwell before Thy face.

3 Were I in heaven without my God,
　　'Twould be no joy to me;
　And, whilst this earth is my abode,
　　I long for none but Thee.

4 What, if the springs of life were broke,
　　And flesh and heart should faint?
　God is my soul's eternal Rock,
　　The Strength of every saint.

5 But to draw near to Thee, my God!
　　Shall be my sweet employ;
　My tongue shall sound Thy works abroad,
　　And tell the world my joy.
　　　　　　　　　　Isaac Watts, 1719.

FOURTH SUNDAY IN LENT.

147

"I will love Thee, O Lord, my Strength."
8s & 7s, 6 lines.

I WILL love Thee,—all my treasure!
  I will love Thee,—all my strength!
I will love Thee—without measure,
  And will love Thee right at length.
Oh, I will love Thee, Light divine,
Till I die and find Thee mine!

2 I will praise Thee, Sun of glory!
  For Thy beams have gladness brought.
I will praise Thee,—will adore Thee,
  For the light I vainly sought:
Will praise Thee that Thy words so blest
Spake my sin-sick soul to rest.

3 In Thy footsteps now uphold me,
  That I stumble not nor stray;
When the narrow way is told me,
  Never let me ling'ring stay,
But come, my weary soul to cheer,
Shine, eternal Sunbeam, here.

4 Be my heart more warmly glowing,
  Sweet and calm the tears I shed;
And its love, its ardor showing,
  Let my spirit onward tread;
Still near to Thee, and nearer still,
Draw this heart, this mind, this will.

5 I will love, in joy and sorrow!
  Crowning joy! will love Thee well!
I will love, to-day, to-morrow,
  While I in this body dwell:
Oh! I will love Thee, Light divine,
Till I die and find Thee mine!

Johann Scheffler (Angelus).
Trans. (Hymns from Land of Luther).

148

"We walk by faith, not by sight."
C. M.

FAITH is the brightest evidence
  Of things beyond our sight,
Breaks through the clouds of flesh and sense
  And dwells in heav'nly light.

2 It sets times past in present view,
    Brings distant prospects home,
  Of things a thousand years ago,
    Or thousand years to come.

3 By faith, we know the worlds were made
    By God's almighty word:
  Abr'am to unknown countries led
    By faith, obeyed the Lord.

4 He sought a city fair and high,
    Built by th' eternal hands;
  And faith assures us, though we die,
    That heavenly building stands.
                        Isaac Watts, 1709.

"Grant that we, who are now righteously afflicted and bowed down by the sense of our sins, may be refreshed and lifted up with the joy of Thy salvation."

149   11s & 10s.

COME, ye disconsolate! where'er ye languish,
  Come to the mercy-seat, fervently kneel;
Here bring your wounded hearts; here tell your anguish;
  Earth has no sorrow, that heaven cannot heal.

2 Joy of the desolate! Light of the straying!
    Hope, when all others die, fadeless and pure!
  Here speaks the Comforter, in God's name saying,
    Earth has no sorrow, that heaven cannot cure.

3 Here see the Bread of life; see waters flowing
    Forth from the throne of God, boundless in love:
  Come to the feast prepared; come, ever-knowing,
    Earth has no sorrow, but heaven can remove.
                        Thomas Moore, 1816, *altered.*

FIFTH SUNDAY IN LENT.

"And having spoiled principalities and powers, He made a show of them openly, triumphing over them."

150   8s, 7s, 6 *lines.*

SING, my tongue, the glorious battle,
  Sing the last, the dread affray;

O'er the cross, the Victor's trophy,
  Sound the glad triumphal lay,
How, the pains of death enduring,
  Earth's Redeemer won the day.

2 Now the thirty years accomplished,
  Which on earth He willed to see;
Born for this, He meets His Passion,
  Gives Himself an offering free;
On the cross the Lamb is lifted,
  There the sacrifice to be.

3 Faithful cross! above all other
  One and only noble Tree!
None in foliage, none in blossom,
  None in fruit thy peer may be,
Sweetest wood, and sweetest iron;
  Sweetest weight is hung on thee!

4 Thou alone wast counted worthy
  This world's ransom to sustain;
That a shipwrecked race for ever
  Might a port of refuge gain,
With the sacred blood anointed
  Of the Lamb for sinners slain.

Venantius Fortunatus, 600.
Translation Compiled.

"*God forbid that I should glory, save in the cross of our Lord Jesus Christ.*"

151 L. M.

THE royal banners forward go;
  The cross shines forth in mystic glow;
Where He in flesh, our flesh who made,
Our sentence bore, our ransom paid.

2 Where deep for us the spear was dy'd,
Life's torrent rushing from His side,
To wash us in that precious flood,
Where mingled water flowed, and blood.

3 Fulfill'd is all that David told
In true prophetic song of old;
Amidst the nations God, saith He,
Hath reigned and triumphed from the tree.

4 O tree of beauty! Tree of light!
O tree with royal purple dight!
Elect on whose triumphal breast
Those holy limbs should find their rest!

5 On whose dear arms, so widely flung,
The weight of this world's ransom hung;
The price of human kind to pay,
And spoil the spoiler of his prey!

6 To Thee, eternal Three in One,
Let homage meet by all be done;
Whom by the cross Thou dost restore,
Preserve and govern evermore.
Venantius Fortunatus, 580.
Trans. John M. Neale.

"And having made peace, through the blood of His cross."

152 L. M.

WE sing the praise of Him who died,
Of Him who died upon the cross;
The sinner's Hope let men deride,
For this we count the world but loss.

2 Inscribed upon the cross we see
In shining letters, "God is love,"
He bears our sins upon the tree,
He brings us mercy from above.

3 The cross! it takes our guilt away,
It holds the fainting spirit up;
It cheers with hope the gloomy day,
And sweetens every bitter cup.

4 It makes the coward spirit brave,
And nerves the feeble arm for fight;
It takes its terror from the grave,
And gilds the bed of death with light.

5 The balm of life, the cure of woe,
The measure and the pledge of love,
The sinner's refuge here below,
The angels' theme in heaven above.

6 To Christ, who won for sinners grace
By bitter grief and anguish sore,
Be praise from all the ransomed race
For ever and for evermore!
Thomas Kelly, 1815.

"By His own blood He entered in once into the holy place, having obtained eternal redemption for us."

153 S. M.

NOT all the blood of beasts,
  On Jewish altars slain,
Could give the guilty conscience peace,
  Or wash away the stain.

2 But Christ, the heavenly Lamb,
  Takes all our sins away;—
A sacrifice of nobler name,
  And richer blood than they.

3 My faith would lay her hand
  On that dear head of Thine,
While, like a penitent, I stand,
  And there confess my sin.

4 My soul looks back to see
  The burdens Thou didst bear,
When hanging on the cursed tree,—
  And hopes her guilt was there.

5 Believing, we rejoice
  To see the curse remove;
We bless the Lamb, with cheerful voice,
  And sing His bleeding love.

Isaac Watts, 1709.

"Ye were not redeemed with corruptible things—: but with the precious blood of Christ, as of a lamb without blemish, and without spot."

154 C. M.

JESUS, with all Thy saints above,
  My tongue would bear her part:
Would sound aloud Thy saving love,
  And sing Thy bleeding heart.

2 Bless'd be the Lamb, my dearest Lord,
  Who bought me with His blood,
And quenched His Father's flaming sword
  In His own vital flood:

3 The Lamb that freed my captive soul
  From Satan's heavy chains,
And sent the Lion down to howl
  Where hell and horror reigns.

4 All glory to the dying Lamb,
   And never-ceasing praise,
 While angels live to know His name,
   Or saints to feel His grace.
                              Isaac Watts, 1707.

"A man shall be as an hiding-place from the wind, and a covert from the tempest."

155   7s, 8 *lines*.

JESUS, Lover of my soul!
   Let me to Thy bosom fly,
 While the nearer waters roll,
   While the tempest still is high;
 Hide me, O my Saviour! hide,
   Till the storm of life is past;
 Safe into the haven guide;
   Oh! receive my soul at last.

2 Other refuge have I none,
   Hangs my helpless soul on Thee:
 Leave, ah! leave me not alone,
   Still support and comfort me:
 All my trust on Thee is stayed,
   All my help from Thee I bring;
 Cover my defenceless head,
   With the shadow of Thy wing.

3 Thou, O Christ! art all I want;
   More than all in Thee I find;
 Raise the fallen, cheer the faint,
   Heal the sick, and lead the blind:
 Just and holy is Thy name;
   I am all unrighteousness;
 False and full of sin I am,
   Thou art full of truth and grace.

4 Plenteous grace with Thee is found,
   Grace to cover all my sin;
 Let the healing streams abound,
   Make and keep me pure within.
 Thou of life the Fountain art,
   Freely let me take of Thee:
 Spring Thou up within my heart,
   Rise to all eternity.
                           Charles Wesley, 1740.

" Sanctified through the offering of the body of Jesus once for all."

156 L. M. 6 *lines.*

O THOU eternal Victim slain,
  A sacrifice for guilty man,
By the eternal Spirit made
An off'ring in the sinner's stead,
Our everlasting Priest art Thou,
Pleading Thy death for sinners now.

2 Eternal Victim, from Thy side,
Thy love did pour a crimson tide,
And still Thy vesture dyed in blood
Gives token of the cleansing flood;
The Lamb for ever slain art Thou,
Pleading Thy death for sinners now.

3 O Lord of lords, and King of kings,
Thou Sun with healing in Thy wings,
Pour down upon our darkened sight
The brightness of Thy living light;
So may we know Thee Victim, Priest,
And find Thee in Thy heavenly feast.

                      Charles Wesley.

SIXTH SUNDAY IN LENT.

" They took branches of palm trees, and went forth to meet Him, and cried, hosanna."

157 L. M.

RIDE on, ride on in majesty!
  Hark, all the tribes hosanna cry!
Thy humble beast pursues his road,
With palms and scattered garments strewed.

2 Ride on, ride on in majesty!
In lowly pomp ride on to die!
O Christ! Thy triumphs now begin,
O'er captive death and conquered sin.

3 Ride on, ride on in majesty!
The wingèd squadrons of the sky
Look down with sad and wond'ring eyes
To see th' approaching sacrifice.

SIXTH SUNDAY IN LENT.

4 Ride on, ride on in majesty!
   Thy last and fiercest strife is nigh:
   The Father, on His sapphire throne
   Expects His own anointed Son!
                        Henry H. Milman, 1827.

"Hosanna to the Son of David."

158　　　C. M.

HOSANNA! raise the pealing hymn
　　To David's Son and Lord;
With cherubim and seraphim,
　　Exalt th' incarnate Word.

2 Hosanna! Sovereign, Prophet, Priest!
　　How vast Thy gifts, how free!
Thy blood our life; Thy word, our feast;
　　Thy name, our only plea.

3 Hosanna! Master! lo! we bring
　　Our off'rings to Thy throne:
Not gold, nor myrrh, nor mortal thing,
　　But hearts to be Thine own.

4 Hosanna! once Thy gracious ear
　　Approved a lisping throng;
Be gracious still, and deign to hear
　　Our poor but grateful song.

5 O Saviour! if redeemed by Thee,
　　Thy temple we behold,
Hosannas through eternity
　　We'll sing to harps of gold.
                        Wm. H. Havergal, 1833.

"Out of the mouths of babes and sucklings hast Thou ordained strength."

159　　　7s & 6s.

GLORY, and laud, and honor,
　　To Thee, Redeemer King!
To whom the lips of children
　　Made sweet Hosannas ring!

2 Thou art the King of Israel;
　　Thou David's royal Son;
Who in the Lord's name comest,
　　The King and blessed one.

3 The company of angels
   Are praising Thee on high;
And mortal men, and all things
   Created, make reply.

4 The people of the Hebrews
   With palms before Thee went;
Our praise, and prayer, and anthems
   Before Thee we present.

5 In hast'ning to Thy Passion
   They raised their hymns of praise:
In reigning 'midst Thy glory,
   Our melody we raise.

6 Thou didst accept their praises;
   Accept the prayers we bring,
Who in all good delightest,
   Thou good and gracious King.
Theodulph, 821.
Trans. Jno. M. Neale, 1856.

"The chastisement of our peace was upon Him; and with His stripes we are healed."

160   C. M.

O THOU who through this holy week
   Didst suffer for us all;
The sick to cure, the lost to seek,
   To raise up them that fall:

2 We cannot understand the woe
   Thy love was pleased to bear:
O Lamb of God, we only know
   That all our hopes were there!

3 Thy feet the path of suffering trod;
   Thy hand the victory won:
What shall we render to our God
   For all that He hath done?

4 To God the Father, God the Son,
   And God the Holy Ghost,
By man on earth be honor done,
   And by the heavenly host.
Jno. M. Neale, 1844.

"And when He had thus spoken, He went before, ascending up to Jersualem."

161   C. M. 8 *lines.*

SEE what unbounded zeal and love
   Inflamed the Saviour's breast,

When steadfast t'wards Jerusalem,
  His urgent way He pressed.
Good-will to man, and zeal for God
  His every thought engross:
· He longs to be baptized with blood,
  He thirsts to reach the cross.

2 With all His sufferings full in view,
  And woes to us unknown,
Forth to the work His Spirit flew,
  'Twas love that urged Him on:
By His obedience unto death
  See Paradise restored:
And fallen man brought face to face
  With His forgiving Lord.

3 Prepare us, Lord, to view Thy cross,
  Who all our griefs hast borne;
To look on Thee, whom we have pierced,
  To look on Thee, and mourn:
While thus we mourn, may we rejoice,
  And as Thy cross we see,
May each exclaim in faith and hope,
  "The Saviour died for me!"   *W. Cowper,*
Altered.

"Mercifully grant that we may be counted worthy to have part both in the fellowship of His sufferings and in the glorious power of His resurrection."

162
L. M.

O THOU pure Light of souls in need,
  True joy of every human breast,
Sower of life's immortal seed,
  Our Saviour and Redeemer blest!

2 What wondrous pity Thee o'ercame,
  To make our guilty load Thine own,
Sinless, to suffer death and shame
  For our trangressions to atone!

3 Thou, bursting Hades open wide,
  Didst all the captive souls unchain;
And thence to Thy dread Father's side
  With glorious pomp ascend again.

4 Jesus! may pity Thee compel
  To heal the wounds of which we die,
And take us in Thy light to dwell,
  Who for Thy blissful presence sigh.

5 Be Thou our Guide, be Thou our Goal;
   Be Thou our pathway to the skies;
   Our joy, when sorrow fills the soul;
   In death, our everlasting prize.
                              Latin Hymn.
                              Trans. E. Caswall.

"*In the Lord have I righteousness and strength.*"

163 L. M.

JESUS, Thy blood and righteousness
    My beauty are, my glorious dress;
   'Midst flaming worlds, in these arrayed,
With joy shall I lift up my head.

2 Bold shall I stand in Thy great day,
  For who aught to my charge shall lay?
  Fully absolved through these I am,
  From sin and fear, from guilt and shame.

3 When from the dust of death I rise
  To claim my mansion in the skies,
  E'en then, this shall be all my plea;
  Jesus hath lived, hath died for me.

4 Thus Abraham, the friend of God,
  Thus all heaven's armies bought with blood,
  Saviour of sinners, Thee proclaim;
  Sinners of whom the chief I am.

5 Jesus, be endless praise to Thee,
  Whose boundless mercy hath for me,
  For me, and all Thy hands have made,
  An everlasting ransom paid.

6 Ah! give to all Thy servants, Lord,
  With power to speak Thy gracious word;
  That all who to Thy wounds will flee,
  May find eternal life in Thee.
                              Zinzendorf, 1739.
                              Trans. J. Wesley, 1740.

"*Behold the Lamb of God.*"

164 L. M.

BEHOLD the sin-atoning Lamb,
    With wonder, gratitude and love!
To take away our guilt and shame,
   See Him descending from above.

2 Our sins and griefs on Him were laid ;
    He meekly bore the mighty load :
Our ransom-price He fully paid,
    In groans and tears, in sweat and blood.

3 To save a guilty world He dies ;
    Sinners, behold the bleeding Lamb !
To Him lift up your longing eyes,
    And hope for mercy in His name.

4 Pardon and peace through Him abound,
    He can the richest blessings give ;
Salvation in His name is found,
    He bids the dying sinner live.

5 Jesus, my Lord, I look to Thee :
    Where else can helpless sinners go ?
Thy boundless love shall set me free
    From all my wretchedness and woe.

"Worthy is the Lamb that was slain to receive power, and riches, and wisdom, and strength, and honor, and glory, and blessing."

165   C. M.

COME, let us join our cheerful songs
    With angels round the throne ;
Ten thousand thousand are their tongues
    But all their joys are one.

2 "Worthy the Lamb that died," they cry,
    "To be exalted thus ; "
"Worthy the Lamb," our lips reply,
    "For He was slain for us."

3 Jesus is worthy to receive
    Honor and power divine ;
And blessings more than we can give,
    Be, Lord, forever Thine.

4 Let all that dwell above the sky,
    And air, and earth, and seas,
Conspire to lift Thy glories high,
    And speak Thine endless praise.

5 The whole creation join in one,
    To bless the sacred name
Of Him that sits upon the throne,
    And to adore the Lamb.

Isaac Watts, 1707.

PASSION WEEK.

"The Lord Jesus, the same night in which He was betrayed, took bread, and when He had given thanks, He brake it, and said, " Take, eat."

166   L. M.

'TWAS on that dark, that doleful night,
   When powers of earth and hell arose
Against the Son of God's delight,
   And friends betrayed Him to His foes:

2 Before the mournful scene began,
   He took the bread, and blest, and brake:
What love through all His actions ran!
   What wondrous words of grace He spake!

3 "This is my body, broke for sin;
   Receive and eat the living food;"
Then took the cup, and blest the wine,
   " 'Tis the new cov'nant in my blood."

4 For us His flesh with nails was torn,
   He bore the scourge, He felt the thorn;
And justice poured upon His head
   Its heavy vengeance in our stead.

5 For us His vital blood was spilt,
   To buy the pardon of our guilt,
When for black crimes of greatest size,
   He gave His soul a sacrifice.

6 "Do this," He cried, "till time shall end,
   In mem'ry of your dying friend;
Meet, at my table, and record
   The love of your departed Lord."

7 Jesus! Thy feast we celebrate,
   We show Thy death, we sing Thy name,
Till Thou return, and we shall eat
   The marriage supper of the Lamb.

                       Isaac Watts, 1707.

"This is my body which is given for you: this do in remembrance of Me."

167   10s.

THIS is My Body, which is given for you;
   Do this—He said and brake—remembering me.
O Lamb of God, our paschal Offering true,
   To us the Bread of Life each moment be.

2 This is My Blood, for sin's remission shed—
    He spake, and passed the wine-stained chalice round:
 So let us drink, and on Life's fulness fed
    With heavenly joy each quickening pulse shall bound.

3 The hour is come! with us in peace sit down;
    Thine own belov'd, O love us to the end;
 Serve us one Banquet ere the night's dark frown
    Veil from our sight the presence of our Friend.

4 Girded with love still wash Thy servants' feet,
    While they submissive wonder and adore;
 Bathed in Thy Blood our spirits every whit
    Are clean—yet cleanse our goings more and more.

5 Some will betray Thee—Master, is it I?
    Leaning upon Thy love, we ask in fear;
 Ourselves mistrusting, earnestly we cry
    To Thee, the Strong, for strength when sin is near.

6 But round us fall the evening shadows dim:
    A saddened awe pervades our darkening sense,
 In solemn choir we sing the parting Hymn,
    And hear Thy Voice—Arise, let us go hence.

C. L. Ford.

"My soul is exceeding sorrowful unto death: tarry ye here and watch."

168   L. M.

'TIS midnight—and on Olive's brow
    The star is dimm'd that lately shone;
'Tis midnight—in the garden now,
    The suff'ring Saviour prays alone.

2 'Tis midnight—and from all remov'd,
    Immanuel wrestles lone with fears;
E'en the disciple that He loved
    Heeds not his Master's griefs and tears.

3 'Tis midnight—and for others' guilt
    The man of sorrows weeps in blood;
Yet He that hath in anguish knelt,
    Is not forsaken by his God.

4 'Tis midnight—and from ether-plains
    Is borne the song that angels know;
Unheard by mortals are the strains
    That sweetly soothe the Saviour's woe.

Wm. B. Tappan, 1829.

"Christ also suffered for us, leaving us an example that ye should follow His steps."

169 L. M.

O LORD, the wilderness to me
A very Paradise shall be,
Since Thou for forty days wast there
In fasting, solitude and prayer.

2 Unworthy though these feet to rest
On ground Thy footsteps once have blest,
The way of sorrows shall be mine,
Made sweet because it first was Thine.

3 Lord, let me find some lowly place
Where I may seek Thy pitying face,
And plead with Thee by Olivet,
By agony and bloody sweat.

4 Some quiet aisle or dim recess
Shall make for me a wilderness;
And surely angels shall be there
To wait on penitence and prayer.

5 Nor is this all: for I would know
The depth of shame, the crown of woe,
Stand by the stricken Mother's side
While Thou art mocked and crucified.

6 And then in hours of saddest gloom
I still will watch around Thy tomb,
Till with the day new joy be born,
And Thou shalt rise on Easter-morn.

7 Oh blessed thought, that faith can see
In every altar, Calvary,
Find there the loving arms outspread,
And fall before the fallen Head.

8 Come! King of kings; come! Light of light:
The Bride awaits the day all bright,
When she shall lift, her mourning o'er,
The shout of paschal joy once more.

William Chatterton Dix.

"Herzliebster Jesu, was hast Du verbrochen?"

170 11s, 11s, 11s & 5s.

ALAS, dear Lord, what law then hast Thou broken,
That such sharp sentence should on Thee be spoken?
Of what great crime hast Thou to make confession—
What dark transgression?

2 They crown His head with thorns, they smite, they scourge Him,
With cruel mockings to the cross they urge Him,
They give Him gall to drink, they still decry Him—
    They crucify Him.

3 Whence come these sorrows, whence this mortal anguish?
It is my sins for which my Lord must languish;
Yes, all the wrath, the woe He doth inherit,
    'Tis I do merit!

4 There was no spot in me by sin untainted,
Sick with its venom all my heart had fainted;
My heavy guilt to hell had well-nigh brought me,
    Such woe it wrought me.

5 O wondrous love! whose depths no heart hath sounded,
That brought Thee here by foes and thieves surrounded;
All worldly pleasures, heedless, I was trying,
    While Thou wert dying!

6 O mighty King! no time can dim Thy glory!
How shall I spread abroad Thy wondrous story?
How shall I find some worthy gift to proffer?
    What dare we offer?

7 For vainly doth our human wisdom ponder—
Thy woes, Thy mercy still transcend our wonder.
Oh how should I do aught that could delight Thee!
    Can I requite Thee?

8 Yet unrequited, Lord I would not leave Thee,
I can renounce whate'er doth vex or grieve Thee,
And quench, with thoughts of Thee and prayers most lowly,
    All fires unholy.

9 But since my strength alone will ne'er suffice me
To crucify desires that still entice me,
To all good deeds, oh let Thy Spirit win me,
    And reign within me!

10 I'll think upon Thy mercy hour by hour,
I'll love Thee so that earth must lose her power;
To do Thy will shall be my sole endeavor
    Henceforth forever.

11 Whate'er of earthly good this life may grant me
I'll risk for Thee,—no shame, no cross shall daunt me;
I shall not fear what man can do to harm me,
    Nor death alarm me.

12 But worthless is my sacrifice, I own it,
  Yet, Lord, for love's sake Thou wilt not disown it;
  Thou wilt accept my gift in Thy great meekness,
      Nor shame my weakness.

13 And when, dear Lord, before Thy throne in heaven
  To me the crown of joy at last is given,
  Where sweetest hymns Thy saints forever raise Thee,
      I too shall praise Thee!

J. Heerman, 1630.
Trans. by Catherine Winkworth.

171
"It is finished."
8s, 7s, 4s.

HARK! the voice of love and mercy,
    Sounds aloud from Calvary!
See! it rends the rocks asunder,
    Shakes the earth, and veils the sky!
        "It is finish'd!"
    Hear the dying Saviour cry!

2 It is finish'd!—O what pleasure
    Do these charming words afford!
  Heav'nly blessings without measure,
    Flow to us from Christ the Lord.
        It is finish'd!
    Saints, the dying words record.

3 Finish'd, all the types and shadows
    Of the ceremonial law!
  Finish'd, all that God has promis'd;
    Death and hell no more shall awe:
        It is finish'd!
    Saints, from hence your comfort draw.

4 Tune your harps anew, ye seraphs!
    Join to sing the pleasing theme;
  All on earth, and all in heav'n
    Join to praise Immanuel's name:
        Hallelujah!
    Glory to the bleeding Lamb!

Jonathan Evans (?) 1787.

"And the sun was darkened, and the vail of the temple was rent in the midst."

172
L. M. 5 *lines.*

CLEFT are the rocks, the earth doth quake,
  The slumberers of the grave awake:

The temple's veil is rent in twain :
For Christ our sacrifice is slain,
And bears of sin and death the pain.

2 Lo! nature's face of beaming light
She veils in darkness at the sight
Of Him, her God, the Crucified :
'Tis man alone that dares deride
The Saviour who for him hath died.

3 The mighty One, the Son of God,
Hath humbly kissed affliction's rod,
That by His stripes we might be healed,
Our pardon by His blood be sealed,
And boundless mercy stand revealed.

4 Oh let us cast each vice away
Which thus the Son of God could slay!
With contrite heart and weeping eye
Behold the Saviour's cross on high,
And every sin and folly fly!

5 So may we join the song of love
Which saints and angels sing above :
All honor, glory, praise to Thee,
Which wert, and art, and art to be,
The Lamb, slain from eternity.

C. Dawson.

"Behold and see, if there be any sorrow like unto my sorrow."

173   *7s, 6s, 8 lines.*

O SACRED Head now wounded,
 With grief and shame weighed down;
Now scornfully surrounded
 With thorns, Thy only crown;
O sacred Head, what glory,
 What bliss, till now, was Thine!
Yet, though despised and gory,
 I joy to call Thee mine.

2 O noblest brow and dearest,
 In other days the world
All feared, when Thou appearedst,
 What shame on Thee is hurl'd!
How art Thou pale with anguish,
 With sore abuse and scorn :
How does that visage languish
 Which once was bright as morn.

3 The blushes late residing
    Upon that holy cheek,
The roses once abiding
    Upon those lips so meek;
Alas! they have departed;
    Wan death has rifled all!
For weak, and broken-hearted
    I see Thy body fall.

4 What Thou, my Lord, hast suffered
    Was all for sinners' gain;
Mine, mine was the trangression,
    But Thine the deadly pain.
Lo! here I fall, my Saviour!
    'Tis I deserve Thy place,
Look on me with Thy favor,
    Vouchsafe to me Thy grace.

5 Receive me, my Redeemer,
    My Shepherd, make me Thine.
Of every good the Fountain,
    Thou art the Spring of mine.
Thy lips with love distilling,
    And milk of truth sincere,
With heaven's bliss are filling
    The soul that trembles here.

6 Beside Thee, Lord, I've taken
    My place—forbid me not!
Hence will I ne'er be shaken
    Though Thou to death be brought.
If pain's last paleness hold Thee,
    In agony opprest—
Then, then will I enfold Thee,
    Within this arm and breast.

7 The joy can ne'er be spoken—
    Above all joys beside;
When in Thy body broken
    I thus with safety hide.
My Lord of life desiring
    Thy glory now to see,
Beside the cross expiring
    I'd breathe my soul to Thee.

8 What language shall I borrow
    To thank Thee, dearest Friend,

For this, Thy dying sorrow,
  Thy pity without end !
O make me Thine forever,
  And should I fainting be,
Lord, let me never, never
  Outlive my love to Thee.

9 And when I am departing,
  O part not Thou from me;
When mortal pangs are darting,
  Come Lord and set me free.
And when my heart must languish
  Amidst the final throe,
Release me from my anguish
  By Thine own pain and woe.

10 Be near me when I'm dying,
  O show Thy cross to me !
And for my succor flying,
  Come, Lord, to set me free.
These eyes new faith receiving
  From Jesus shall not move,
For he, who dies believing,
  Dies safely through Thy love.
        Paul Gerhardt, 1656.
        Trans. J. W. Alexander, 1859.

"O Lamb of God, that takest away the sin of the world, have mercy upon us."

174   *German Choral.*

O LAMB of God, who bleeding,
  Upon the cross didst languish,
Nor scorn, nor malice heeding,
  So patient in Thine anguish.
On Thee our guilt was lying;
Thou savedst us by dying.
  Have mercy on us, Lord Jesus.

2 O Lamb of God, who bleeding, &c.
  Grant us Thy peace, Lord Jesus.
        Nikolaus Decius, 1523.
        Trans. T. C. Porter, 1859.

"He was wounded for our transgressions."

175   *8s & 7s, 6 lines.*

NOW, my soul ! Thy voice upraising,
  Tell, in sweet and mournful strain,

How the Crucified, enduring
    Grief, and wounds, and dying pain,
Freely of His love was offered,
    Sinless was for sinners slain.

2 See! His hands and feet are fastened;
    So He makes His people free:
Not a wound whence blood is flowing
    But a fount of grace shall be;
Yea, the very nails which nail Him
    Nail us also to the tree.

3 Through His heart the spear is piercing,
    Though His foes have seen Him die;
Blood and water thence are streaming
    In a tide of mystery,
Water from our guilt to cleanse us,
    Blood to win us crowns on high.

4 Jesus! may those precious fountains
    Drink to thirsting souls afford;
Let them be our cup and healing,
    And at length our full reward;
So a ransomed world shall ever
    Praise Thee, its redeeming Lord.
              Santolius Maglorianus, 1650.
                  Trans: *Hy. Wm. Baker, 1861.*

" What things were gain to me those I counted loss for Christ."

176   L. M.

WHEN I survey the wondrous cross,
    On which the Prince of glory died,
My richest gain I count but loss,
    And pour contempt on all my pride.

2 Forbid it, Lord, that I should boast,
    Save in the death of Christ, my God;
All the vain things that charm me most,
    I sacrifice them to His blood.

3 See from His head, His hands, His feet,
    Sorrow and love flow mingled down!
Did e'er such love and sorrow meet,
    Or thorns compose so rich a crown?

4 Were the whole realm of nature mine,
    That were a present far too small:
Love so amazing, so divine,
    Demands my soul, my life, my all.   *Isaac Watts*, 1707.

"He bore our sins in His own body on the tree."

177   7s.

O THOU Majesty divine!
    Jesus! on that cross of Thine!
Who can prove his love to Thee
By such a test of agony?

2 Show me, Lord, Thy wounds, I pray,
Let me love for love repay;
Let Thy blood, thus shed for me,
Now my life and healing be.

3 What in me is wounded yet,
What doth still disease beget,
Dearest Saviour, make it whole,
Lord, restore this sin-sick soul.

4 Lord, my heart would feel and know
All Thine agony and woe,
Each deep wound, that I may be
Wholly crucified with Thee.

5 Gracious Jesus, Saviour dear!
Guilty though I be, give ear;
Spurn me not, though vile, I pray,
From Thy blessed cross away.

6 Lying at Thy mercy-seat,
Lo! with tears I wash Thy feet;
Pity on my misery take,
Jesus, for Thy mercy's sake.

7 From Thy cross, uplifted high,
O Belovèd, cast Thine eye:
Turn me to Thee, heart and soul;
By Thy sorrows make me whole.

8 Here I'll mourn with my last breath,
O'er my sins, and o'er Thy death;
Jesus, Lamb of God, Thy cross
Saves me from eternal loss.

"Thou hast loved us, and washed us from our sins in Thine own blood."

178   7s & 6s.

O JESUS, in Thy torture
    Nailed to the bitter tree,
My soul's true Guide and Nurture
I yearn to be with Thee.

2 How can I taste of pleasure
   Whilst Thou dost hang in pain,
Jesus mine only Treasure,
   Mine everlasting Gain?

3 O Jesus, may Thy sadness,
   Thine agony and tears,
Win for my spirit gladness
   Throughout the endless years.

4 With Thine own body feed me,
   Life to my soul accord,
Then to Thy pierc'd heart lead me,
   And hide me there, O Lord.

5 And in my dying hour
   By those sharp wounds I pray,
Lord, may Thy passion's power
   Wash all my sins away.

Latin Hymn of XV. Century.
Trans :—?

"*Ye are come to the blood of sprinkling, that speaketh better things than that of Abel.*"

179
6s & 5s.

GLORY be to Jesus,
   Who, in bitter pains,
Poured for me the life-blood
   From His sacred veins!

2 Grace and life eternal
   In that blood I find;
Blest be His compassion
   Infinitely kind.

3 Blest through endless ages
   Be the precious stream,
Which from endless torments
   Did the world redeem.

4 Abel's blood for vengeance
   Pleaded to the skies;
But the blood of Jesus
   For our pardon cries.

5 Oft as it is sprinkled
   On our guilty hearts,
Satan in confusion
   Terror-struck departs.

6 Oft as earth exulting
    Wafts its praise on high,
  Angel-hosts rejoicing
    Make their glad reply.

7 Lift ye then your voices;
    Swell the mighty flood;
  And with saints and angels
    Praise the precious blood.
Italian Hymn.
Trans. E. Caswall, 1849.

"And I, if I be lifted up from the earth, will draw all men unto Me."

180   8s & 7s.

SWEET the moments, rich in blessing,
    Which before the cross I spend,
Life, and health, and peace possessing,
    From the sinner's dying Friend!

2 Here I'll sit, forever viewing
    Mercy's streams in streams of blood:
  Precious drops! my soul bedewing,
    Plead, and claim my peace, with God.

3 Truly blessèd is the station,
    Low before His cross to lie,
  While I see divine compassion
    Floating in His languid eye.

4 Here it is I find my heaven,
    While upon the Lamb I gaze;
  Love I much?—I've much forgiven—
    I'm a miracle of grace.

5 Love and grief my heart dividing,
    With my tears His feet I'll bathe;
  Constant still in faith abiding,—
    Life deriving from His death.
James Allen, 1757.
Altered by Walter Shirley, 1776.

"O Death, I will be thy plagues: O grave, I will be thy destruction."

181   L. M.

TO Christ, whose cross repaired our loss,
    All laud and praise from man are due:
Be He the song of every tongue
    The earth's wide bound and heavèn through!

2 That mighty throe of Thy last woe;
   Thy precious blood so freely poured;
Our hearts subdue Thy grace to sue,
   O Jesus Christ, Redeemer, Lord!

3 Who, by the power of that dark hour,
   The reign of sin hast trodden down,
Grant holy peace and full release,
   Redeemer of a world forlorn!

4 Who in the grave—that new-made cave—
   O heavenly King, didst mortal lie:
Teach us to rest safe on Thy breast,
   For Thee to live, in Thee to die.

5 Whom Thou didst call from guilty thrall,
   Vouchsafe in danger to defend,
And lead us on to Thy blest throne,
   The seat of joys that never end.

F. Oakeley.

"Who is this that cometh from Edom, with dyed garments from Bozrah?"

182   8s & 7s, 8 *lines.*

WHO is this that comes from Edom?
   Clad in robes with carnage stain'd;
Bringing victory and freedom
   By His martial prowess gain'd?
'Tis the Captain of salvation
   Who is conquering in the fight,
Rescuing a lost creation
   By His unassisted might.

2 Lord, the course Thou art pursuing
   Is a course of glorious gain;
But the work which Thou art doing
   Is a work of bitter pain;
In a Passion-tide beginning,
   It will lead to bright renown;
By it Thou a way art winning
   To an everlasting crown.

3 Through Thy cloud of shame and sorrow
   Brilliant gleams of light appear;
Whence we hope and comfort borrow
   In our griefs and struggles here;
Thou dost conquer death by dying;
   By Thy death we ever live;

And to us in darkness lying
  Thou dost endless glory give.

4 Cruel hands of sinners bound Thee,
    Thou a sinful world hast freed;
  They with thorns in mockery crown'd Thee,
    Placing in Thy hand a reed;
  Now a starry crown Thou wearest,
    Heavenly King, almighty Lord;
  Sceptre of the world Thou bearest,
    And by angels art adored.
              C. Wordsworth.

"Wash me, and I shall be whiter than snow."

183 C. M.

FOR ever here my rest shall be,
    Close to Thy wounded side;
  This all my hope and all my plea—
    For me the Saviour died!

2 My dying Saviour and my God,
    Fountain for guilt and sin,
  Sprinkle me ever with Thy blood,
    And cleanse and keep me clean.

3 Wash me, and make me thus Thine own;
    Wash me, and mine Thou art;
  Wash me, but not my feet alone,
    My hands, my head, my heart.

4 Th' atonement of Thy blood apply,
    Till faith to sight improve;
  Till hope in full fruition die,
    And all my soul be love.
              Charles Wesley, 1740.

" We bless Thee for all the pains Thou hast suffered, for every drop of blood Thou hast shed, for every word of comfort Thou hast spoken on the cross."

184 7s, 8 *lines.*

BY the blood that flowed from Thee
    In Thy bitter agony;
  By the traitor's guileful kiss
  Filling up Thy bitterness;
    Jesus, Saviour, hear our cry:
    Thou wert suffering once as we:
  Hear the loving litany
    We Thy children sing to Thee.

2 By the cords that, round Thee cast,
Bound Thee to the pillar fast;
By the scourge so meekly borne;
By Thy purple robe of scorn;
  Jesus, Saviour, hear our cry: &c.

3 By the thorns that crowned Thy head;
By the sceptre of a reed;
By Thy foes on bending knee
Mocking at Thy royalty;
  Jesus, Saviour, hear our cry: &c.

4 By the people's cruel jeers;
By the holy women's tears;
By Thy footsteps faint and slow,
Weighed beneath Thy cross of woe:
  Jesus, Saviour, hear our cry: &c.

5 By the nails and pointed spear;
By Thy desolation drear;
By Thy dying prayer which rose
Begging mercy for Thy foes;
  Jesus, Saviour, hear our cry: &c.

6 By the darkness thick as night,
Blotting out the sun from sight;
By the cry with which in death
Thou didst yield Thy parting breath;
  Jesus, Saviour, hear our cry: &c.   *F. W. Faber.*

EASTER EVE.

" And there was Mary Magdalene and the other Mary, sitting over against the sepulchre."

185   *7s, 6 lines.*

RESTING from His work to-day
  In the tomb the Saviour lay;
Still He slept, from head to feet
Shrouded in the winding-sheet,
Lying in the rock alone,
Hidden by the sealèd stone.

2 Late at even there was seen
Watching long the Magdalene;
Early, ere the break of day,
Sorrowful she took her way
To the holy garden glade,
Where her buried Lord was laid.

3 So with Thee, till life shall end
  I would solemn vigil spend;
  Let me hew Thee, Lord, a shrine
  In this rocky heart of mine,
  Where in pure embalmèd cell
  None but Thou may ever dwell.

4 Myrrh and spices will I bring,
  True affection's offering;
  Close the door from sight and sound
  Of the busy world around;
  And in patient watch remain
  Till my Lord appear again.

  Thos. Whytehead, 1842.

"*He went and preached unto the spirits in prison.*"

186
L. M.

JESUS, the Author of our life!
  As Thine our burden and our strife:
  As Thine it was to die and rise,
  So Thine the grave and Paradise.

2 O Lord, who blest the Sabbath-day,
  Lo, at Thy tomb for rest we pray:
  Here rest from our own work; and there
  The perfect rest with Thee to share.

3 O God the Word, who flesh wast made
  And in the grave for sinners laid:
  With Thee this mortal frame we trust;
  O guard and glorify our dust.

4 O soul of Christ, so freely breathed,
  And to the Father's hand bequeathed,
  Draw us with hearts' desire to Thee,
  When we among the dead are free.

5 Dread Preacher, who to fathers old
  Didst wonders in the gloom unfold:
  Thy perfect creed, O may we learn
  In Eden, waiting Thy return.

6 They saw Thy day and heard Thy voice,
  And in Thy glory did rejoice;
  And Thou didst break their prison bars,
  And lead them high above the stars.

7 "Captivity led captive" then
  Was sung by angels and by men:

EASTER EVE.

 Grant us the same to sing by faith,
 Both now, and at the hour of death.

8 Our souls and bodies, Lord, receive,
 To Thine own blessed Easter-eve:
 All our beloved in mercy keep,
 As one by one they fall asleep. *J. Keble.*

"For he that is entered into his rest he also hath ceased from his own works, as God did from His."

187   10s & 6s.

REST, weary Son of God: and I with Thee,
 Rest in that rest of Thine.
My weariness was Thine; Thou bearest it,
 And now Thy rest is mine.

2 Thy life on earth was one sad weariness;
 Nowhere to lay Thy head.
Thy days were toil and heat; Thy lonely nights
 Sought some cold mountain bed.

3 How calmly in that tomb Thou liest now,
 Thy rest how still and deep!
O'er Thee in love the Father rests: He gives
 To His belovèd sleep.

4 On Bethel-pillow now Thy head is laid,
 In Joseph's rock-hewn cell;
Thy watchers are the angels of Thy God:
 They guard Thy slumbers well.

5 Rest, weary Son of God: Thy work is done,
 And all Thy burdens borne;
Rest on that stone, till the third sun has brought
 Thine everlasting morn.

6 Then to a higher, brighter, truer rest,
 Upon the throne above,
Rise, weary Son of Man, to carry out
 Thy glorious work of love.
      Horatius Bonar, 1868.

"And Joseph wrapped the body in a clean linen cloth, and laid it in his own tomb, which he had hewn out in the rock."

188   *German Choral.*

REST of the weary! Thou
 Thyself art resting now,
Where lowly in Thy sepulchre Thou liest.

From out her deathly sleep
My soul doth start, to weep
So sad a wonder, that Thou Saviour diest!

2 Thy bitter anguish o'er,
To this dark tomb they bore
Thee, Life of life,—Thee, Lord of all creation !
The hollow rocky cave
Must serve Thee for a grave,
Who wast Thyself the Rock of our salvation!

3 O Prince of Life ! I know
That when I too lie low,
Thou wilt at last my soul from death awaken ;
Wherefore I will not shrink
From the grave's awful brink ;
The heart that trusts in Thee shall ne'er be shaken.

4 To me the darksome Tomb
Is but a narrow room,
Where I may rest in peace, from sorrow free.
Thy death shall give me power
To cry in that dark hour,
O Death, O Grave, where is your victory?

5 The grave can nought destroy,
Only the flesh can die,
And e'en the body triumphs o'er decay :
Clothed by Thy wondrous might
In robes of dazzling light,
This flesh shall burst the grave at that last day.

6 My Jesus, day by day,
Help me to watch and pray,
Beside the tomb where in my heart Thou'rt laid.
Thy bitter death shall be
My constant memory,
My guide at last into death's awful shade.

Solomon Frank, 1711.
Trans. Catherine Winkworth.

"*Weeping may endure for a night, but joy cometh in the morning.*"

189 *7s & 8s.*

SILENCE in the house of prayer ;
Low our Lord in earth lies sleeping ;
Silence, silence, everywhere,
While the saints their watch are keeping.

EASTER SUNDAY.

2 He at earliest morn shall rise;
   Now in mystic peace He slumbers;
Flow, ye plaintive melodies;
   Ring, ye still recurring numbers.

3 Sweet it seems to sit and wake
   By that tomb in garden lonely,
Knowing He can ne'er forsake,
   This a passing trial only.

4 Though for us His soul doth seek
   That mysterious world of spirits,
He shall rise to cheer the weak;
   Hope and joy His Church inherits.

5 So Lent's latest vigil now
   Keep we with a tempered sadness:
Easter-morn! speed quickly thou,
   And transform this grief to gladness.

6 Silence in the house of prayer;
   Low our Lord in earth lies sleeping;
Silence, silence, everywhere,
   While the saints their watch are keeping.

Arthur T. Gurney.

EASTER SUNDAY.

"Christ our Passover is crucified for us; therefore let us keep the feast."

190   L. M.

THE Lamb's high banquet called to share
   In robes of saintly white we sing:
And through the Red Sea safely brought
   We triumph sound to Christ our King!

2 He gives His body, on the cross
   Consumed with love, to be our food:
And drinking of His roseate blood
   We live upon the living God.

3 Th' avenging angel passes o'er
   The blood drops on the lintel spread:
The waters, cleft for Israel's hosts,
   Soon close to whelm th' Egyptian dead.

4 Now Christ, the Lamb without a stain,
   Is slain our Paschal Lamb to be:

His flesh is our oblation made,
   The leaven of sincerity.
5 Hail, purest Victim heaven could find
   The powers of hell to overthrow:
Thou hast the chains of death destroyed,
   Thou dost the prize of life bestow.

6 Hail, Victor Christ! Hail, risen King,
   To Thee alone belongs the crown:
Thy power the heavenly gates unbarred,
   And dragged the Prince of darkness down.

7 O Jesus, from the death of sin
   Keep us, we pray; so shalt Thou be
The everlasting Paschal joy
   Of all the souls new-born in Thee.

Latin Hymn.
Trans. E. Caswall.

191 *"The glory of the Lord is risen upon thee."*
D. C. M.

AWAKE, glad soul! awake! awake!
   Thy Lord hath risen long;
Go to His grave, and with thee take
   Both tuneful heart and song;
Where Life is waking all around,
   Where Love's sweet voices sing,
The first bright Blossom may be found
   Of an Eternal Spring.

2 To Angels' sleepless eyes alone
   Did heav'n the boon accord;
Their hands had roll'd away the stone
   And deck'd their rising Lord;
And still within the solemn shade
   Of Death they sat and shone,
To point where lately He was laid,
   And tell how He was gone.

3 O Love! which lightens life's distress,
   Love, death cannot destroy;
O Grave! whose very emptiness
   To faith is full of joy:
Let but that Love our hearts supply
   From heaven's Eternal Spring,
Then Grave, where is thy victory?
   And Death, where is thy sting?

I

4 The shade and gloom of life are fled
   This Resurrection Day;
Henceforth in Christ are no more dead,
   The grave hath no more prey:
In Christ we live, in Christ we sleep,
   In Christ we wake and rise;
And the sad tears Death makes us weep
   He wipes from all our eyes.

5 And every bird, and every tree,
   And every opening flower,
Proclaim His glorious victory,
   His Resurrection-power:
The folds are glad, the fields rejoice,
   With vernal verdure spread,
The little hills lift up their voice,
   And shout that Death is dead.

6 Then wake, glad heart! awake! awake!
   And seek thy risen Lord,
Joy in His Resurrection take
   And comfort in His word;
And let thy life, through all its ways,
   One long thanksgiving be,
Its theme of joy, its song of praise,
   Christ died and rose for me.   *J. S. B. Monsell, 1867.*

"Because I live, ye shall live also."

192   7s, 8s, 7s, 8s, 7s, 7s.

JESUS lives, and so shall I.
   Death, Thy sting is gone forever:
He who deigned for me to die,
   Lives, the bands of death to sever.
He shall raise me with the just:
Jesus is my Hope and Trust.

2 Jesus lives and reigns supreme;
   And, His kingdom still remaining,
I shall also be with Him,
   Ever living, ever reigning.
God has promised; be it must:
Jesus is my Hope and Trust.

3 Jesus lives, and God extends
   Grace to each returning sinner.
Rebels He receives as friends,
   And exalts to highest honor.
God is true as He is just;
Jesus is my Hope and Trust.

4 Jesus lives, and by His grace,
  Victory o'er my passions giving,
 I will cleanse my heart and ways,
  Ever to His glory living.
 Th' weak He raises from the dust:
 Jesus is my Hope and Trust.

5 Jesus lives, and I am sure
  Naught shall e'er from Jesus sever:
 Satan's wiles and Satan's power,
  Pain or pleasures, ye shall never!
 Christian armor cannot rust:
 Jesus is my Hope and Trust.

6 Jesus lives, and death is now
  But my entrance into glory:
 Courage! then, my soul, for thou
  Hast a crown of life before thee;
 Thou shalt find thy hopes were just;
 Jesus is the Christian's trust.
  Chr. F. Gellert, 1757.
  Trans: Unknown.

*"Ye seek Jesus of Nazareth which was crucified: He is risen;
He is not here."*

193 7s.

CHRIST the Lord is risen to-day,
  Sons of men and angels say;
Raise your joys and triumphs high,
Sing, ye heavens, and earth reply.

2 Love's redeeming work is done,
 Fought the fight, the battle won;
 Lo! the sun's eclipse is o'er,
 Lo! he sets in blood no more.

3 Vain the stone, the watch, the seal,
 Christ hath burst the bonds of hell;
 Death in vain forbids Him rise,
 Christ hath opened Paradise.

4 Lives again our glorious King!
 "Where, O death, is now thy sting?"
 Once He died our souls to save,
 "Where's thy vict'ry, boasting grave?"

5 Soar we now where Christ hath led,
 Foll'wing our exalted Head:
 Made like Him, like Him we rise,
 Ours the cross, the grave, the skies.
  Charles Wesley, 1739.

EASTER SUNDAY.

"*He was dead, and behold He is alive forevermore.*"

194 7s, 8 lines.

AT the Lamb's high feast we sing
Praise to our victorious King,
Who hath washed us in the tide
Flowing from His piercèd side:
Praise we Him, whose love divine
Gives His guests His blood for wine,
Gives His body for the feast;
Love the Victim—Love the Priest.

2 Where the Paschal blood is poured
Death's dark angel sheathes his sword;
Israel's hosts triumphant go
Through the wave that drowns the foe.
Praise we Christ, whose blood was shed,
Paschal Victim, Paschal Bread:
With sincerity and love
Eat we manna from above.

3 Mighty Victim from the sky,
Hell's fierce powers beneath Thee lie:
Thou hast conquered in the fight;
Thou hast brought us life and light.
Now no more can death appal,
Now no more the grave enthral:
Thou hast opened Paradise,
And in Thee Thy saints shall rise.

4 Easter triumph, Easter joy—
Sin alone can this destroy:
From sin's power do Thou set free
Souls new-born, O Lord, in Thee.
Hymns of glory and of praise,
Father unto Thee we raise;
Risen Lord, all praise to Thee,
With the Spirit, ever be.

Latin Hymn.
Trans. R. Campbell, 1850.

"*Oh death where is thy sting? oh grave where is thy victory?*"

195 7s, 6s, 8 lines.

THE Lord of life is risen,
Sing, Easter heralds, sing;
He bursts His rocky prison,
Wide let the triumph ring.

In death no longer lying,
  He rose, the Prince, to-day;
Life of the dead and dying
  He triumphed o'er decay.

2 The Lord of life is risen,
    And love no longer grieves;
  In ruin lies death's prison,
    Sing, heralds, Jesus lives.
  We hear Thy blessed greeting:
    Salvation's work is done!
  We worship Thee, repeating:
    "Life for the dead is won!"

3 Around Thy tomb, O Jesus,
    How sweet the Easter breath;
  Hear we not in the breezes,
    "Where is Thy sting, O Death?"
  Dark hell flies in commotion,
    The heavens their anthems sing;
  While far o'er earth and ocean,
    Glad hallelujahs ring!

4 O publish this salvation,
    Ye heralds, through the earth;
  To every buried nation
    Proclaim the day of birth.
  Till, rising from their slumbers
    In long and ancient night,
  The countless heathen numbers
    Shall hail the Easter light.

5 Hail! hail! our Jesus risen!
    Sing, ransomed brethren, sing!
  Through death's dark, gloomy prison,
    Let Easter chorals ring.
  Haste, haste, ye captive legions
    Accept your glad reprieve;
  Come forth from sin's dark regions—
    In Jesus' kingdom live.

J. P. Lange, 1851.
Trans. H. Harbaugh.

"The Lord is risen indeed."

196 S. M.

"THE Lord is ris'n indeed;"
  The grave hath lost its prey;
With Him shall rise the ransom'd seed
  To reign in endless day.

2 "The Lord is ris'n indeed;"
   He lives, to die no more;
   He lives, His people's cause to plead,
   Whose curse and shame He bore.

3 "The Lord is ris'n indeed;"
   Attending angels, hear;
   Up to the courts of heav'n, with speed,
   The joyful tidings bear.

4 Then take your golden lyres,
   And strike each cheerful chord;
   Join all the bright, celestial choirs,
   To sing our risen Lord.
                    Thomas Kelly, 1804.

"I am He that liveth and was dead; and behold I am alive forevermore, Amen; and have the keys of hell and death."

197   8s, 7s, 8 *lines.*

HALLELUJAH! Hallelujah!
   Hearts to heaven and voices raise;
Sing to God a hymn of gladness,
Sing to God a hymn of praise.
He who on the cross a victim
For the world's salvation bled,
Jesus Christ, the King of glory,
Now is risen from the dead.

2 Now the iron bars are broken,
   Christ from death to life is born,
   Glorious life, and life immortal
   On this holy Easter morn:
   Christ has triumphed and we conquer
   By His vict'ry o'er the grave;
   Quicken'd with Him by the Spirit,
   We the life eternal have.

3 Christ is risen, Christ the first-fruits
   Of the holy harvest-field,
   Which will all its full abundance
   At His second coming yield;
   Men the golden ears of harvest
   With their heads before Him wave,
   Ripened by His glorious sunshine,
   From the furrows of the grave.

4 Christ is risen, we are risen.
   Shed upon us heav'nly grace,

EASTER SUNDAY. 135

    Rain and dew and streams of glory
    From the brightness of Thy face,
    That we, with our hearts in heavèn,
    Here on earth may fruitful be,
    And by angel hands be gather'd,
    And be ever, Lord, with Thee.
              Christopher Wordsworth, altered.

"*If ye then be risen with Christ, seek those things which are above.*"

198   7s, 8s, 7s, 8s, 4s.

    JESUS lives! no longer now
      Can thy terrors, Death, appal us:
    Jesus lives! by this we know
      Thou, O Grave, can'st not enthral us.
        Alleluia!

2 Jesus lives! henceforth is death
    But the gate of life immortal:
This shall calm our trembling breath,
    When we pass its gloomy portal.
      Alleluia!

3 Jesus lives! for us He died:
    Then, alone to Jesus living,
Pure in heart may we abide,
    Glory to our Saviour giving.
      Alleluia!

4 Jesus lives! our hearts know well
    Nought from us His love shall sever;
Life, nor death, nor powers of hell
    Tear us from His keeping ever.
      Alleluia!

5 Jesus lives! to Him the throne
    Over all the world is given:
May we go where He is gone,
    Rest and reign with Him in heaven.
      Alleluia!
               C. E. Gellert, 1757.
             Trans. Frances E. Cox, 1841.

"*Alleluia.*"

199

THE strain upraise of joy and praise, Alleluia!
    To the glory of their King
Shall the ransomed people sing Alleluia!

3 And the choirs that dwell on high
Shall re-echo through the sky Alleluia!

4 They through the fields of Paradise that roam,
   The blessed ones, repeat through that bright home Alleluia!
5 The planets glitt'ring on their heavenly way,
   The shining constellations, join, and say Alleluia!
6 Ye clouds that onward sweep!
   Ye winds on pinions light!
   Ye thunders echoing loud and deep!
   Ye lightnings, wildly bright!
   In sweet consent unite your Alleluia!
7 Ye floods and ocean billows!
   Ye storms and winter snow!
   Ye days of cloudless beauty!
   Hoar frost and summer glow!
   Ye groves that wave in spring,
   And glorious forests, sing Alleluia!
8 First let the birds with painted plumage gay,
   Exalt their great Creator's praise, and say Alleluia!
9 Then let the beasts of earth with varying strain,
   Join in creation's hymn, and cry again Alleluia!
10 Here let the mountains thunder forth, sonorous Alleluia!
    There let the valleys sing in gentler chorus, Alleluia!
11 Thou jubilant abyss of ocean, cry Alleluia!
    Ye tracts of earth and continents, reply Alleluia!
12 To God, who all creation made,
    The frequent hymn be duly paid: Alleluia!
13 This is the strain, the eternal strain, the Lord of all things
       loves: Alleluia!
    This is the song, the heav'nly song, that Christ Himself ap-
       proves: Alleluia!
14 Wherefore we sing, both heart and voice awaking, Alleluia!
    And children's voices echo, answer making, Alleluia!
15 Now from all men be outpour'd
    Alleluia to the Lord;
    With Alleluia evermore
    The Son and Spirit we adore.
16 Praise be done to the Three in One.
    Alleluia! Alleluia! Alleluia! Alleluia.
                                        Godescalcus, 950.
                                    Trans: Jno M. Neale, 1851.

"*The first begotten of the dead, and the prince of the kings of
the earth.*"

200   8s & 7s, 8 *lines.*

ALLELUIA, sing to Jesus,
   His the sceptre, His the throne;

Alleluia, His the triumph,
  His the victory alone ;
Hark the songs of peaceful Zion
  Thunder like a mighty flood ;
Jesus out of every nation
  Hath redeemed us by His blood.

2 Alleluia, Bread of angels
    Thou on earth our Food, our Stay,
  Alleluia, here the sinful
    Flee to Thee from day to day;
  Intercessor, Friend of sinners,
    Earth's Redeemer, plead for me,
  Where the songs of all the sinless
    Sweep across the crystal sea.

3 Alleluia, King eternal,
    Thee the Lord of lords we own ;
  Alleluia, born of Mary,
    Earth Thy footstool, heav'n Thy throne :
  Thou within the veil hast entered,
    Robed in flesh, our great High Priest ;
  Thou on earth both Priest and Victim
    In the Eucharistic Feast.
                              W. C. Dix.

"The angel of the Lord descended from heaven, and came and rolled back the stone from the door, and sat upon it."

201   H. M.

YES, the Redeemer rose,
    The Saviour left the dead ;
  And o'er our hellish foes
    High raised His conquering head :
  In wild dismay, the guards around
  Fall to the ground, and sink away.

2 Lo ! the angelic bands
    In full assembly meet,
  To wait His high commands
    And worship at His feet :
  Joyful they come, and wing their way,
  From realms of day to Jesus' tomb.

3 Then back to heaven they fly,
    And the glad tidings bear ;
  Hark ! as they soar on high,
    What music fills the air !

Their anthems say, "Jesus, who bled,
Hath left the dead; He rose to-day."

4 Ye mortals! catch the sound,—
    Redeemed by Him from hell;
And send the echo round
    The globe on which you dwell;
Transported cry, "Jesus, who bled,
Hath left the dead, no more to die."

5 All hail! triumphant Lord!
    Who sav'st us with Thy blood:
Wide be Thy name adored,
    Thou rising, reigning God!
With Thee we rise, with Thee we reign
And empires gain, beyond the skies.

Philip Doddridge, 1740.

EASTER MONDAY.

"Behold two of them went that same day to a village called Emmaus."

202 7s.

WHEN two friends on Easter-day
    To Emmaus bent their way,
On that Paschal eventide
Christ was walking at their side.

2 Then their hearts within them glow'd
When Himself to them He show'd
In the Scripture, as a King
Glorified by suffering.

3 Thou art ever with us, Lord,
Walking in Thy holy word;
And Thy voice, O Saviour dear,
In that word we ever hear;

4 What the holy prophets meant
In the ancient Testament,
Thou art opening to our view,
Lord, forever in the New.

5 And Thy presence, Lord, we feel
When we at Thy table kneel;
When we feed upon Thee there,
We too at Emmaus are.

6 Though not kenn'd by carnal eye,
Yet we know Thee ever nigh;
Though Thou art much further gone
Even to Thy heavenly throne;

7 Yet we, Lord, behold Thy face
Ever in the means of grace:
There Thou walkest by our side,
There Thou with us dost abide.

Christopher Wordsworth.

"Abide with us: for it is toward evening and the day is far spent."

203 10s.

ABIDE with me; fast falls the eventide:
The darkness deepens; Lord! with me abide;
When other helpers fail, and comforts flee,
Help of the helpless! Oh! abide with me.

2 Swift to its close ebbs out life's little day;
Earth's joys grow dim; its glories pass away;
Change and decay in all around I see:
O Thou who changest not! abide with me.

3 I need Thy presence every passing hour;
What, but Thy grace, can foil the Tempter's pow'r?
Who, like Thyself, my Guide and Stay can be?
Through cloud and sunshine, Oh! abide with me.

4 I fear no foe with Thee at hand to bless;
Ills have no weight, and tears no bitterness;
Where is death's sting? where, grave! thy victory?
I triumph still, if Thou abide with me.

5 Hold Thou Thy cross before my closing eyes;
Shine through the gloom, and point me to the skies;
Heav'n's morning breaks, and earth's vain shadows flee:
In life and death, O Lord! abide with me.

Henry Francis Lyte, 1847.

"Abide in me and I in you."

204 C. M.

'ABIDE with us,' the shades of eve
Are falling fast around;
'Far spent' the day—O do not leave
The souls Thy love has found!

2 O leave us!—tho' slow of heart
  To trust Thy plighted word;
  Abide, nor evermore depart,
  Abide with us, O Lord!

3 The solemn joy, the awful fear,
  The hallow'd hush of peace,
  The consciousness that Thou art near,
  We would not these should cease.

4 They came to us with glad accord
  This blessed Easter-tide,
  They will 'abide with us,' O Lord
  If Thou with us abide.

J. S. B. Monsell, 1857.

"*He is Lord of all.*"

205 C. M.

ALL hail! the power of Jesus' name,
  Let angels prostrate fall,
Bring forth the royal diadem,
  And crown Him Lord of all.

2 Crown Him, ye morning stars of light,
  Who fixed this floating ball;
  Now hail the strength of Israel's might,
  And crown Him Lord of all.

3 Crown Him, ye martyrs of our God,
  Who from His altar call;
  Extol the stem of Jesse's rod
  And crown Him Lord of all.

4 Ye chosen seed of Israel's race,
  Ye ransomed from the fall,
  Hail Him who saves you by His grace,
  And crown Him Lord of all.

5 Hail Him, ye heirs of David's line,
  Whom David, Lord did call;
  The God incarnate! Man divine!
  And crown Him Lord of all.

6 Sinners, whose love can ne'er forget
  The wormwood and the gall;
  Go, spread your trophies at His feet,
  And crown Him Lord of all.

7 Let every kindred, every tribe
  On this terrestrial ball,
  To Him all majesty ascribe,
  And crown Him Lord of all.

8 O that with yonder sacred throng,
  We at His feet may fall;
  We'll join the everlasting song,
  And crown Him Lord of all.
                Edward Perronet, 1780, *altered.*

FIRST SUNDAY AFTER EASTER.

"Then were the disciples glad when they saw the Lord."

206   L. M.

THAT Easter-tide with joy was bright,
  The sun shone out a fairer light,
When to their longing eyes restor'd,
Th' Apostles saw their risen Lord.

2 He bade them see His hands, His side,
  Where yet the glorious wounds abide;
  Oh, tokens true, which made it plain
  Their Lord indeed was ris'n again.

3 Jesus, the King of righteousness,
  Do Thou Thyself our hearts possess,
  That we may give Thee all our days
  The tribute of our grateful praise.

4 O Lord of all, with us abide
  In this our joyful Easter-tide;
  From every weapon death can wield
  Thine own redeem'd forever shield.

"Then came Jesus, the doors being shut, and stood in the midst, and said, 'Peace be unto you.'"

207   7s.

CALM they sit with closèd door
  Shutting out the city's din;
Tenant of the tomb no more
  See the Saviour enter in;

2 Spirit-like behold Him glide
    To each saintly wond'ring guest,
  Show His piercèd hands and side,
    Breathe His peace in every breast.

3 What though years have rolled away,
 Since, triumphant from the tomb,
Jesus, at the close of day,
 Sought that quiet, upper room.

4 Oft from Zion's heavenly hill
 Seeks He yet His faithful few,
Bides with them in spirit still,
 Shows each glorious wound anew.

5 Mighty Lord, descend, we pray,
 Where Thy fond disciples meet;
Many a Magdalene to-day
 Fain would her Deliv'rer greet:

6 Many a Thomas scarce can dare
 Own Thee for His God and Lord;
Come and banish doubt and care
 With Thy true almighty Word.

"He that believeth on the Son of God hath the witness in himself."

208   7s, 8s, 7s, 8s, 7s, 7s.

JESUS, my eternal Trust,
 And my Saviour, ever liveth;
This I know; and deep and just
 Is the peace this knowledge giveth;
Calm though death's long night be fraught
Still with many an anxious thought.

2 Hope's strong chain, around me bound,
 Still shall twine my Saviour grasping;
And my hand of faith be found,
 As death left it, Jesus clasping;
No assault the foe can make,
E'er that deathless clasp shall break!

3 I am flesh, and therefore duly
 Dust and ashes must become;
This I know, but know as truly,
 He will wake me from the tomb,
That with Him, whate'er betide,
I may evermore abide!

4 God Himself in that best place,
 Shall a glorious body give me;
I shall see His blissful face,
 To His heav'ns He'll receive me;
To His joyful presence raise,
Ever upon Christ to gaze!

SECOND SUNDAY AFTER EASTER.

5 Then these eyes my Lord shall know,
   My Redeemer, and my Brother;
In His love my soul shall glow,
   I myself, and not another!
Then from this rejoicing heart
Every weakness shall depart.
Louisa Henrietta of Brandenburg, 1653.
Trans. Elizabeth Charles?

"We see Jesus who was made a little lower than the angels, for the suffering of death, crowned with glory and honor."

209   C. M.

HOSANNA to the Prince of light,
   Who clothed Himself in clay,
Entered the iron gates of death,
   And tore the bars away.

2 Death is no more the king of dread,
   Since our Immanuel rose:
He took the tyrant's sting away,
   And vanquished all our foes.

3 See how the Conq'ror mounts aloft,
   And to His Father flies,
With scars of honor in His flesh,
   And triumph in His eyes!

4 Raise your devotion, mortal tongues,
   To reach His blessed abode:
Sweet be the accents of your songs
   To our incarnate God.

5 Bright angels! strike your loudest strings,
   Your sweetest voices raise;
Let heaven, and all created things,
   Sound our Immanuel's praise.
Isaac Watts, 1707.

SECOND SUNDAY AFTER EASTER.

"The Lord is my shepherd; I shall not want."

210   S. M.

THE Lord my Shepherd is,
   I shall be well supplied;
Since He is mine, and I am His,
   What can I want beside?

2 He leads me to the place
   Where heav'nly pasture grows,
  Where living waters gently pass,
   And full salvation flows.

3 If e'er I go astray,
   He doth my soul reclaim,
  And guides me in His own right way
   For His most holy Name.

4 While He affords His aid
   I cannot yield to fear;
  Though I should walk through death's dark shade,
   My Shepherd's with me there.

5 In spite of all my foes
   Thou dost my table spread;
  My cup with blessings overflows
   And joy exalts my head.

6 The bounties of Thy love
   Shall crown my foll'wing days;
  Nor from Thy house will I remove,
   Nor cease to speak Thy praise.

Isaac Watts, 1719.

"I am the good shepherd."

211
L. M.

JESUS, the shepherd of the sheep,
  Thy little flock in safety keep;
The flock for which Thou cam'st from heav'n,
The flock for which Thy life was giv'n.

2 O guard Thy sheep from beasts of prey,
  And guide them that they never stray:
  Cherish the young, sustain the old,
  Let none be feeble in Thy fold.

3 Secure them from the scorching beam,
  And lead them to the living stream:
  In verdant pastures let them lie,
  And watch them with a shepherd's eye.

4 O may Thy sheep discern Thy voice,
  And in its sacred sound rejoice:
  From strangers may they ever flee,
  And know no other guide but Thee.

5 Lord, bring Thy sheep that wander yet,
And let the number be complete
Then let Thy flock from earth remove,
And occupy the fold above. *Thomas Kelly.*

"I know that my Redeemer liveth."

212 L. M.

HE lives, the great Redeemer lives,
What joy the blest assurance gives:
And now, before His Father, God,
Pleads the full merit of His blood.

2 Repeated crimes awake our fears,
And justice, armed with frowns, appears;
But in the Saviour's lovely face,
Sweet mercy smiles, and all is peace.

3 Hence, then, ye black despairing thoughts,
Above our fears, above our faults,
His pow'rful intercessions rise,
And guilt recedes, and terror dies.

4 In ev'ry dark, distressful hour,
When sin and Satan join their power,
Let this dear hope repel the dart,
That Jesus bears us on His heart.

5 Great Advocate, almighty Friend!
On Him our humble hopes depend:
Our cause can never, never fail,
For Jesus pleads, and must prevail.

Anne Steele, 1760.

"For ye were as sheep going astray; but are now returned unto the Shepherd and Bishop of your souls."

213 H. M.

GREAT Prophet of my God,
My tongue would bless Thy name:
By Thee the joyful news
Of our salvation came:
The joyful news of sins forgiven,
Of hell subdued, and peace with heaven.

2 Be Thou my Counsellor,
My Pattern, and my Guide:
And through this desert land
Still keep me near Thy side:
O let my feet ne'er run astray,
Nor rove, nor seek the crooked way.

3 I love my Shepherd's voice:
   His watchful eyes shall keep
 My wandering soul among
   The thousands of His sheep;
 He feeds His flock, He calls their names,
 His bosom bears the tender lambs.
                              Isaac Watts, 1709.

"The God of peace who brought again from the dead our Lord Jesus, the great Shepherd of the sheep, through the blood of the everlasting covenant, make you perfect."

214 7s.

NOW may He, who, from the dead,
   Brought the Shepherd of the sheep,
 Jesus Christ, our King and Head,
   All our souls in safety keep!

2 May He teach us to fulfil
   What is pleasing in His sight;
 Perfect us in all His will,
   And preserve us day and night!

3 To that dear Redeemer's praise
   Who the covenant sealed with blood,
 Let our hearts and voices raise
   Loud thanksgivings to our God.
                              John Newton, 1779.

"He shall feed his flock like a shepherd."

215 L. M.

JESUS, my Shepherd, let me share
   Thy guiding hand, Thy tender care;
 And let me ever find in Thee,
 A refuge and a rest for me.

2 O lead me ever by Thy side,
 Where fields are green, and waters glide;
 And be Thou still, where'er I be,
 A refuge and a rest for me.

3 While I this barren desert tread,
 Feed Thou my soul on heavenly bread;
 'Mid foes and fears Thee may I see,
 A refuge and a rest for me.

4 Anoint me with Thy gladdening grace,
 To cheer me in the heavenly race;
 Cause all my gloomy doubts to flee,
 And make my spirit rest in Thee.

5 When death shall end this mortal strife,
  Bring me through death to endless life;
  Then, face to face, beholding Thee,
  My refuge and my rest shall be.

THIRD SUNDAY AFTER EASTER.

"For to this end Christ both died and rose and revived, that He might be Lord both of the dead and the living."

216 8s, 7s, 8s, 7s, 8s, 8s, 7s.

THE Lord of Might from Sinai's brow
    Gave forth His voice of thunder:
And Israel lay on earth below,
    Outstretched in fear and wonder:
Beneath His feet was pitchy night,
And at His left hand and His right
    The rocks were rent asunder.

2 The Lord of Love on Calvary,
    A meek and suffering stranger,
  Upraised to heaven His languid eye,
    In nature's hour of danger:
  For us He bore the weight of woe,
  For us He gave His blood to flow,
    And met His Father's anger.

3 The Lord of Love, the Lord of Might,
    The King of all created,
  Shall back return to claim His right,
    On clouds of glory seated:
  With trumpet-sound and angel-song,
  And hallelujahs loud and long,
    O'er death and hell defeated. *Reginald Heber.*

"A little while, and ye shall see me, because I go to the Father."

217 L. M.

LET me be with Thee where Thou art,
    My Saviour, my eternal Rest:
  Then only will this longing heart
    Be fully and for ever blest.

2 Let me be with Thee where Thou art,
    Thy unveiled glory to behold:
  Then only will this wandering heart
    Cease to be treach'rous, faithless, cold.

3 Let me be with Thee where Thou art,
    Where spotless saints Thy name adore:
  Then only will this sinful heart
    Be evil and defiled no more.

4 Let me be with Thee where Thou art,
    Where none can die, where none remove:
  Then neither death nor life will part
    Me from Thy presence and Thy love.
                      Charlotte Elliott, 1836.

"I beseech you as strangers and pilgrims, abstain from fleshly lusts."

218   C. M.

SAVED by Thy blood, the Red Sea pass'd,
    Our foes o'erthrown by Thee,
  Strangers in this world's wilderness,
    And pilgrims, Lord, are we.

2 But Thou art with us; in the night
    Thy shining pillar leads,
  In scorching sands Thy streams refresh,
    Thy heav'nly manna feeds.

3 Thy church, O Saviour, holds the Law
    By Thy dread Godhead given,
  Preaches Thy word, and taught by Thee
    Dispenses grace from heaven.

4 O keep us far from fleshly lusts;
    For, cleans'd, O Lord by Thee,
  Strangers in this world's wilderness,
    And pilgrims here are we;

5 Obedient to Thy will, O Lord,
    And by Thy bounty blest,
  So may we reach the promised land,
    The Canaan of our Rest.   *Christopher Wordsworth.*

"Your heart shall rejoice, and your joy no man taketh from you."

219   H. M.

REJOICE! the Lord is King!—
    Your God and King adore;
  Mortals! give thanks, and sing,
    And triumph evermore:
  Lift up your hearts,—lift up your voice,
  Rejoice! again, I say, rejoice!

2 His kingdom cannot fail;
    He rules o'er earth and heaven;

The keys of death and hell
  Are to our Jesus given:
Lift up your hearts,—lift up your voice,
Rejoice! again, I say, rejoice!

3 He all His foes shall quell,
    Shall all our sins destroy;
  And every bosom swell
    With pure seraphic joy:
  Lift up your hearts,—lift up your voice,
  Rejoice! again, I say, rejoice!

4 Rejoice in glorious hope;
    Jesus, the Judge, shall come,
  And take His servants up
    To their eternal home:
  We soon shall hear th' archangel's voice,
  The trump of God shall sound, rejoice!
                                Charles Wesley, 1746.

"Wait on the Lord: be of good courage, and He shall strengthen thy heart."

220   C. M.

THE Lord of glory is my light,
    And my salvation too;
  God is my strength; nor will I fear
    What all my foes can do.

2 One privilege my heart desires;
    O grant me an abode,
  Among the churches of Thy saints,
    The temples of my God!

3 There shall I offer my requests,
    And see Thy beauty still;
  Shall hear Thy messages of love,
    And there inquire Thy will.

4 When troubles rise, and storms appear,
    There may His children hide;
  God has a strong pavilion, where
    He makes my soul abide.

5 Now shall my head be lifted high
    Above my foes around,
  And songs of joy and victory
    Within Thy temple sound.   *Isaac Watts*, 1719.

221

"I go to prepare a place for you."
S. M.

"Forever with the Lord!"
  Amen, so let it be:
Life from the dead is in that word,
  And immortality.

2 Here in the body pent,
    Absent from Him I roam,
  Yet nightly pitch my moving tent
    A day's march nearer home.

3 My Father's house on high,
    Home of my soul, how near
  At times to Faith's foreseeing eye
    Thy golden gates appear!

4 My thirsty spirit faints
    To reach the land I love,
  The bright inheritance of saints,
    Jerusalem above!

5 I hear at morn and even,
    At noon and midnight hour,
  The choral harmonies of heaven
    Earth's Babel tongues o'erpower.

6 "Forever with the Lord!"
    Father, if 'tis Thy will,
  The promise of that faithful word,
    E'en here to me fulfil.

7 So, when my latest breath
    Shall rend the veil in twain,
  By death I shall escape from death,
    And life eternal gain.

8 Knowing as I am known,
    How shall I love that word,
  And oft repeat before the throne,
    "Forever with the Lord!" *James Montgomery*, 1835.

222

"Lo I am with you alway, even unto the end of the world."
8s, 7s, 8 lines.

"Always with us, always with us:"—
  Words of cheer and words of love;
Thus the risen Saviour whispers,
  From His dwelling-place above.
With us, when we toil in sadness,
  Sowing much and reaping none;
Telling us that in the future
  Golden harvests shall be won:

2 With us, when the storm is sweeping
    O'er our pathway dark and drear ;
Waking hope within our bosoms,
    Stilling every anxious fear :
With us, in the lonely valley,
    When we cross the chilling stream ;
Lighting up the steps to glory,
    With salvation's radiant beam.
          Edwin H. Nevin, 1858.

FOURTH SUNDAY AFTER EASTER.

"It is expedient for you that I go away; for if I go not away, the Comforter will not come unto you."

223   8*s*, 6*s*, 8*s*, 4*s*.

OUR blest Redeemer, ere He breathed
    His tender last farewell,
A Guide, a Comforter, bequeathed
    With us to dwell.

2 He came sweet influence to impart,
    A gracious, willing Guest,
While He can find one humble heart
    Wherein to rest.

3 And His that gentle voice we hear,
    Soft as the breath of even,
That checks each thought, that calms each fear,
    And speaks of heaven.

4 And every virtue we possess,
    And every conquest won,
And every thought of holiness,
    Are His alone.

5 Spirit of purity and grace,
    Our weakness, pitying, see :
O make our hearts Thy dwelling-place,
    And worthier Thee.   *Harriet Auber*, 1829.

"Every good gift and every perfect gift is from above, and cometh down from the Father of Lights."

224   L. M.

FATHER of lights ! to Thee we pray,
    Guide us and cheer us on our way ;
Lift up Thy countenance divine,
And on our heavenward journey shine.

2 The joys of earth are brief and vain,
   Their glistening spangles quickly wane,
   Thy light no change or shadow knows,
   But with eternal splendor glows.

3 Thou, Lord, who didst on Sinai's hill
   In cloud and thunder speak Thy will,
   And didst with Thine Almighty hand
   Inscribe on stone Thy dread command;

4 Write now the law, which love imparts,
   Upon the tables of our hearts;
   With Thy free Spirit us inspire,
   Illume with light, and warm with fire.

5 No mirror, where with flickering ray
   The evanescent shadows play,
   No, but a faithful chart, O Lord,
   To us is Thine unerring word;

6 There with eyes riveted we trace
   The roads and rivers of Thy grace,
   Which bear the pilgrim on his way
   To realms of everlasting day.

7 Lord, give us grace with faith to read
   And in our lives show forth our creed;
   Like Christ, to visit in distress
   The widow and the fatherless;

8 Not by the lures of sin beguiled,
   Not by the stains of sin defiled;
   But walking in the light of love
   To Thy Jerusalem above.

C. Wordsworth.

"*I will not leave you comfortless.*"

225 L. M.

THOU, who dost build for us on high,
   A house beyond the shining sky:
Draw us, O Christ, to Thee above,
And bind us there with cords of love!

2 Thou Source of good, most gracious Lord;
   Thyself shalt be our great reward:
   In Thee we wake from life's brief night
   Translated into endless light.

3 If Thou dost love us, leave us not:
But send down from that pure calm spot
The Holy Comforter to prove
Thy guardian care, Thy fostering love.

4 Thou who shalt come our Judge to be,
Jesus, all glory be to Thee:
Save us, O Lord, we humbly pray—
Thy servants save, on that great day.

5 Then shall we see Thee as Thou art,
With open face and joyful heart:
Enraptured love Thee, and adore
World without end, for evermore.
Isaac Williams, altered.

" Grant us grace to raise our thoughts and affections from earth to heaven, and to breathe continually after Thy presence."

226 6s.

THERE is a blessed Home
Beyond this land of woe,
Where trials never come,
Nor tears of sorrow flow;

2 Where faith is lost in sight,
And patient hope is crowned,
And everlasting light
Its glory throws around.

3 There is a land of peace,
Good angels know it well;
Glad songs that never cease
Within its portals swell;

4 Around its glorious throne,
Ten thousand saints adore
Christ, with the Father One
And Spirit, evermore.

5 O joy all joys beyond,
To see the Lamb who died,
And count each sacred wound
In hands, and feet, and side;

6 To give to Him the praise
Of every triumph won,
And sing through endless days
The great things He hath done.

7 Look up ye saints of God,
    Nor fear to tread below
  The path your Saviour trod
    Of daily toil and woe;

8 Wait but a little while
    In uncomplaining love,
  His own most gracious smile
    Shall welcome you above.
                    Henry W. Baker, 1861.

" In my Father's house are many mansions : I go to prepare a place for you."

227   8s, 7s, 8 *lines.*

JESUS, who hath gone before us
    Heavenly mansions to prepare,—
  See Him, who is ever pleading
    For us with prevailing prayer;
  See Him, who with sound of trumpet
    And with His angelic train,
  Summoning the world to judgment,
    On the clouds will come again.

2 Raise us up from earth to heaven,
    Give us wings of faith and love,
  Gales of holy aspirations
    Wafting us to realms above;
  That, with hearts and minds uplifted,
    We with Christ our Lord may dwell,
  Where He sits enthroned in glory
    In His heavenly citadel.

3 So at last, when He appeareth,
    We from out our graves may spring,
  With our youth renewed like eagles,
    Flocking round our heavenly King,
  Caught up on the clouds of heaven,—
    And may meet Him in the air,
  Rise to realms where He is reigning,
    And may reign for ever there.
                        C. Wordsworth.

"Blessed is the man that trusteth in Thee."

228   L. M.

JESUS, my Lord, 'tis sweet to rest
  Upon Thy tender loving breast,
  Where deep compassions ever roll
  Towards my helpless, weary soul.

2 Thy love, My Saviour, dries my tears,
  Expels my griefs, and calms my fears;
  Sheds light and gladness o'er my heart,
  And bids each anxious thought depart.

3 Blest foretaste this of joys to come
  In Thy eternal, heavenly home;
  Where I shall see Thy smiling face,
  And know Thy rich, unfathomed grace.

4 That grace sustains my spirit now,
  Though still a pilgrim here below;
  That grace suffices, comforts, guides,
  Upholds, defends, preserves, provides.

5 Yes, Thou art with me, O my God,
  To bear me on to Thy abode,
  Where I shall never cease to prove
  Thy deep, divine, unfailing love.

6 Help me to praise Thee day by day,
  Till earth's dark scenes are passed away,
  Till in Thine own unclouded light
  Thy glory satisfies my sight.

H. B. 1862.

FIFTH SUNDAY AFTER EASTER.

"Ask and ye shall receive."

229 C. M.

LORD, in Thy name Thy servants plead,
  And Thou hast sworn to hear:
Thine is the harvest, Thine the seed,
  The fresh and fading year.

2 Our Hope, when autumn winds blew wild,
    We trusted, Lord, with Thee;
  And still, now spring has on us smiled,
    We wait on Thy decree.

3 The former and the latter rain,
    The summer sun and air,
  The green ear, and the golden grain,
    All Thine, are ours by prayer.

4 Thine too by right, and ours by grace,
    The spirit's growth unseen;

  The hopes that soothe, the fears that brace,
   The love that shines serene.

5 So grant the precious fruits brought forth
  By sun and moon below,
That Thee in Thy new heaven and earth
  We never may forego.

John Keble, 1857.

"Bless the Lord, oh my soul, and forget not all His benefits."

230   8*s*, 7*s*. 8 *lines.*

FATHER, blessing ev'ry seed-time,
  And refreshing all the soil,
Ripening the gracious harvest
  For which all Thy servants toil.
O Thou Source of every blessing
  Shower'd daily from above,
Hearken to our lips confessing
  Our thanksgiving for Thy love.

2 Here we bless Thy hand that gave us
  Thought and feeling, life and limb;
Bless Thy Son, who died to save us,
  In our glad and joyous hymn;
Bless Thy Spirit, who doth make us
  Fit to worship as we ought:
Father, leave not nor forsake us,
  Till into Thy garner brought.

3 With Thy dews and sunshine tend us,
  Through life's long and changeful year;
From the Enemy defend us,
  Lest the tares of sin appear.
Let Thine eye and hand the keepers
  Of our souls for ever be,
Till Thine angel harvest-reapers
  Sheaves of glory bind for Thee.

Judith Madan.

" These things have I spoken, that in Me ye might have peace."

231   C. M.

IF Christ is mine, then all is mine,
  And more than angels know;
Both present things and things to come,
  And grace and glory too.

2 If Christ is mine, let friends forsake,
  And earthly comforts flee;

He, the full source of every good,
  Is more than all to me.

3 If Christ is mine, unharmed I pass
    Through death's dark dismal vale,
  He'll be my comfort and my stay,
    When heart and flesh shall fail.

4 O Christ, assure me Thou art mine;
    I nothing want beside;
  My soul shall at the Fountain live,
    When all the streams are dried.
                    Benj. Beddome, 1776, *altered.*

'*I leave the world and go unto the Father.*'

232   C. M.

THE head, that once was crown'd with thorns,
    Is crown'd with glory now;
  A royal diadem adorns
    The mighty Victor's brow.

2 The highest place that heaven affords
    Is His—is His by right;
  "The King of kings, and Lord of lords,"
    And heaven's eternal Light:

3 The Joy of all who dwell above,
    The Joy of all below,
  To whom He manifests His love,
    And grants His name to know;

4 To them the cross, with all its shame,
    With all its grace, is given;
  Their name,—an everlasting name;
    Their joy,—the joy of heaven.

5 They suffer with their Lord below,
    They reign with Him above;
  Their profit and their joy—to know
    The mystery of His love.

6 The cross He bore is life and health,—
    Though shame and death to Him;
  His people's hope, His people's wealth,
    Their everlasting theme.   *Thomas Kelly*, 1820.

"*Pure religion and undefiled before God and the Father is this,
To visit the fatherless and widows in their affliction.*"

233   C. M.

JESUS, my Lord, how rich Thy grace!
    Thy bounties how complete!

How shall we count the matchless sum?
  How pay the mighty debt?

2 High on a throne of radiant light
  Dost Thou exalted shine;
What can our poverty bestow,
  When all the worlds are Thine?

3 But Thou hast brethren here below,
  The partners of Thy grace,
And wilt confess their humble names
  Before Thy Father's face.

4 In them Thou mayest be clothed and fed,
  And visited and cheered;
And in their accents of distress
  Our Saviour's voice is heard.

5 Thy face, with reverence and with love,
  We in Thy poor would see;
O may we minister to them,
  And in them, Lord, to Thee.

          Philip Doddridge, 1740, *altered.*

*"In the world ye shall have tribulation: but be of good cheer;
I have overcome the world."*

234   8s, 7s.

JESUS, o'er the grave victorious,
  Conq'ring death, and conq'ring hell,
Reign Thou in Thy might all glorious;
  Heav'n and earth Thy triumph swell.

2 Saints in Thee approach the Father
  Asking in Thy name alone;
He, in Thee, with love increasing,
  Gives, and glorifies the Son.

3 Down to earth in all its darkness
  From the Father Thou didst come;
Seeking sinners in their blindness,
  Calling earth's poor exiles home;

4 By a life of love and labor
  Doing all the Father's will;
Giving to each suppliant suff'rer
  Precious balm for every ill;

5 Patient ever in well-doing,
  Moving on in steps of blood,
Through the grave to heights of glory,
  Reconciling us with God.

6 Here, in Thee, is peace forever;
  We can tribulation bear;
  Kiss Thy cross, with rapture knowing
    Thou hast conquered suff'ring there.
                          E. E. Higbee, 1873.

ASCENSION DAY.

*" He was received up into heaven and sat on the right hand
        of God."*

235   7s.

HAIL the day that sees Him rise,
  Ravished from our wishful eyes;
Christ, awhile to mortals given,
Reascends His native heaven.

2 There the pompous triumph waits;
  Lift up your heads, eternal gates!
  Wide unfold the radiant scene;
  Take the King of glory in!

3 Him though highest heaven receives,
  Still He loves the earth He leaves;
  Though returning to His throne,
  Still He calls mankind His own.

4 See! He lifts His hands above!
  See! He shows the prints of love!
  Hark! His gracious lips bestow
  Blessings on His church below!

5 Still for us His death He pleads;
  Prevalent, He intercedes;
  Near Himself prepares our place,
  Harbinger of human race.

6 There we shall with Thee remain,
  Partners of Thine endless reign;
  There Thy face unclouded see,
  Find our heav'n of heav'ns in Thee.
                          Charles Wesley, 1739.

*" Lift up your heads, O ye gates; even lift them up, ye everlasting
      doors; and the King of glory shall come in."*

236   L. M.

OUR Lord is risen from the dead,
  Our Jesus is gone up on high;
The pow'rs of hell are captive led,
  Dragged to the portals of the sky.

2 There His triumphal chariot waits,
 And angels chant the solemn lay:
"Lift up your heads, ye heav'nly gates!
 Ye everlasting doors, give way!"

3 "Loose all your bars of massy light,
 And wide unfold the radiant scene;
He claims these mansions as His right;
 Receive the King of glory in."

4 "Who is the King of glory! Who?"—
 "The Lord, that all our foes o'ercame,
The world, sin, death, and hell o'erthrew;
 And Jesus is the Conq'ror's name.

5 Lo! His triumphal chariot waits,
 And angels chant the solemn lay:
"Lift up your heads, ye heav'nly gates!
 Ye everlasting doors, give way!"

6 "Who is this King of glory? Who?"—
 "The Lord of glorious power possest;
The King of saints and angels too,
 God over all, for ever blest!
Charles Wesley, 1741.

"Who is this King of glory? The Lord, strong and mighty, the Lord mighty in battle."

237 *8s & 7s. 8 lines.*

SEE, the Conqueror mounts in triumph!
 See, the King in royal state,
Riding on the clouds, His chariot,
 To His heav'nly palace gate!
Hark! the choirs of angel voices
 Joyful alleluias sing,
And the portals high are lifted
 To receive their heav'nly King.

2 Who is this that comes in glory,
 With the trump of jubilee?
Lord of battles, God of armies,
 He has gained the victory;
He, who on the cross did suffer,
 He, who from the grave arose,
He has vanquished sin and Satan,
 He by death has spoiled His foes.

3 Thou hast raised our human nature,
 In the clouds to God's right hand;

There we sit in heav'nly places,
  There with Thee in glory stand;
Jesus reigns, adored by angels;
  Man with God is on the throne;
Mighty Lord! in Thine ascension,
  We by faith behold our own.
                      Christopher Wordsworth, 1863.

"This Man, after He had offered one sacrifice for sins, forever sat down on the right hand of God."

238   L. M.

O SAVIOUR, who for man hast trod
  The wine-press of the wrath of God,
Ascend, and claim again on high
Thy glory left for us to die.

2 A radiant cloud is now Thy seat,
  And earth lies stretched beneath Thy feet;
  Ten thousand thousands round Thee sing,
  And share the triumph of their King.

3 The angel-host enraptured waits:
  "Lift up your heads, eternal gates!"
  O God-and-Man! The Father's throne
  Is now for evermore Thine own.

4 Our great High Priest and Shepherd, Thou
  Within the veil art entered now,
  To offer there Thy precious blood
  Once poured on earth a cleansing flood.

5 And thence the Church, Thy chosen Bride,
  With countless gifts of grace supplied,
  Through all her members draws from Thee
  Her hidden life of sanctity.

6 O Christ, our Lord, of Thy dear care
  Thy lowly members heaven-ward bear;
  Be ours with Thee to suffer pain,
  With Thee for evermore to reign.
                           Latin Hymn.
                Trans: J. Chandler, altered.

"Having an high priest over the house of God, let us draw near with a true heart, in full assurance of faith."

239   L. M.

WHERE high the heav'nly temple stands,
  The house of God not made with hands,
A great High Priest our nature wears,
The Guardian of mankind appears.

2 He, who for men their surety stood,
  And poured on earth His precious blood,
  Pursues in heaven His mighty plan,
  The Saviour and the Friend of man.

3 Jesus, who suffered here below,
  Feels sympathy with human woe,
  And still remembers in the skies,
  His tears, His prayers, His agonies.

4 In every pang that rends the heart,
  The Man of sorrows had a part;
  Touched with the feeling of our grief
  He to the sufferer sends relief.

5 With boldness, therefore, at the throne
  Let us make all our sorrows known,
  And ask the aid of heav'nly power
  To help us in the evil hour.   *Michael Bruce.*

"And when He had spoken these things, while they beheld, He was taken up, and a cloud received Him out of their sight."

240   8s, 7s.

TO the throne He left, victorious
  Lo! our King ascends on high:
Ransomed by His Passion glorious,
  Let us raise our glorious cry.

2 Forty days from death uprisen,
  He His chosen ones did guide;
Gave them power to loose from prison
  All the souls for whom He died.

3 In the three-fold Name baptizing,
  They were sent the world to bless;
Told to witness of His rising,
  Through all lands His name confess.

4 Then, as they looked on adoring,
  Angels, clad in robes of white,
Spake to them, when He, high soaring,
  Passed in glory out of sight.

5 "So shall He who thus ascended,
  Come once more, as then He rose;
All the world's great conflict ended,
  He triumphant o'er His foes!"

6 At Thy coming, Lord, we pray Thee,
  Grant us joys that never fade;

ASCENSION DAY.

    While life lasts may we obey Thee,
      Turn to Thee for strength and aid;

7. Then shall we, the strain upraising,
      Joyous Alleluias sing;
    Through th' eternal ages praising
      Thee our everlasting King.
E. H. Plumptre.

"Thou hast crowned him with glory and honor."

241   8s, 7s, & 4s.

LOOK, ye saints!—the sight is glorious:
    See the "Man of Sorrows" now!
From the fight returned victorious,
    Every knee to Him shall bow:
      Crown Him! crown Him!
Crowns become the Victor's brow.

2 Crown the Saviour! angels! crown Him!
    Rich the trophies Jesus brings;
In the seat of power enthrone Him,
    While the heav'nly concave rings:—
      Crown Him! crown Him!
Crown the Saviour, "King of kings!"

3 Sinners in derision crowned Him,
    Mocking thus the Saviour's claim;
Saints and angels! crowd around Him,
    Own His title, praise His name:
      Crown Him! crown Him!
Spread abroad the Victor's fame.

4 Hark! those bursts of acclamation!
    Hark! those loud, triumphant chords!
Jesus takes the highest station;
    Oh! what joy the sight affords!
      Crown Him! crown Him!
"King of kings, and Lord of lords."
Thomas Kelly, 1809.

"Now is come salvation and strength and the kingdom of our God and the power of His Christ."

242   C. M.

BEHOLD the glories of the Lamb
    Amid His Father's throne;
Prepare new honors for His name
    And songs before unknown.

2 Let elders worship at His feet,
   The church adore around,
With vials full of odors sweet,
   And harps of sweeter sound.

3 Now to the Lamb that once was slain
   Be endless blessings paid ;
Salvation, glory, joy, remain
   For ever on Thy head.

4 Thou hast redeem'd our souls with blood,
   Hast set the prisoners free,
Hast made us kings and priests to God,
   And we shall reign with Thee.

5 The worlds of nature and of grace
   Are put beneath Thy power ;
Then shorten these delaying days,
   And bring the promised hour.

Isaac Watts, 1696.

"Seek those things which are above where Christ sitteth on the right hand of God."

243
8s, 7s.

CHRIST, above all glory seated,
   King triumphant, strong to save!
Dying, Thou hast death defeated,
   Buried, Thou hast spoiled the grave.

2 Thou art gone, where now is givèn
   What no mortal might could gain,
On th' eternal throne of heavèn,
   In Thy Father's power to reign.

3 There Thy kingdoms all adore Thee,
   Heaven above and earth below !
While the depths of hell before Thee,
   Trembling and amazèd bow.

4 We, O Lord, with hearts adoring
   Follow Thee beyond the sky ;
Hear our prayers Thy grace imploring,
   Lift our souls to Thee on high.

5 So, when Thou again in glory
   On the clouds of heaven shalt shine,
We Thy flock may stand before Thee,
   Owned for evermore as Thine.

6 Hail! all hail! in Thee confiding,
   Jesus, Thee shall all adore,
In Thy Father's might abiding,
   With One Spirit evermore.
Latin Hymn 5*th century.*
Trans. ?

SUNDAY AFTER ASCENSION.

"Let Thy priests be clothed with righteousness and let Thy saints shout for joy."

244   7*s,* 6 *lines.*

GLORY, glory to our King!
   Crowns unfading wreathe His head:
Jesus is the name we sing—
   Jesus, risen from the dead;
Jesus, Conqueror o'er the grave;
Jesus, mighty now to save.

2 Jesus is gone up on high,
   Angels come to meet their King;
Shouts triumphant rend the sky,
   While the Victor's praise they sing!
"Open now ye heav'nly gates!
'Tis the King of glory waits."

3 Now behold Him high enthroned,
   Glory beaming from his face.
By adoring angels owned,
   God of holiness and grace:
O for hearts and tongues to sing,
Glory, glory to our King!

4 Jesus, on Thy people shine;
   Warm our hearts and tune our tongues,
That with angels we may join,
   Share their bliss and swell their songs:
Glory, honor, praise and power,
Lord! be Thine for evermore.
Thomas Kelly, 1804.

"Leave us not orphans in our weary mortal state."

245   S. M.

THOU art gone up on high,
   To realms beyond the skies;
And round Thy throne unceasingly
   The songs of praise arise:

2 But we are ling'ring here,
   With sin and care oppressed;
   Lord, send Thy promis'd Comforter
   And lead us to our rest.

3 Thou art gone up on high:
   But Thou didst first come down,
   Through earth's most bitter misery
   To pass unto Thy crown;

4 And girt with grief and fears
   Our onward course must be;
   But only let this path of tears
   Lead us at last to Thee.

5 Thou art gone up on high;
   But Thou shalt come again,
   With all the bright ones of the sky
   Attendant in Thy train.

6 Lord, by Thy saving power,
   So make us live and die,
   That we may stand in that dread hour
   At Thy right hand on high.

Emma Toke, 1851.

"Send unto us the Comforter who may guide us always in the way of truth and peace."

246
L. M.

O JESUS! Lord of heav'nly grace,
   Redeemer of our guilty race,
On Thee our waiting eyes we bend,
The saint's delight, the sinner's friend.

2 What wondrous love prevailed on Thee
   The Bearer of our sins to be;
   Thyself in sacrifice to give,
   That sinners might not die, but live!

3 Now crushed is Satan's doleful reign,
   And broken is the tyrant's chain:
   And Thou art, in Thy meet abode,
   A Conq'ror on the throne of God.

4 O let Thy clemency prevail
   To heal the losses we bewail:
   O cheer us with Thy beaming face,
   Enrich us with Thy gifts of grace.

5 Be Thou our guide, be Thou our goal,
Our joy, when sorrow fills the soul;
In life, our pathway to the skies,
In death, our everlasting prize.

"Why stand ye gazing up into heaven? This same Jesus shall so come in like manner as ye have seen Him go into heaven."

247 7*s.*

MASTER, Lord, to Thee we cry,
On Thy throne exalted high:
See Thy faithful servants, see!
Ever gazing up to Thee.

2 Grant, though parted from our sight,
High above yon azure height,
Grant our hearts may thither rise,
Following Thee beyond the skies.

3 Ever may we upwards move,
Wafted on the wings of love;
Looking when our Lord shall come,
Longing for our heavenly home:

4 There may we with Thee remain,
Partners of Thine endless reign;
There Thy face unclouded see,
Find our heaven of heavens in Thee;

5 There before Thy footstool fall;
There confess Thee Lord of all;
And, while endless ages last,
There our crowns before Thee cast.
Charles Wesley.

"Set your affections upon things which are above."

248 C. M.

O JESUS, who art gone before
To Thy blest realms of light:
O, thither may our spirits soar,
And wing their upward flight.

2 Make us to those delights aspire,
Which spring from love to Thee:
Which pass the carnal heart's desire,
Which faith alone can see;

3 Where God to those whom He doth own,
His secret doth reveal;
And is Himself their joy and crown,
And all in all doth fill.

4 To guide us to Thy glories, Lord,
      To lift us to the sky;
    O may Thy Holy Ghost be pour'd
      Upon us from on high. *Latin Hymn.*
                           Trans. by J. Chandler.

"Father, I will that they also whom Thou hast given Me be with Me where I am."

249　　　　　　C. M.

THE golden gates are lifted up,
    The doors are opened wide,
  The King of Glory is gone in
    Unto His Father's side.

  2 Thou art gone up before us, Lord,
      To make for us a place,
    That we may be where now Thou art,
      And look upon God's face.

  3 And ever on our earthly path
      A gleam of glory lies,
    A light still breaks behind the cloud
      That veiled Thee from our eyes.

  4 Lift up our hearts, lift up our minds,
      Let Thy dear grace be given,
    That while we wander here below,
      Our treasure be in heaven.

  5 That where Thou art at God's right hand,
      Our hope, our love may be,
    Dwell Thou in us, that we may dwell
      For evermore in Thee.

" But when the Comforter is come whom I will send unto you from the Father."

250　　　　　　7s.

MIGHTY Saviour, gracious King,
    Now Thy waiting people bless;
  Thou that dost deliverance bring,
    Come to reign in righteousness.

  2 Thou dost heavenly light impart:
      Tune the ear to Zion's song;
    Teach and guide the wayward heart,
      Loose and prompt the stamm'ring tongue.

  3 Pour Thy Spirit from on high;
      Come, Thy mourning Church to bless;

SUNDAY AFTER ASCENSION.

  Streams of life and joy supply;
   Fill the world with righteousness;
4 Light shall then possess Thine own,
  Holy quiet, perfect peace;
  And where heav'nly seed is sown,
   Thou wilt give the blest increase.
        Edward Osler?

251
"*Let all the world bow down before Him.*"
L. M.

OH! for a sweet, inspiring ray,
  To animate our feeble strains,
From the bright realms of endless day,
  The blissful realms, where Jesus reigns!

2 There, low before His glorious throne,
  Adoring saints and angels fall;
And, with delightful worship, own
  His smile their bliss, their heav'n, their all.

3 Immortal glories crown His head,
  While tuneful hallelujahs rise,
And love, and joy, and triumph spread
  Through all th' assemblies of the skies.

4 He smiles,—and seraphs tune their songs
  To boundless rapture, while they gaze;
Ten thousand, thousand joyful tongues
  Resound His everlasting praise.

5 There, all the fav'rites of the Lamb
  Shall join at last the heav'nly choir:
Oh! may the joy-inspiring theme,
  Awake our faith and warm desire.

6 Dear Saviour! let Thy Spirit seal
  Our interest in that blissful place;
Till death remove this mortal veil
  And we behold Thy lovely face.
        Anne Steele, 1760.

252
"*Let all the angels of God worship Him.*"
C. M.

BEYOND the glitt'ring starry skies,
  Far as th' eternal hills,
There, in the boundless worlds of light
  Our dear Redeemer dwells.

2 Legions of angels round His throne
  In countless armies shine;

    At His right hand, with golden harps,
      They offer songs divine.

3 "Hail, glorious Prince of Peace," they cry,
    "Whose unexampled love
  Moved Thee to quit those blissful realms,
    And royalties above."

4 Through all His travels here below,
    They did His steps attend:
  Oft wondering how, or where, at last
    This mystic scene would end.

5 They saw His heart transfix'd with wounds,
    And viewed the crimson gore;
  They saw Him break the bars of death,
    Which none e'er broke before.

6 They brought His chariot from above,
    To bear Him to His throne;
  Clapped their triumphant wings, and cried,
    "The glorious work is done."

        Dan'l Turner and James Fanch, 1776.

WHITSUNDAY.

"And suddenly there came a sound from heaven as of a rushing mighty wind."

253   C. M.

WHEN God of old came down from heaven,
    In power and wrath He came;
Before His feet the clouds were riven,
    Half darkness and half flame.

2 But when He came the second time,
    He came in power and love;
  Softer than gale at morning prime
    Hovered His holy Dove.

3 The fires that rushed on Sinai down
    In sudden torrents dread,
  Now gently light a glorious crown
    On every sainted head.

4 And as on Israel's awe-struck ear
    The voice exceeding loud,
  The trump, that angels quake to hear,
    Thrill'd from the deep, dark cloud:

5 So, when the Spirit of our God
   Came down His flock to find,
 A voice from heav'n was heard abroad,
   A rushing, mighty wind.

6 It fills the Church of God; It fills
   The sinful world around;
 Only in stubborn hearts and wills
   No place for It is found.

7 Come Lord, come Wisdom, Love, and Power,
   Open our hearts to hear;
 Let us not miss th' accepted hour
   Save, Lord, by love or fear. *John Keble*, 1827.

"He will reprove the world of sin, and of righteousness, and of judgment."

254 S. M.

C OME, Holy Spirit, come,
   Let Thy bright beams arise,
 Dispel the darkness from our minds,
   And open all our eyes.

2 Revive our drooping faith,
   Our doubts and fears remove,
 And kindle in our breasts the flame
   Of never-dying love.

3 Convince us of our sin,
   Then lead to Jesus' blood,
 And to our wond'ring view reveal
   The secret love of God.

4 'Tis Thine to cleanse the heart,
   To sanctify the soul,
 To pour fresh life in every part,
   And new-create the whole.

5 Dwell therefore in our hearts,
   Our minds from bondage free;
 Then we shall know, and praise, and love
   The Father, Son, and Thee!
                    Joseph Hart, 1759.

"But the fruit of the Spirit is love, joy, peace, long-suffering, gentleness, goodness, faith."

255 C. P. M.

C OME, Holy Spirit, from above,
   And from the realms of light and love

Thine own bright rays impart.
Come, Father of the fatherless,
Come, Giver of all happiness,
Come, Lamp of every heart.

2 O Thou, of comforters the best,
O Thou, the soul's most welcome guest,
O Thou, our sweet repose,
Our resting-place from life's long care,
Our shadow from the world's fierce glare,
Our solace in all woes.

3 O Light divine, all light excelling;
Fill with Thyself the inmost dwelling
Of souls sincere and lowly;
Without Thy pure divinity,
Nothing in all humanity,
Nothing is strong or holy.

4 Wash out each dark and sordid stain;
Water each dry and arid plain,
Raise up the bruisèd reed.
Enkindle what is cold and chill,
Relax the stiff and stubborn will,
Guide those that guidance need.

5 Give to the good, who find in Thee
The Spirit's perfect liberty,
Thy seven fold power and love.
Give virtue strength its crown to win,
Give struggling souls their rest from sin,
Give endless peace above.

Robert II. of France.
Trans. A. P. Stanley, 1873.

"Neither will I hide my face any more from them: for I have poured out my Spirit upon the house of Israel."

256   L. M.

SPIRIT of mercy, truth, and love,
O shed Thine influence from above;
And still from age to age convey
The wonders of this sacred day.

2 In every clime, by every tongue,
Be God's surpassing glory sung:
Let all the listening earth be taught
The wonders by our Saviour wrought.

3 Unfailing Comfort, heavenly Guide,
  Still o'er Thy holy Church preside;
  Still let mankind Thy blessings prove,
  Spirit of mercy, truth, and love.
  R. W. Ryle, 1842.

"By the washing of regeneration and renewing of the Holy Ghost."

257   7s.

GRACIOUS Spirit! Love divine!
  Let Thy light within me shine;
  All my guilty fears remove,
  Fill me full of heaven and love.

2 Speak Thy pardoning grace to me,
  Set the burdened sinner free;
  Lead me to the Lamb of God;
  Wash me in His precious blood.

3 Life and peace to me impart,
  Seal salvation on my heart;
  Breathe Thyself into my breast,
  Earnest of immortal rest.

4 Let me never from Thee stray,
  Keep me in the narrow way;
  Fill my soul with joy divine,
  Keep me, Lord! forever Thine.
  John Stocker, 1776.

"Mercifully grant unto us this same gift of the Spirit, to renew, illuminate, refresh, and sanctify our dying souls, to be over us and around us like the light and dew of heaven."

258   L. M.

O HOLY GHOST, Thy heav'nly dew
  The hearts of sinners can renew;
  Thou dost within our hearts abide,
  And still to holy action guide.

2 Thou mak'st the soul with joy to sing
  When sorrow's clouds are deepening:
  With Jesus Christ Thou mak'st us one,
  Earnest of heav'n from God's high throne.

3 Best gift of God, and man's true Friend,
  Into my inmost soul descend:
  The mind of Jesus Christ impart,
  And consecrate to Thee my heart.

4 Teach me to do my Father's will,
  To lie beneath His guidance still;
  Lighten my mind, and O incline
  My heart to make His pleasure mine.

5 From spot and blemish make me pure,
  My future bliss in heaven secure:
  When lost in darkness, give me light,
  And cheer me through death's dreary night.
                        Lavater, 1770.
                    Trans. Frances E. Cox.

"*The Spirit itself maketh intercession for us with groanings which cannot be uttered.*"

259   7s.

GRANTED is the Saviour's prayer;
  Hail, O gracious Comforter,
Promise of our parting Lord,
To His throne in heav'n restored.

2 God, the everlasting God,
  Makes with mortals His abode:
  He, whom heav'n cannot contain,
  Dwelleth in the heart of man.

3 There He helps our feeble moans,
  Deepens our imperfect groans;
  Intercedes in silence there,
  Sighs th' unutterable prayer.

4 Holy Ghost, our hearts inspire,
  Lighten there Thy heav'nly fire;
  Day by day our life renew,
  Thou the Gift and Giver too.

5 Brood Thou o'er our nature's night:
  Kindle darkness into light.
  Spread Thy overshadowing wings:
  Order from confusion springs.

6 Pain, and sin, and sorrow cease;
  Thee we taste, and all is peace;
  Joy divine in Thee we prove,
  Light of Truth, and Fire of love.   *John Wesley.*

"*Sending down Thy Holy Ghost on the day of Pentecost to establish the Church as the home of His continual presence and power among men.*"

260   8s, 7s, 8 *lines.*

WHEN the faithful were assembled
  On the day of Pentecost,

Rush'd the wind, the place it trembled;
  Came from heaven the Holy Ghost;
Golden showers of consecration,
  Tongues of fire were on them shed;
And that holy dedication
  Made an altar of each head.

2 Now the festive Pentecostal
    Harvest-home of souls they keep;
  With his sickle each apostle
    Whitening fields goes forth to reap;
  God with holy flame from heaven
    Writes on hearts the law of love;
  Jubilee of sins forgiven
    Sounds its trumpet from above.

3 Holy Ghost, Divine Creator,
    Who didst on the waters move;
  Holy Ghost, Regenerator,
    Author of all life and love;
  Holy Ghost, Illuminator,
    Who didst then with fire baptize;
  Holy Ghost, great Renovator,
    Come, the world evangelize.

4 With the kneeling congregation,
    Thou art in the House of Prayer;
  Laver of regeneration
    Is o'ershadowed by Thee there;
  Thou dost shed at Confirmation
    From Thy wing a gift of grace;
  Eucharistic celebration
    Has revealings of Thy face.

5 Strengthen, warm, and purify us;
    From the bands of sin release;
  Comfort, counsel, sanctify us;
    Give us love, and joy, and peace;
  Patience, faith, and resignation
    Breathe upon us with Thy breath;
  Give us heavenly consolation
    In the solemn hour of death.

6 So when earth with fruit aboundeth,
    And shall angel-reapers see,
  And the great Archangel soundeth
    God's eternal Jubilee,

WHITSUNDAY.

We may join their gratulation;
To the Father and the Son
And the Spirit, adoration
Ever be, blest Three in One.
Christopher Wordsworth.

"By Thy glorious resurrection and ascension and by the coming of the Holy Ghost, good Lord, deliver us."

261   7s.

BY the first bright Easter-day,
When the stone was rolled away;
By the glory round Thee shed
At Thy rising from the dead;
   King of glory, hear our cry;
   Make us soon Thy joys to see,
Where enthroned in majesty
   Countless angels sing to Thee.

2 By Thy parting blessing given,
As Thou didst ascend to heaven;
By the cloud of living light
That received Thee out of sight;
   King of glory, hear our cry; &c.

3 By that rushing sound of might
Coming down from heaven's height;
By the cloven tongues of flame
That on Thy Apostles came;
   King of glory, hear our cry; &c.

4 Only Victim we can plead,
Great High Priest to intercede,
Showing that which can alone
For the sin of man atone;
   Lamb of God, hear our cry; &c.

5 In the dreadful judgment-day,
When the world shall pass away;
Be the merciful decree
That our Friend the Judge shall be:
   King of glory, hear our cry; &c.
Frederick W. Faber.

WHITMONDAY.

"Who through the Holy Ghost hast made Thy one catholic Church to be the body of Christ."

262 L. M.

WE bless Thee for Thy Church, O Lord,
  Called from the world, and sealed Thine own,
One by the faith of Thy pure word,
  By Thy baptismal laver one.

2 We bless Thee for Thy Church, where Thou
  Dost sanctify the soul from sin,
And cleanse Thine image, marred till now,
  By holy rite, from guilt within.

3 We bless Thee for Thy Church, which sends
  Thy truth remotest tribes among,
And scattered members comprehends
  From every people, kindred, tongue.

4 We bless Thee for Thy Church, which, placed
  Aloft, by signs conspicuous known,
Is on Thine own apostles based,
  And Jesus Christ the Corner-stone.

5 We pray that on that sacred site,
  In symbols pure, with safeguards true,
Our souls may evermore unite,
  And peace, by Thee ordained, ensue.

6 To Thee by saints in earth and heaven,
  By seraph-choir and angel-host,
Be blessing, honor, glory given,
  O Father, Son, and Holy Ghost.
                    Hymn. Christ.

"The Holy Ghost fell on all them which heard the word."

263 L. M.

O SPIRIT of the living God!
  In all Thy plenitude of grace,
Where'er the foot of man hath trod,
  Descend on our apostate race.

2 Give tongues of fire, and hearts of love
  To preach the reconciling word;
Give power and unction from above,
  Where'er the joyful sound is heard.

M

3 Be darkness, at Thy coming, light;
   Confusion, order in Thy path;
Souls without strength inspire with might,
   Bid mercy triumph over wrath.

4 O Spirit of the Lord! prepare
   All the round earth her God to meet;
Breathe Thou abroad like morning air,
   Till hearts of stone begin to beat.

5 Baptize the nations far and nigh;
   The triumphs of Thy cross record;
The name of Jesus glorify,
   Till every kindred call Him Lord.
James Montgomery, 1825.

"The love of God is shed abroad in our hearts by the Holy Ghost."

264   C. M.

COME, Holy Spirit, heavenly Dove!
   With all Thy quickening powers;
Kindle a flame of sacred love,
   In these cold hearts of ours.

2 Look how we grovel here below,
   Fond of these trifling toys!
Our souls can neither fly nor go,
   To reach eternal joys.

3 In vain we tune our formal songs,
   In vain we strive to rise;
Hosannas languish on our tongues,
   And our devotion dies.

4 Dear Lord! and shall we ever live
   At this poor dying rate?
Our love so faint, so cold to Thee,
   And Thine to us so great?

5 Come, Holy Spirit, heavenly Dove!
   With all Thy quickening powers;
Come, shed abroad a Saviour's love,
   And that shall kindle ours.
Isaac Watts, 1709.

"As many as are led by the Spirit of God, they are the sons of God."

265   L. M.

COME, gracious Spirit, heavenly Dove,
   With light and comfort from above;
Be Thou our Guardian, Thou our Guide,
O'er every thought and step preside.

2 Conduct us safe, conduct us far
  From every sin and hurtful snare;
  Lead to Thy word that rules must give,
  And teach us lessons how to live.

3 The light of truth to us display,
  And make us know and choose Thy way;
  Plant holy fear in every heart,
  That we from God may ne'er depart.

4 Lead us to Christ, the living Way,
  Nor let us from His precepts stray;
  Lead us to holiness, the road
  That we must take to dwell with God.

5 Lead us to heaven that we may share
  Fulness of joy for ever there:
  Lead us to God, our final rest,
  To be with Him for ever blest.
                    Simon Browne, 1720, *altered.*

TRINITY SUNDAY.

"Who hast made Thyself known in the work of man's redemption as the mystery of the ever adorable Trinity, Father Son and Holy Ghost."

266　　　　　L. M.

O HOLY, holy, holy Lord!
  Bright in Thy deeds and in Thy name,
Forever be Thy name adored,
  Thy glories let the world proclaim!

2 O Jesus, Lamb once crucified
    To take our load of sins away,
  Thine be the hymn that rolls its tide
    Along the realms of upper day!

3 O Holy Spirit! from above,
    In streams of light and glory given,
  Thou source of ecstacy and love,
    Thy praises ring through earth and heaven!

4 O God Triune! to Thee we owe
    Our every thought, our every song;
  And ever may Thy praises flow
    From saint and seraph's burning tongue.
              James Wallis Eastburne, 1819.

"And they rest not day and night, saying, Holy, holy, holy, Lord God Almighty, which was, and is, and is to come."

267 11s, 12s, 12s, 10s.

HOLY, Holy, Holy! Lord God Almighty!
　　Early in the morning our song shall rise to Thee:
Holy, Holy, Holy! merciful and mighty;
　　God in Three Persons, Blessed Trinity!

2 Holy, Holy, Holy! all the saints adore Thee,
　　Casting down their golden crowns around the glassy sea;
Cherubim and Seraphim falling down before Thee,
　　Which wert, and art, and evermore shalt be.

3 Holy, Holy, Holy! though the darkness hide Thee,
　　Though the eye of sinful man Thy glory may not see,
Only Thou art Holy: there is none beside Thee,
　　Perfect in power, in love, and purity.

4 Holy, Holy, Holy! Lord God Almighty!
　　All Thy works shall praise Thy name, in earth, and sky, and sea:
Holy, Holy, Holy! merciful and mighty;
　　God in Three Persons, Blessed Trinity!

　　　　　　　　　　　　Reginald Heber, 1827.

"We worship and adore Thy glorious name, joining in the song of the Cherubim and Seraphim."

268 7s, 8s, 7s, 8s, 7s, 7s.

THEE, O God, we humbly praise,
　　Thee as Lord and King confessing;
All the earth its homage pays:
　　Honor, power, glory, blessing,
Ever giveth unto Thee,
Father of eternity.

2 All the angels join the hymn,
　　All the powers of heaven replying,
Cherubim to Seraphim,
　　With unwearied voices crying:
Holy, holy, holy Lord,
God of hosts, be Thou adored.

3 Thee, the Apostles' glorious choir,
　　Prophets ranked in goodly number,
Martyrs robed in white attire,
　　Praise, and never sleep nor slumber;
Loud their hallelujahs rise
Rolling through the vaulted skies.

4 Father! Thee, the Church doth own,
   Wide through every land and nation,
With Thy true and only Son,
   Worthy of all adoration,
And the Holy Spirit—Her
Everlasting Comforter!

5 King, O Christ, ere time began
   In the Father's glory reigning,
Thou, to rescue fallen man,
   Neither birth nor death disdaining,
Hast to all believers giv'n
Entrance through the gate of heav'n.

6 Seated now at God's right hand,
   Thou shalt come as Judge: before Thee
When the quick and dead shall stand,
   Help Thy servants, we implore Thee;
Make them with Thy saints to shine,
In eternal glory Thine.

7 Save Thy people, Lord, we pray;
   Bless Thy heritage forever;
Rule and lift them up alway;
   Thee we magnify, and never
Cease to praise Thy holy name,
Through all ages still the same.

8 Lord! this day, from every ill
   Guard us till the evening closes;
Lord! have mercy on us still, .
   As in Thee our hope reposes;
All my trust is stayed on Thee,
Let me ne'er confounded be. *Ambrose.*
Trans. Thomas C. Porter, 1859.

"To Thee all angels cry aloud: the heavens and all the powers therein."

269   7s, 6 lines.

HOLY, Holy, Holy Lord,
   God of Hosts, Eternal King,
By the heavens and earth adored;
Angels and archangels sing,
Chanting everlastingly
To the Blessed Trinity.

2 Thousands, tens of thousands, stand,
   Spirits blest, before Thy throne,
Speeding thence at Thy command,

And when Thy behests are done,
Singing everlastingly
To the Blessed Trinity.

3 Cherubim and Seraphim,
Veil their faces with their wings;
Eyes of angels are too dim
To behold the King of kings,
While they sing eternally
To the Blessed Trinity.

4 Thee apostles, prophets Thee,
Thee the noble martyr-band,
Praise with solemn jubilee,
Thee the Church in every land;
Singing everlastingly
To the Blessed Trinity.

5 In Thy name baptized are we,
With Thy blessing are dismiss'd;
And thrice-holy chant to Thee
In the holy Eucharist;
Life is one Doxology
To the Blessed Trinity.

Christopher Wordsworth.

"Go ye, therefore, and teach all nations, baptizing them in the name of the Father, and of the Son, and of the Holy Ghost."

270　　　　　　　C. M.

THOU, Lord, baptiz'd in Thine own blood,
　　And buried in the grave,
Didst raise Thyself to endless life,
　　Omnipotent to save.

2 Baptiz'd into Thy death we died,
　　Were buried, rose with Thee;
That we might live with Thee to God,
　　And ever blest may be.

3 Thee, ris'n in triumph from the grave,
　　Did Thine apostles see;
And hear Thy words: "All power is given
　　In heaven and earth to Me;

4 "Go forth into the world,—Go forth,
　　And all evangelize;
Go forth into the world, and all
　　Into One name baptize."

5 O may the world Thy temple be,
   A living temple, Lord!
Growing in light, and life, and love;
   A paradise restored!
Christopher Wordsworth.

"Reveal in us, we beseech Thee, the full power of this faith, into which we have been planted by baptism."

271   C. M.

SEND us Thy showers of grace, that we,
   Grafted in Thee—the Vine,
May there abide, and may our lives
   With golden fruitage shine.

2 Baptiz'd in Christ we died to sin,
   And to new life were born;
O may we rise, and hail with joy
   The Resurrection's morn.

3 Baptiz'd in Christ we put on Christ,
   And then were cloth'd in light;
O may we keep that garment pure,
   And ever walk in white.

4 So may we stand with saints in bliss,
   That white-rob'd company,
Before the everlasting throne,
   And render thanks to Thee.

5 To Father, Son, and Holy Ghost,
   One God and Persons Three,
Whose name we bear, in whom we live
   Eternal glory be.
Christopher Wordsworth.

FIRST SUNDAY AFTER TRINITY.

"Beloved, let us love one another; for love is of God."

272   C. M.

OUR God is love: and all His saints
   His image bear below;
The heart with love to God inspir'd,
   With love to man will glow.

2 O may we love each other, Lord,
   As we are loved of Thee:
For none are truly born of God,
   Who live in enmity.

3 Heirs of the same immortal bliss,
   Our hopes and fears the same,
The cords of love our hearts should bind,
   The law of love inflame.

4 So shall the vain contentious world
   Our peaceful lives approve,
And wondering say, as they of old,
   "See how these Christians love." *Thos. Cotterill?*

"He who loveth not, knoweth not God; for God is love."

273   7s. 6 lines.

SINCE we kept the Saviour's birth,
   Half the yearly course is flown;
We have followed Him on earth,
   We have traced Him to His throne:
Grateful now we stand, and greet
Our salvation wrought complete.

2 What one sweetest flower and best
   Decks the garden of the Spouse?
What one gem beyond the rest
   Sparkles on the Victor's brows?
What one strain in heaven above
Swells the chorus? God is Love!

3 Thou who lovedst us on high,
   Looking from the seats of bliss,
Then, to take our misery,
   Passedst through a world like this,
Of Thy Spirit, Lord, impart;
Warm with love each grateful heart!

4 To the brethren evermore,
   To the neighbor dwelling by,
To the outcast at our door,
   To the needy when they cry,
Grant us each in love to be
As Thy Church hath learned of Thee.
        Henry Alford, 1866, altered.

"Breathe into us that divine charity, which is the fulfilling of the law."

274   L. M.

O THOU, descended from above,
   The pure celestial fire impart.
Kindle a flame of sacred love
   On the cold altar of my heart.

2 There let it for Thy glory burn
   With inextinguishable blaze;
And, trembling, to its source return,
   In humble prayer and fervent praise.

3 Jesus! confirm my heart's desire
   To work, and speak, and think for Thee.
Still let me guard the holy fire,
   And still stir up Thy gift in me:

4 Ready for all Thy perfect will,
   My acts of faith and love repeat,
Till death Thy endless mercies seal,
   And make my sacrifice complete.
              Charles Wesley, 1762, altered.

"*And this commandment have we from Him, that he who loveth God love his brother also.*"

275   C. M.

O FOUNT of good, to own Thy love
   Our thankful hearts incline:
What can we render, Lord, to Thee,
   When all the worlds are Thine?

2 But Thou hast needy brethren here,
   Partakers of Thy grace,
Whose names Thou wilt Thyself confess
   Before the Father's face.

3 In each sad accent of distress
   Thy pleading voice is heard;
In them Thou may'st be clothed and fed,
   And visited and cheer'd.

4 Help us then, Lord, Thy yoke to wear,
   To joy to do Thy will;
Each other's burdens gladly bear,
   And love's sweet law fulfil.

5 Thy face with reverence and with love
   We in Thy poor would see;
And while we minister to them,
   Would do it as to Thee.   *Philip Doddridge.*

"*Beloved, if God so loved us, we ought also to love one another.*"

276   C. M.

FATHER of mercies, send Thy grace
   All powerful from above,
To form in our obedient souls
   The image of Thy love.

2 O may our sympathizing breast
   That generous pleasure know,
Freely to share in others' joy,
   And weep for others' woe.

3 Whene'er the helpless sons of grief
   In low distress are laid,
Soft be our hearts their pains to feel,
   And swift our hands to aid.

4 So Jesus looked on dying men,
   Enthroned above the skies;
And when He saw their lost estate,
   Felt His compassion rise.

5 Since Christ, to save our guilty souls,
   On wings of mercy flew,
We, whom the Saviour thus hath loved,
   Should love each other too.
Philip Doddridge, 1740, altered.

"Herein is love, not that we loved God, but that He loved us."

277   S. M.

OUR heavenly Father calls,
   And Christ invites us near,
With both our friendship shall be sweet,
   And our communion dear.

2 God pities all our griefs;
   He pardons every day;
Almighty to protect our souls,
   And wise to guide our way.

3 How large His bounties are!
   What various stores of good,
Diffused from our Redeemer's hand,
   And purchased with His blood!

4 Jesus, our living Head!
   We bless Thy faithful care;
Our Advocate before the throne,
   And our Forerunner there.

5 Here fix, my roving heart!
   Here wait, my warmest love!
Till the communion be complete
   In nobler scenes above.
Philip Doddridge, 1740.

SECOND SUNDAY AFTER TRINITY.

"We know that we have passed from death unto life, because we love the brethren."

278 8s & 7s.

LORD, in Thy kingdom there shall be
  No aliens from each other,
But, even as he loves himself
  Each saint shall love his brother.

2 When in Thy courts we meet below,
  To mourn our sinful living,
And with one mingling voice repeat
  Confession, creed, thanksgiving;

3 Make us to hear in each sweet word
  Thy Holy Spirit calling
To union with Thy Church and Thee,
  That heav'nly bond forestalling.

4 One baptism and one faith have we,
  One Spirit sent to win us;
One Lord, one Father, and one God
  Above, and through, and in us.

5 Never, by schism or by sin,
  May we this union sever,
Till all, to perfect stature grown,
  Are one with Thee forever.
  Hymn. Christ.

"That we should believe on the name of His Son, Jesus Christ, and love one another."

279 S. M.

BLEST be the tie that binds
  Our hearts in Christian love!
The fellowship of kindred minds
  Is like to that above.

2 Before our Father's throne
  We pour our ardent prayers;
Our fears, our hopes, our aims are one,
  Our comforts and our cares.

3 We share our mutual woes,
  Our mutual burdens bear;
And often for each other flows
  The sympathizing tear.

4 When we asunder part,
 It gives us inward pain;
But we shall still be joined in heart
 And hope to meet again.

5 This glorious hope revives
 Our courage by the way;
While each in expectation lives,
 And longs to see the day.

6 From sorrow, toil, and pain,
 And sin, we shall be free;
And perfect love, and friendship, reign
 Through all eternity.
John Fawcett, 1772.

"*A certain man made a supper and bade many.*"

280 7s, 6s, 7s, 6s, 7s, 7s, 7s, 6s.

JESUS, Master of the feast!
 The feast itself Thou art;
Now receive Thine every guest,
 And comfort every heart!
Give us living bread to eat.
 Manna that from heaven comes down;
See us waiting at Thy feet,
 And make Thy favor known.

2 In this earthly wilderness
 Thou hast a table spread,
Richly filled with every grace
 Our fainting souls can need:
Still sustain us by Thy love,
 Still Thy servants' strength repair,
Till we reach Thy courts above,
 And feast for ever there.
Charles Wesley, 1745, *altered*.

"*And the bread which I give is my flesh which I will give for the life of the world.*"

281 C. M.

LET us adore th' eternal Word,
 'Tis He our souls hath fed;
Thou art our living Stream, O Lord,
 And Thou th' immortal Bread.

2 Blest be the Lord that gives His flesh,
  To nourish dying men;
And often spreads His table fresh,
  Lest we should faint again.

3 Our souls shall draw their heavenly breath
  Whilst Jesus finds supplies;
Nor shall our graces sink to death,
  For Jesus never dies.

4 The God of mercy be ador'd,
  Who calls our souls from death,
Who saves by His redeeming Word
  And new-creating breath.
                              Isaac Watts.

"I dwell in the high and holy place, with him also that is of a contrite and humble spirit."

282   C. M.

MY God, how wonderful Thou art,
  Thy majesty how bright;
How beautiful Thy mercy-seat,
  In depths of burning light.

2 How dread are Thine eternal years,
  O everlasting Lord;
By saints and angels day and night
  Incessantly adored.

3 O how I fear Thee, living God,
  With deepest, tenderest fears;
And worship Thee with trembling hope,
  And penitential tears.

4 Yet I may love Thee too, O Lord,
  Almighty as Thou art,
For Thou hast stooped to ask of me
  The love of my poor heart.

5 No earthly father loves like Thee,
  No mother, e'er so mild,
Bears and forbears as Thou hast done
  With me Thy sinful child.

6 Father of Jesus, love's Reward!
  What rapture will it be
Prostrate before Thy throne to lie
  And gaze, and gaze on Thee?
                       Frederick W. Faber, 1849.

"Shine powerfully into our hearts by Thy Spirit, and draw us with the cords of Thy constraining grace."

283　　　　L. M.

AMIDST a world of hopes and fears,
　A world of cares, and toils, and tears,
Where foes alarm, and dangers threat,
And pleasures kill, and glories cheat:

2 Send down, O Lord! a heavenly ray,
To guide me in the doubtful way;
And o'er me hold Thy shield of power,
To guard me in the dang'rous hour.

3 Teach me the flatt'ring paths to shun,
In which the thoughtless many run,
Who for a shade the substance miss,
And grasp their ruin in their bliss.

4 May never pleasure, wealth, or pride,
Allure my wand'ring soul aside;
But through this maze of mortal ill,
Safe lead me to Thy heav'nly hill.

5 There glories shine, and pleasures roll,
That charm, delight, transport the soul,
And every longing wish shall be
Possess'd of boundless bliss in Thee.

Unit. Coll.

THIRD SUNDAY AFTER TRINITY.

"There is joy in the presence of the angels over one sinner that repenteth."

284　　　　7s.

WHEN, this goodly world to frame,
　Th' Lord of might and mercy came,
Shouts of joy were heard on high,
And the stars sang from the sky:

2 When of love the midnight beam
Dawn'd on the towers of Bethlehem,
Then, along the echoing hill,
Angels sang; "On earth good will."

3 When the sheep, that went astray,
Turns again to Zion's way;
When the soul, by grace subdued,
Sobs its prayer of gratitude;

4 Then the heav'nly hosts above,
   Filled with holy joy and love,
   Strike the loud and rapt'rous strain
   From their golden harps again.
                    Reginald Heber, altered.

"He was lost and is found."

285 S. M.

HARK, through the courts of heaven
   Voices of angels sound,
"He that was dead now lives again,
   He that was lost is found!"

2 God of unfailing grace,
   Send down Thy Spirit now,
Raise the dejected soul to hope,
   And make the lofty bow.

3 In countries far from home,
   On earthly husks we feed;
Back to our Father's home, O Lord,
   Our wandering footsteps lead.

4 Then at each soul's return
   The heavenly harp shall sound,
"He that was dead now lives again,
   He that was lost is found!"
                    Henry Alford, 1844.

"If we walk in the light as He is in the light, we have fellowship one with another."

286 C. P. M.

MAY we Thy precepts, Lord, fulfil,
   To do on earth our Father's will,
      As angels do above.
To walk in Christ, the living Way,
With all Thy children, and obey
   The law of Christian love.

2 So may we join Thy name to bless,
Thy grace adore, Thy power confess,
   From sin and strife to flee:
One is our calling, one our name,
The end of all our hope the same,
   A crown of life with Thee.

3 Spirit of life, of joy, and peace,
Unite our hearts, our joy increase;
Thy gracious help supply:
To every soul the blessing give,
In Christian fellowship to live,
In joyful hope to die. *Edward Osler.*

"Perfect and fulfil in us the work of Thy converting grace."

287 L. M.

MY Hope, my All, my Saviour Thou!
To Thee, lo! now my soul I bow;
I feel the bliss Thy wounds impart,
I find Thee, Saviour! in my heart.

2 Be Thou my Strength, be Thou my Way;
Protect me through my life's short day:
In all my acts may wisdom guide,
And keep me, Saviour! near Thy side.

3 Correct, reprove, and comfort me;
As I have need, my Saviour be:
And if I would from Thee depart,
Then clasp me, Saviour! to Thy heart.

4 In fierce temptation's darkest hour,
Save me from sin and Satan's power;
Tear every idol from Thy throne,
And reign, my Saviour! reign alone.

5 My suffering time will soon be o'er;
Then shall I sigh and weep no more;
My ransomed soul shall soar away,
To sing Thy praise in endless day.

"Casting all your care upon Him for He careth for you."

288 7s.

FATHER of eternal grace!
Glorify Thyself in me;
Meekly beaming in my face,
May the world Thine image see.

2 Happy only in Thy love,
Poor, unfriended, or unknown;
Fix my thoughts on things above,
Stay my heart on Thee alone.

3 Humble, holy, all-resigned
  To Thy will,—Thy will be done!—
Give me, Lord! the perfect mind
  Of Thy well-belovèd Son.

4 Counting gain and glory loss,
  May I tread the path He trod;
Die with Jesus on the cross,
  Rise with Him, to Thee, my God!

James Montgomery, 1808.

"Are they not all ministering spirits, sent forth to minister for them who shall be heirs of salvation?"

289   C. M.

GIVE us, O Lord, the eye of faith
  The inner world to see,
Then, holy angels we shall view
  And their blest ministry.

2 Angelic faces we shall see,
  Angelic wings o'erspread
Above Thy holy altar, Lord,
  And Thee, the living Bread.

3 And we shall hear angelic harps,
  And heav'nly minstrelsy,
When one repenting sinner turns
  With contrite heart to Thee.

4 And when we see the deepening calm,
  And watch the quiv'ring breath
That trembles on the lips in prayer
  Of holy saints in death;

5 Then angel-ministers will be
  Unveilèd to our eyes,
Waiting to waft the faithful soul
  In peace to Paradise.

6 O give us grace as angels here
  To live in holy love;
That the last trump may summon us
  To bliss with them above.

Christopher Wordsworth.

"O God, the Lord, strong to deliver and mighty to save, who hast been the refuge and dwelling-place of Thy people in all generations."

290   L. M.

HEALTH of the weak, to make them strong!
  Refuge of sinners, and their song!

Comfort of each afflicted breast!
Haven of hope in realms of rest!

2 Lord of the patriarchs gone before!
Light of the prophets' learned lore!
Deign from Thy throne to look on me,
And hear my lowly Litany.

3 Lead me, O Spirit, to the Son,
To taste and feel what He has done:
To lay me low before His cross,
And reckon all besides as dross;

4 To speak, and think, and will, and move,
And love, as Thou would'st have me love:
O, look upon this bended knee,
And hear my heart's own Litany.
Matthew Brydges.

FOURTH SUNDAY AFTER TRINITY.

"For I reckon that the sufferings of this present time are not worthy to be compared with the glory which shall be revealed in us."

291 8*s*, 7*s*.

JESUS, I my cross have taken,
  All to leave and follow Thee;
Destitute, despised, forsaken,
  Thou, from hence, my all shalt be.

2 Perish every fond ambition,
  All I've sought, or hoped, or known;
Yet how rich is my condition!
  God and heaven are still my own.

3 Go, then earthly fame and treasure!
  Come, disaster, scorn, and pain!
In Thy service pain is pleasure,
  With Thy favor, loss is gain!

4 I have called Thee, Abba, Father!
  I have stayed my heart on Thee!
Storms may howl and clouds may gather,
  All must work for good to me.

5 Man may trouble and distress me,
  'Twill but drive me to Thy breast;
Life with trials hard may press me,
  Heaven will bring me sweeter rest.

6 Oh! 'tis not in grief to harm me,
　　While Thy love is left to me;
　Oh! 'twere not in joy to charm me,
　　Were that joy unmixed with Thee.
7 Take, my soul, thy full salvation;
　　Rise o'er sin, and fear, and care;
　Joy to find, in every station,
　　Something still to do or bear.
8 Haste then on from grace to glory,
　　Armed by faith, and winged by prayer;
　Heaven's eternal day's before thee,
　　God's own hand shall guide thee there.
　　　　　　　　　　Henry Francis Lyte, 1833.

292

"My grace is sufficient for thee."
6s & 4s.

MY faith looks up to Thee,
　　Thou Lamb of Calvary,
　　　Saviour divine;
Now hear me while I pray;
Take all my guilt away;
O let me from this day
　　　Be wholly Thine!

2 May Thy rich grace impart
　　Strength to my fainting heart,
　　　My zeal inspire;
　As Thou hast died for me,
　O may my love to Thee
　Pure, warm, and changeless be
　　　A living fire.

3 While life's dark maze I tread,
　　And griefs around me spread,
　　　Be Thou my guide;
　Bid darkness turn to day,
　Wipe sorrow's tears away,
　Nor let me ever stray
　　　From Thee aside.

4 When ends life's transient dream,
　　When death's cold, sullen stream
　　　Shall o'er me roll;
　Blest Saviour! then in love
　Fear and distrust remove;
　O bear me safe above,
　　　A ransomed soul.　　*Ray Palmer*, 1830.

FOURTH SUNDAY AFTER TRINITY.

"Vouchsafe unto us such an abiding sense of the reality and glory of those things which Thou hast prepared for them that love Thee, as may serve to raise us above the vanity of this present world."

293   8s, 7s, 8s, 7s, 7s, 7s.

ON the fount of life eternal
   Gazing wistful and athirst;
Yearning, straining, from the prison
   Of confining flesh to burst;
Here the soul an exile sighs
For her native Paradise.

2 Who can paint that lovely city,
   City of true peace divine,
Whose pure gates forever open
   Each in pearly splendor shine;
Whose abodes of glory clear
Nought defiling cometh near?

3 There no stormy winter rages;
   There no scorching summer glows;
But through one perennial spring-tide,
   Blooms the lily with the rose;
And the Lamb, with purest ray,
Scatters round eternal day.

4 There the saints of God, resplendent
   As the sun in all his might,
Evermore rejoice together,
   Crowned with diadems of light;
And from peril safe at last,
Reckon up their triumphs past.

5 There in strains harmonious blending,
   They their sweetest anthems sing;
And, on harps divinely thrilling,
   Glorify their glorious King;
Aided by whose arm of might,
They were victors in the fight.

6 Look, O Jesus, on Thy soldiers,
   Worn and wounded in the fight;
Grant, O grant us, rest for ever,
   In Thy beatific sight;
And Thyself our guerdon be
Through a long eternity.

E. Caswall.

"If so be that we suffer with Him, that we may be also glorified together."

294 S. M.

OH, what, if we are Christ's,
  Is earthly shame or loss?
Bright shall the crown of glory be
  When we have borne the cross.

2 Keen was the trial once,
    Bitter the cup of woe,
  When martyred saints, baptized in blood,
    Christ's sufferings shared below.

3 Bright is their glory now,
    Boundless their joy above,
  Where on the bosom of their God
    They rest in perfect love.

4 Lord, may that grace be ours,
    Like them in faith to bear
  All that of sorrow, grief, or pain
    May be our portion here:

5 Enough, if Thou at last
    The word of blessing give,
  And let us rest in Thine own home,
    Where saints and angels live.
                        Henry W. Baker, 1852.

"For we know that the whole creation groaneth and travaileth in pain together until now."

295 C. M.

LIGHT of the lonely pilgrim's heart,
  Star of the coming day!
Arise, and with Thy morning beams
  Chase all our griefs away!

2 Come, blessed Lord! let every shore
    And answering island sing
  The praises of Thy royal Name,
    And own Thee as their King.

3 Bid the whole earth, responsive now
    To the bright world above,
  Break forth in sweetest strains of joy
    In memory of Thy love.

4 Jesus! Thy fair creation groans,
　The air, the earth, the sea,
　In unison with all our hearts,
　And calls aloud for Thee.

5 Thine was the cross with all its fruits
　Of grace and peace divine:
　Be Thine the crown of glory now,
　The palm of victory Thine!
Edward Denny, 1848.

"Be ye therefore merciful, as your Father also is merciful."

296   C. M.

WHAT grace, O Lord, and beauty shone
　Around Thy steps below;
What patient love was seen in all
　Thy life and death of woe!

2 For ever on Thy burdened heart
　A weight of sorrow hung,
Yet no ungentle murmuring word
　Escaped Thy silent tongue.

3 Thy foes might hate, despise, revile,
　Thy friends unfaithful prove;
Unwearied in forgiveness still,
　Thy heart could only love.

4 O give us hearts to love like Thee,
　Like Thee, O Lord, to grieve
Far more for other's sins than all
　The wrongs that we receive.

5 One with Thyself, may every eye
　In us, Thy brethren, see
The gentleness and grace that spring
　From union, Lord, with Thee.
Edward Denny, 1839.

FIFTH SUNDAY AFTER TRINITY.

"Cause Thy Church to arise and shine, O Lord, and let her ministers be clothed with righteousness and salvation."

297   L. M.

O GUARDIAN of the Church divine,
　The sevenfold gifts of grace are Thine,
And kindled by Thy hidden fires
The soul to highest aims aspires.

2 Thy ministers, O Lord, endue
  With wisdom, and their zeal renew;
  Turn all their weakness into might,
  O Thou the source of life and light.

3 Spirit of truth, on us bestow
  The faith in all its power to know;
  That with the saints of ages gone,
  And those to come, we may be one.

4 Protect Thy Church from every foe,
  And peace, the fruit of love, bestow;
  Convert the world, make all confess
  Thy mercy, truth, and righteousness.
                    T. Chamberlain, altered.

"*Even as Christ also loved the Church, and gave Himself for it.*"

298 6s.

WE love the place, O God,
  Wherein Thine honor dwells;
The joy of Thine abode
  All earthly joy excels.

2 It is the House of prayer,
    Wherein Thy servants meet;
  And Thou, O Lord, art there
    Thy chosen flock to greet.

3 We love the sacred font;
    For there the Holy Dove
  To pour is ever wont
    His blessing from above.

4 We love Thine altar, Lord;
    O what on earth so dear?
  For there, in faith adored,
    We find Thy presence near.

5 We love the word of life,
    The word that tells of peace,
  Of comfort in the strife,
    And joys that never cease.

6 We love to sing below
    For mercies freely given;
  And O! we long to know
    The triumph-song of heaven.

7 Lord Jesus, give us grace
   On earth to love Thee more,
  In heaven to see Thy face,
   And with Thy saints adore.
                              W. H. Bullock, 1854.

"Finally be ye all of one mind, having compassion one of another."

299   7s.

JESUS, Lord, we look to Thee,
  Let us in Thy name agree;
  Show Thyself the Prince of Peace,
  Bid all strife forever cease.

2 Make us of one heart and mind,
  Courteous, pitiful, and kind,
  Lowly, meek, in thought and word,
  Altogether like our Lord.

3 Let us for each other care,
  Each the other's burden bear,
  To Thy Church the pattern give,
  Show how true believers live.

4 Free from anger and from pride,
  Let us thus in God abide:
  All the depths of love express,
  All the heights of holiness.   *Charles Wesley.*

"Love as brethren, be pitiful, be courteous."

300   C. M.

LORD, as to Thy dear cross we flee,
   And plead to be forgiven,
  So let Thy life our pattern be,
   And form our souls for heaven.

2 Help us, through good report and ill,
   Our daily cross to bear,
  Like Thee, to do our Father's will,
   Our brethren's griefs to share.

3 Let grace our selfishness expel,
   Our earthliness refine,
  And kindness in our bosoms dwell,
   As free and true as Thine.

4 If joy shall at Thy bidding fly,
   And grief's dark day come on,
  We, in our turn, would meekly cry
   Father! Thy will be done!

5 Should friends misjudge, or foes defame,
   Or brethren faithless prove,
  Then, like Thine own, be all our aim
   To conquer them by love.

6 Kept peaceful in the midst of strife,
   Forgiving and forgiven,
  O may we lead the pilgrim's life,
   And follow Thee to heaven.
                    John Hampden Gurney, 1838.

301

"Who shall separate us from the love of Christ?"
                  S. M.

DEAR Saviour, we are Thine
   By everlasting bands;
Our hearts, our souls, we would resign
   Entirely to Thy hands.

2 To Thee we still would cleave
   With ever-growing zeal;
  If millions tempt us Christ to leave,
   O let them ne'er prevail.

3 Thy Spirit shall unite
   Our souls to Thee, our Head;
  Shall form us to Thine image bright,
   And teach Thy paths to tread.

4 Death may our souls divide
   From these abodes of clay:
  But love shall keep us near Thy side,
   Through all the gloomy way.

5 Since Christ and we are one,
   Why should we doubt or fear?
  If He in heaven has fixed His throne,
   He'll fix His members there.
                           P. Doddridge.

302

"O pray for the peace of Jerusalem: they shall prosper that love Thee."
                  S. M.

I LOVE Thy kingdom, Lord,
   The house of Thine abode;
The Church our blest Redeemer sav'd
   With His own precious blood.

2 I love Thy Church, O God!
　　Her walls before Thee stand,
　Dear as the apple of Thine eye,
　　And graven on Thy hand.

3 For her my tears shall fall;
　　For her my prayers ascend:
　To her my cares and toils be giv'n,
　　Till toils and cares shall end.

4 Beyond my highest joy
　　I prize her heav'nly ways,
　Her sweet communion, solemn vows,
　　Her hymns of love and praise.

5 Jesus, Thou Friend divine,
　　Our Saviour, and our King,
　Thy hand from every snare and foe,
　　Shall great deliv'rance bring.

6 Sure as Thy truth shall last,
　　To Zion shall be given
　The brightest glories earth can yield,
　　And brighter bliss of heaven.
Timothy Dwight, 1800.

"For the eyes of the Lord are over the righteous."

303　　　　　S. M.

MY spirit on Thy care,
　　Blest Saviour, I recline,
Thou wilt not lead me to despair,
　　For Thou art love divine.

2 In Thee I place my trust;
　　On Thee I calmly rest;
　I know Thee good—I know Thee just,
　　And count Thy choice the best.

3 Whate'er events betide,
　　Thy will They all perform;
　Safe in Thy breast my head I hide
　　Nor fear the coming storm.

4 Let good or ill befall,
　　It must be good for me;
　Secure of having Thee in all,
　　Of having all in Thee.
Henry Francis Lyte, 1834.

SIXTH SUNDAY AFTER TRINITY.

" For whether we live, we live unto the Lord; and whether we die, we die unto the Lord."

304 S. M.

JESUS! I live to Thee,
  The loveliest and best;
My life in Thee, Thy life in me,
  In Thy blest love I rest.

2 Jesus! I die to Thee,
  Whenever death shall come;
To die in Thee, is life to me.
  In my eternal home.

3 Whether to live or die,
  I know not which is best;
To live in Thee, is bliss to me,
  To die is endless rest.

5 Living or dying, Lord,
  I ask but to be Thine;
My life in Thee, Thy life in me
  Makes heaven forever mine.

  Henry Harbaugh.

" Therefore we are buried with him by baptism into death."

305 10s.

O LOVING Jesus, for us crucified,
  We, who are Thine, together with Thee died;
We, Lord, with Thee were buried in the grave,
When Thy baptismal waters us did lave.

2 O mighty Jesus, who for us art risen,
We, who are Thine, then rose from sin's dark prison;
We, by Thy help, death's iron bars did break,
New life is ours, and glory, for Thy sake.

3 O Conqueror Jesus, who art mounted high,
Bearing with Thee Thy members to the sky,
Lift us, O lift us, in Thy glorious flight,
From earth to realms of everlasting light.

4 O King of glory, from Thy throne above
Who didst the Spirit send of peace and love,
His silver wings a heavenward course will hold;
Give us those wings, and feathers as of gold.

5 O God Triune, baptiz'd in Thy dear name,
  We pray for heavenly light and holy flame,
  That firm in faith, and walking in Thy love,
  We may Thee ever praise in bliss above.
                                    Christopher Wordsworth.

"Likewise reckon ye also yourselves to be dead indeed unto sin."

306   C. M.

BROUGHT to the font with holy care,
  And washed from nature's shame,
We join the flock of Christ, and bear
  The Christian's sacred name.

2 Blest privilege! but all in vain
    Our new and heavenly birth,
  If we the truth of God profane,
    And cleave to things of earth.

3 Lord, since Thy holy name we bear,
    Like sons we would obey,
  Mark Thy commands with filial fear,
    And keep Thy perfect way.

4 So, Lord, the inward grace impart,
    And bless the outward sign,
  That love, abiding in our heart,
    In all our life may shine.   *Edward Osler.*

"Let this grace reign in us, as the power of a new heavenly life."

307   L. M.

GOD of all power, and truth, and grace,
  Which shall from age to age endure;
Whose word, when heaven and earth shall pass,
  Remains and stands forever sure;

2 That I Thy mercy may proclaim,
    That all mankind Thy truth may see;
  Hallow Thy great and glorious name,
    And perfect holiness in me.

3 Purge me from every sinful blot,
    My idols all be cast aside,
  Cleanse me from every sinful thought,
    From all the filth of self and pride.

4 Give me a new, a perfect heart,
    From doubt, and fear, and sorrow free;
  The mind which was in Christ impart,
    And let my spirit cleave to Thee.

"Except your righteousness shall exceed the righteousness of the Scribes and Pharisees, ye shall in no case enter into the kingdom of heaven."

308 L. M.

NO more, my God! I boast no more,
   Of all the duties I have done;
I quit the hopes I held before,
   To trust the merits of Thy Son.

2 Now for the love I bear His name,
   What was my gain, I count but loss;
My former pride I call my shame,
   And nail my glory to His cross.

3 Yes, and I must, and will, esteem
   All things but loss for Jesus' sake;
Oh! may my soul be found in Him,
   And of His righteousness partake.

4 The best obedience of my hands
   Dares not appear before Thy throne;
But faith can answer Thy demands,
   By pleading what my Lord has done.

Isaac Watts, 1709.

"And they shall be mine, saith the Lord of Hosts, in that day when I make up my jewels."

309 7s.

THINE for ever! God of love,
   Hear us from Thy throne above;
Thine for ever may we be,
   Here and in eternity.

2 Thine for ever! Lord of life,
   Shield us through our earthly strife:
Thou, the Life, the Truth, the Way,
   Guide us to the realms of day.

3 Thine for ever! O how blest
   They who find in Thee their rest;
Saviour, Guardian, heavenly Friend,
   O protect us to the end.

4 Thine for ever! Saviour, keep
   These Thy frail and trembling sheep;
Safe alone beneath Thy care
   Let us all Thy goodness share.

  5 Thine for ever! Thou our Guide,
   All our wants by Thee supplied,
   All our sins by Thee forgiven,
   Led by Thee from earth to heaven.
Mary Fawler Maude, 1848.

SEVENTH SUNDAY AFTER TRINITY.

" But now being made free from sin, and become servants to God, ye have your fruit unto holiness."

310   C. M.

O THOU, the Lord and Life of those
 Who rest their hope in Thee;
Whose love, from everlasting woes,
 Hath set Thy people free;

2 Thine agony and death display
 The curse our guilt should bear,
Thy resurrection points the way
 To bliss that we may share.

3 To Thee, O Lord, we lift our heart,
 Thy mercy we implore;
Help us to choose the better part,
 And go, and sin no more.

4 Help us the Saviour to confess,
 In whom our life we see;
And oh! may fruits of holiness
 Prove that we live to Thee.
W. J. Hall's Collection.

"But the gift of God is eternal life through Jesus Christ, our Lord."

311   S. M.

TO God the only wise,
 Our Saviour and our King,
Let all the saints below the skies
 Their humble praises bring.

2 'Tis His Almighty love,
 His counsel and His care,
Preserves us safe from sin and death,
 And every hurtful snare.

3 He will present our souls,
 Unblemished and complete,
Before the glory of His face,
 With joys divinely great.

4 Then all the chosen seed
  Shall meet before the throne,
  Shall bless the conduct of His grace,
  And make His wonders known.

5 To our Redeemer God
  Wisdom and power belongs,
  Immortal crowns of majesty,
  And never-ending songs. *Isaac Watts*, 1709.

" Cause the comfort of Thy heavenly grace to abound in us, as the earnest and pledge of joys to come."

312 C. M.

FATHER! whate'er of earthly bliss
  Thy sovereign will denies,
Accepted at Thy throne of grace,
  Let this petition rise:

2 Give me a calm, a thankful heart,
  From every murmur free;
  The blessings of Thy grace impart,
  And let me live to Thee.

3 Let the sweet hope, that Thou art mine,
  My path of life attend;
  Thy presence through my journey shine,
  And crown my journey's end. *Anne Steele*, 1760.

" He that eateth Me, even he shall live by Me."

313 L. M.

JESUS, Thou Joy of loving hearts,
  Thou Fount of life, Thou Light of men,
From the best bliss that earth imparts,
  We turn unfilled to Thee again.

2 Thy truth unchanged hath ever stood;
  Thou savest those that on Thee call;
  To them that seek Thee, Thou art good
  To them that find Thee, All in all.

3 We taste Thee, O Thou living Bread,
  And long to feast upon Thee still:
  We drink of Thee, the Fountain-head,
  And thirst our souls from Thee to fill.

4 Our restless spirits yearn for Thee,
  Where'er our changeful lot is cast;
  Glad, when Thy gracious smile we see,
  Blest, when our faith can hold Thee fast.

5 O Jesus, ever with us stay!
   Make all our moments calm and bright:
Chase the dark night of sin away,
   Shed o'er the world Thy holy light.
Bernard of Clairvaux, 1153.
Trans. Ray Palmer, 1858.

"This is that bread which came down from heaven."

314   *7s & 6s, 8 lines.*

O BREAD, to pilgrims given,
   O Food, that angels eat,
O Manna, sent from heaven,
   For heaven-born natures meet!
Give us, for Thee long pining,
   To eat till richly filled;
Till, earth's delights resigning,
   Our every wish is stilled.

2 O Water, life-bestowing,
   From out the Saviour's heart!
A fountain purely flowing,
   A fount of love Thou art;
Oh! let us, freely tasting,
   Our burning thirst assuage!
Thy sweetness, never wasting,
   Avails from age to age.

3 Jesus! this feast receiving,
   We Thee unseen adore;
Thy faithful word believing,
   We take, and doubt no more;
Give us, Thou true and loving!
   On earth to live in Thee;
Then, death the veil removing,
   Thy glorious face to see.
Latin Hymn.
Trans. Ray Palmer, 1858.

EIGHTH SUNDAY AFTER TRINITY.

"My meditation of Him shall be sweet."

315   C. M.

MY Saviour, my Almighty Friend!
   When I begin Thy praise,
Where will the growing numbers end:
   The numbers of Thy grace?

2 Thou art my everlasting trust;
   Thy goodness I adore;
And since I knew Thy graces first,
   I speak Thy glories more.

3 My feet shall travel all the length
   Of the celestial road,
And march with courage in Thy strength
   To see my Father, God.

4 When I am filled with sore distress
   For some surprising sin,
I'll plead Thy perfect righteousness,
   And mention none but Thine.

5 How will my lips rejoice to tell
   The vict'ries of my King!
My soul, redeemed from sin and hell,
   Shall Thy salvation sing.

6 My tongue shall all the day proclaim
   My Saviour, and my God,
His death hath brought my foes to shame,
   And saved me by His blood.

7 Awake, awake my tuneful powers,
   With this delightful song,
I'll entertain the darkest hours,
   Nor think the season long.

Isaac Watts, 1719.

"But ye have received the Spirit of adoption, whereby we cry, Abba Father."

316 C. M.

SOVEREIGN of all the worlds on high,
   Allow my humble claim;
Nor, while a worm would raise its head,
   Disdain a Father's name.

2 My Father, God! how sweet the sound!
   How tender, and how dear!
Not all the harmony of heav'n
   Could so delight the ear.

3 Come, sacred Spirit, seal the name
   On my expanding heart,
And show that in Jehovah's grace
   I share a filial part.

4 Cheered by a signal so divine,
   Unwav'ring, I believe;
And Abba, Father, humbly cry,
   Nor can the sign deceive.

P. Doddridge.

"And if children, then heirs; heirs of God, and joint heirs with Christ."

317 7s.

BLESSED are the sons of God;
   They are bought with Jesus' blood,
They are ransom'd from the grave,
Life eternal they shall have.

2 They are justified by grace,
   They enjoy a solid peace;
All their sins are washed away,
They shall stand in God's great day.

3 They produce the fruits of grace
   In the works of righteousness!
Born of God, they hate all sin,
God's pure word remains within.

4 They have fellowship with God,
   Through the Mediator's blood;
One with God, through Jesus one,
Glory is in them begun.

5 They alone are truly blest;
   Heirs with God, joint heirs with Christ;
They with love and peace are fill'd,
They are by His Spirit sealed.

Jos. Humphreys, 1743.

"For as many as are led by the Spirit of God, they are the sons of God."

318 C. M.

THE whole creation groans and waits
   Till we, who love Thee, Lord,
Shall stand within Thy temple gates,
   And shine—the sons of God.

2 The sons of God,—how bright they shine!
   No mortal eye can see;
We sinners shall be made divine!
   We shall be one with Thee!

3 One with the Lord and all His saints!
  Thy nature in our own!
  Thy crown our rich inheritance!
  Heirs to Thy royal throne!

4 Thy throne no joy to us would bring,
  If we from Thee were riven;
  For all our joy is in our King,
  And Thou art all our heaven.

"We will be glad and rejoice in Thee; we will remember Thy love."

319 S. M.

MY God! permit my tongue
  This joy, to call Thee mine;
And let my early cries prevail,
  To taste Thy love divine.

2 My thirsty fainting soul
    Thy mercy doth implore;
  Not travelers in desert lands,
    Can pant for water more.

3 For life, without Thy love,
    No relish can afford:
  No joy can be compared to this,
    To serve and please the Lord.

4 In wakeful hours at night,
    I call my God to mind;
  I think how wise Thy counsels are,
    And all Thy dealings kind.

5 Since Thou hast been my help,
    To Thee my spirit flies;
  And on Thy watchful providence
    My cheerful hope relies.

6 The shadow of Thy wings
    My soul in safety keeps;
  I follow where my Father leads,
    And He supports my steps.
                    Isaac Watts, 1719.

NINTH SUNDAY AFTER TRINITY.

"And they thirsted not when He led them through the desert."

320 L. M. 6 *lines.*

CAPTAIN of Israel's host, and Guide
  Of all who seek their home above:

Beneath Thy shadow we abide,
　The cloud of Thy protecting love:
Our strength, Thy grace: our rule, Thy word:
Our end, the glory of the Lord.

2 By Thine unerring Spirit led,
　We shall not in the desert stray:
By Thy paternal bounty fed,
　We shall not lack in all our way:
As far from danger as from fear,
While Thine almighty love is near.
Charles Wesley.

"In the day also He led them with a cloud and all the night with a light of fire."

321 C. M.

FORTH to the land of promise bound,
　Our desert-path we tread;
God's fiery pillar for our guide,
　His Captain at our head.

2 E'en now we faintly trace the hills,
　And catch their distant blue;
And the bright city's gleaming spires
　Rise dimly on our view.

3 Soon, when the desert shall be crossed,
　The flood of death past o'er,
Our pilgrim hosts shall safely land
　On Canaan's peaceful shore.

4 There love shall have its perfect work,
　And prayer be lost in praise;
And all the servants of our God
　Their endless anthems raise.
Henry Alford, 1827.

"Illuminate our minds by Thy heavenly grace, and fill them with the pure wisdom which cometh from above, that we may walk before Thee in simplicity and godly sincerity all our days."

322 L. M.

COME, O Creator, Spirit blest!
　And in our souls take up Thy rest;
Come, with Thy grace and heavenly aid,
To fill the hearts Thy power hath made.

2 Come, Holy Ghost, to Thee we cry:
O highest gift of God most high!
O Fount of life! O Fire of love!
Anointing Spirit from above!

3 Thou in Thy bounteous gifts art known,
Thee, Finger of God's hand, we own;
The promise of the Father Thou!
Our tongues with truth and power endow.

4 Kindle our senses from above,
And make our hearts o'erflow with love;
With patience firm, and virtue high,
The weakness of our flesh supply.

5 Far from us drive the foe we dread,
And grant us Thy true peace instead;
So shall we not, with Thee to guide,
Turn from the path of life aside.

6 O may Thy grace on us bestow,
The Father and the Son to know,
And Thee through endless time confess'd
Of Both th' eternal Spirit blest.

Charlemagne.
Trans. E. Caswall, altered.

"*So He fed them according to the integrity of His heart, and guided them by the skilfulness of His hands.*"

323 L. M.

IN all our wand'rings here below
We see Thee, Lord, where'er we go;
When waters flow from smitten rock,
Thy blood supplies Thy thirsting flock.

2 Thy word, and holy festival,
Thy Church—we see Thee in them all;
When manna from the heav'ns refresh,
Then Jesus feeds us with His flesh.

3 In all the gleams of grace divine
We see Thy holy presence shine;
Beneath the cloud baptiz'd are we,
And Jesus leads us through the sea.

4 No arm can save us from the foe
But Thine,—no other hope we know;
We lean not on ourselves;—Thy rod
Is all our trust, Thou Son of God.

 5 In all our long and weary way,
  Pilgrims of Canaan, lest we stray,
  Be Thou our Guide, Thy grace afford
  And make us Thine in will and word.

 6 So may we through life's desert go,
  And come where fruits of Eshcol grow;
  Gain the rich promise of Thy word
  And rest forever with the Lord.
       C. Wordsworth, altered.

"Not taking counsel of the world or of the flesh, but aiming and endeavoring in all things only to know and do Thy will."

324 10s, 4s, 10s, 4s, 10s, 10s.

LEAD, kindly Light, amid the encircling gloom,
  Lead Thou me on:
The night is dark, and I am far from home,
  Lead Thou me on.
Keep Thou my feet; I do not ask to see
The distant scene; one step enough for me.

 2 I was not ever thus, nor prayed that Thou
   Shouldst lead me on;
 I loved to choose and see my path; but now
   Lead Thou me on.
 I loved the garish day: and, spite of fears,
 Pride ruled my will; remember not past years.

 3 So long Thy power hath blest me, sure it still
   Will lead me on
 O'er moor and fen, o'er crag and torrent, till
   The night is gone,
 And with the morn those angel faces smile,
 Which I have loved long since, and lost awhile.
       Jno H. Newman.

"Now all these things happened unto them for ensamples."

325 S. M.

O LORD, refresh Thy flock;
 Athirst to Thee we cry:
Thou art the spiritual Rock,
 Whence we must drink or die.

 2 Preserve us, Lord, from death:
  Thou art the Lamb, whose blood
 Sprinkled on Israel's doors in faith
  A token was for good.

3 With many a bitter thought
 Of cherished sin subdued,
'Tis meet that, drest in pilgrim garb,
 We take Thee for our food.

4 Away the signs are cast,
 And now Thyself we see;
Yet let each sign that cheered the past
 Still lift our hearts to Thee. *Jos. Anstice.*

TENTH SUNDAY AFTER TRINITY.

"Jesus wept."

326 S. M.

DID Christ o'er sinners weep,
 And shall our cheeks be dry?
Let floods of penitential grief
 Burst forth from every eye.

2 The Son of God in tears
 The angels wondering see:
Hast Thou no wonder, O my soul?
 He shed those tears for Thee.

3 He wept that we might weep,
 Might weep our sin and shame;
He wept to show His love for us,
 And bid us love the same.

4 Then tender be our hearts,
 Our eyes in sorrow dim,
Till every tear from every eye
 Is wiped away by Him.
      Benj. Beddome, 1787.

"If thou hadst known, even thou, at least in this thy day, the things which belong unto thy peace."

327 S. M.

PAST is her day of grace;
 Her cup of wrath o'erflows:
Yet Jesus views the guilty place,
 And weeps her coming woes.

2 "If thou hadst known, e'en thou,
 At least in this thy day,
The message of thy peace—but now
 Thine hour is pass'd away."

 3 And doth the Saviour weep
  Over His people's sin,
 Because they will not let Him keep
  The souls He died to win?

 4 Ye hearts that love the Lord,
  If at this sight ye burn,
 See that in thought, in deed, in word,
  Ye hate what made Him mourn!

John Keble.

"*Now concerning spiritual gifts, brethren, I would not have you ignorant.*"

328 S. M.

O HOLY SPIRIT! come
 And Jesus' love declare;
Oh! tell us of our heavenly home,
 And guide us safely there.

 2 Our unbelief remove,
  By Thine almighty breath;
 Oh! work the wondrous work of love,
  The mighty work of faith.

 3 Thy sceptre, Lord! extend,
  Pity our deep distress;
 Thou art the contrite sinner's Friend,
  Thy waiting servants bless.

 4 We bless Thee for Thy grace,
  And Thine almighty power;
 We bless Thee for Thy holy place,
  And this accepted hour.

Oswald Allen, 1862.

"*Open ye the gates, that the righteous nation, which keepeth the truth, may enter in.*"

329 L. M.

LIFT up your heads, ye mighty gates!
 Behold! the King of glory waits!
The King of kings is drawing near,
The Saviour of the world is here.

 2 Life and salvation doth He bring,
 Wherefore rejoice, and gladly sing:
 Eternal praise, my God! to Thee!
 Creator! wise is Thy decree.

3 Fling wide the portals of your heart,
  Make it a temple, set apart
  From earthly use for heaven's employ,
  Adorned with prayer, and love, and joy.

4 So shall your Sovereign enter in,
  And new and nobler life begin;
  Eternal praise, my God! be Thine,
  For word, and deed, and grace divine.

5 Redeemer! come; I open wide
  My heart to Thee; here, Lord! abide;
  Let me Thine inner presence feel,
  Thy grace and love in me reveal.

6 Thy Holy Spirit guide us on,
  Until our glorious goal be won!
  Eternal praise, eternal fame,
  Be offered, Saviour! to Thy name!
  George Weisel, 1635.
Trans. *Cath. Winkworth*, 1855.

"*He beheld the city and wept over it.*"

330 C. M.

WHEN scorn'd by Zion, David's Son
  Looked down from Olivet,
The countenance of Christ was sad,
  Those eyes with tears were wet.

2 O precious tears, most precious blood,
    More costly than the dew
  That falls on Hermon's hill, and rains
    That Carmel's flowers renew.

3 For from those tears and precious blood,
    As from prolific showers,
  A blessed garden soon will bloom
    Of heavenly passion-flowers.

4 Thou, Lord, wilt rise from Calvary;
    And through Gethsemane
  From Zion pass to Olivet,
    For glorious victory.

5 Another Zion from that mount,
    O Lord, Thou wilt behold,
  Thy heavenly Zion, ever bright
    ·With precious stones and gold.

6 O weep with Christ on Olivet,
  That ye with Christ may rise;
  Ye sow in tears, to reap with Him
  A harvest in the skies.   *Christopher Wordsworth.*

"Come unto Me all ye that labor and are heavy laden, and I will give you rest."

331   L. M.

DEAR Lord! I give my heart to Thee,
  Its throbs of grief will never cease,
Till yearning faith be taught to see
  In Christ, the risen Prince of Peace.

2 My time is flitting day by day,
  Sad conscience weaves, in restless loom,
A shroud, whose dusky lines portray
  The travails of eternal gloom.

3 The bitter fruits of wasted years,
  The empty store of worldly gain,
Hope's blighted flowers, rank with tears,
  And mem'ry's ashes mix'd with pain;

4 This weighty sum of life I bring
  To Calv'ry's gleaming, lofty tree;
Lo! at its foot, the load I fling,
  And to its arms for refuge flee.

5 My guilt—the spear that pierced Thy side,
  My death once swelled Thy dying cry;
Oh cleanse my sins in mercy's tide,
  Still ebbing earthward from the sky.

6 Thine eye doth read the soul's distress,
  When, mourning for Thy peace, it pleads,
Let Thy forgiveness, Jesus, bless,
  And fill my spirit's piteous needs.
                              R. S. Mathews, 1859.

ELEVENTH SUNDAY AFTER TRINITY.

"A new heart will I give you, and a new spirit will I put within you."

332   C. M.

O FOR a heart to praise my God,
  A heart from sin set free!
A heart that's sprinkled with Thy blood,
  So freely shed for me!

2 A heart resign'd, submissive, meek;
  My dear Redeemer's throne;
Where only Christ is heard to speak
  Where Jesus reigns alone!

3 A humble, lowly, contrite heart,
  Believing, true, and clean;
Which neither life nor death can part
  From Him that dwells within!

4 A heart in every thought renewed,
  And full of love divine,
Perfect, and right, and pure, and good;
  A copy, Lord, of Thine!

5 Thy nature, gracious Lord, impart;
  Come quickly from above;
Write Thy new name upon my heart,
  Thy new, best name of love.
                    Charles Wesley, 1742.

333
"God be merciful to me a sinner."
                    C. M.

LORD, like the publican I stand,
  And lift my heart to Thee;
Thy pardoning grace, O God, command;
  Be merciful to me.

2 I smite upon my anxious breast,
  O'erwhelmed with agony!
O save my soul by sin oppressed;
  Be merciful to me.

3 My guilt, my shame, I all confess,
  I have no hope nor plea
But Jesus' blood and righteousness;
  Be merciful to me.

4 Here at Thy cross I still would wait,
  Nor from its shelter flee,
Till Thou, O God, in mercy great,
  Art merciful to me.
                    T. Raffles, 1831.

334
"But by the grace of God I am what I am."
                    C. M.

ALL that I was—my sin, my guilt,
  My death was all my own:
All that I am, I owe to Thee,
  My gracious God! alone.

2 The evil of my former state
   Was mine, and only mine;
The good in which I now rejoice,
   Is Thine, and only Thine.

3 The darkness of my former state,
   The bondage, all was mine;
The light of life, in which I walk,
   The liberty, is Thine.

4 Thy grace first made me feel my sin,
   It taught me to believe;
Then, in believing, peace I found,
   And now I live, I live.

5 All that I am, e'en here on earth,
   All that I hope to be,
When Jesus comes, and glory dawns,
   I owe it, Lord! to Thee.

Horatius Bonar, 1850.

"*He that humbleth himself shall be exalted.*"

335   C. M.

HOLY and rev'rend is the name
   Of our eternal King;
"Thrice holy Lord!" the angels cry;
"Thrice holy!" let us sing.

2 Holy is He in all His works,
   And truth is His delight;
But sinners and their wicked ways
   Shall perish from His sight.

3 The deepest rev'rence of the mind,
   Pay, O my soul, to God;
Lift with Thy hands a holy heart
   To His sublime abode.

4 With sacred awe pronounce His name,
   Whom words nor thoughts can reach;
A broken heart shall please Him more
   Than the best forms of speech.

5 Thou holy God! preserve my soul
   From all pollution free;
The pure in heart are Thy delight,
   And they Thy face shall see.

John Needham, 1768.

"O Lord, open Thou my lips; and my mouth shall show forth Thy praise."

336   8s & 7s, 8 lines.

LORD, with glowing heart I'd praise Thee
 For the bliss Thy love bestows;
For the pardoning grace that saves me,
 And the peace that from it flows:
Help, O God, my weak endeavor;
 This dull soul to rapture raise;
Thou must light the flame, or never
 Can my love be warmed to praise.

2 Praise, my soul, the God that sought Thee,
 Wretched wand'rer, far astray;
Found thee lost, and kindly brought thee
 From the paths of death away;
Praise, with love's devoutest feeling
 Him who saw thy guilt-born fear,
And, the light of hope revealing,
 Bade the blood-stained cross appear.

3 Lord, this bosom's ardent feeling
 Vainly would my life express;
Low before Thy footstool kneeling,
 Deign Thy suppliant's prayer to bless;
Let Thy grace, my soul's chief treasure,
 Love's pure flame within me raise;
And, since words can never measure,
 Let my life show forth Thy praise.
      Francis Scott Key, 1826.

"O come, let us worship and bow down; let us kneel before the Lord our Maker."

337   S. M.

COME, sound His praise abroad,
 And hymns of glory sing;
Jehovah is the sovereign God,
 The universal King.

2 He formed the deeps unknown,
 He gave the seas their bound;
The watery worlds are all His own,
 And all the solid ground.

3 Come, worship at His throne,
 Come, bow before the Lord;
We are His work, and not our own,
 He formed us by His word.

4 To-day attend His voice,
    Nor dare provoke His rod;
  Come, like the people of His choice,
    And own your gracious God.

5 But if your ears refuse
    The language of His grace,
  And hearts grow hard like stubborn Jews,
    That unbelieving race;

6 The Lord, in vengeance dressed,
    Will lift His hand and swear,
  " Ye that despise my promised rest,
    Shall have no portion there."
                        Isaac Watts, 1719.

TWELFTH SUNDAY AFTER TRINITY.

"For if the ministration of condemnation be glory, much more doth the ministration of righteousness exceed in glory."

338   C. M.

NOT to the terrors of the Lord,
    The tempest, fire, and smoke;
  Not to the thunder of that word,
    Which God on Sinai spoke.

2 But we are come to Zion's hill,
    The city of our God,
  Where milder words declare His will,
    And spread His love abroad.

3 Behold th' innumerable host
    Of angels clothed in light!
  Behold the spirits of the just,
    Whose faith is turned to sight!

4 Behold the blessed assembly there,
    Whose names are writ in heaven;
  And God, the Judge of all, declares
    Their vilest sins forgiven!

5 The saints on earth and all the dead
    But one communion make;
  All join in Christ, their living Head,
    And of His grace partake.

6 In such society as this
  My weary soul would rest;
The man that dwells where Jesus is
  Must be forever blest.   *Isaac Watts,* 1709.

"How shall not the ministration of the Spirit be rather glorious?"

339   C. M.

MOSES from Sinai brings the Law,
  His face with glory gleams;
The people's eyes bedimmed by sin,
  Are dazzled by its beams.

2 To shroud the glory of the Law,
  Brilliant with heavenly grace;
And spare their feeble eyes, he puts
  A veil upon his face.

3 Beam with Thy Spirit on our hearts,
  Take off the veil, that we
May see the glory of the Law,
  Jesus, revealed in Thee.

4 Lord, if the Law, on stones engraven,
  Did with such splendor shine,
How should we dare to gaze upon
  Thy countenance divine?

5 If, in the twilight dim, the law
  Gleamed with such lustre bright,
How glorious is the noon-day sun
  Of evangelic Light!

6 Thou sayest, "Without holiness
  No eye shall look on Thee,"
And "Blessed are the pure in heart,
  For they God's face shall see."

7 O, therefore, cleanse our sullied hearts,
  Soften these hearts of stone,
That we may see Thee, and may know
  As we, O Lord, are known.   *C. Wordsworth.*

"My soul doth magnify the Lord."

340   C. P. M.

OH! could I speak the matchless worth,
  Oh! could I sound the glories forth,
    Which in my Saviour shine!
I'd soar, and touch the heavenly strings,
And vie with Gabriel, while he sings
    In notes almost divine.

2 I'd sing the precious blood He spilt,
  My ransom from the dreadful guilt
    Of sin and wrath divine:
  I'd sing His glorious righteousness,
  In which all-perfect, heavenly dress
    My soul shall ever shine.

3 I'd sing the characters He bears,
  And all the forms of love He wears,
    Exalted on His throne:
  In loftiest songs of sweetest praise,
  I would to everlasting days,
    Make all His glories known.

4 Well,—the delightful day will come,
  When He, dear Lord! will bring me home,
    And I shall see His face:
  There, with my Saviour, brother, friend,
  A blessed eternity I'll spend,
    Triumphant in His grace.
                    Samuel Medley, 1789.

*"Work in us such inward conformity with His holy patience,
as may cause us to have part also in His glorious power."*

341   L. M.

MY dear Redeemer, and my Lord!
    I read my duty in Thy word;
But in Thy life the law appears
Drawn out in living characters.

2 Such was Thy truth, and such Thy zeal,
  Such deference to Thy Father's will,
  Such love and meekness, so divine,
  I would transcribe, and make them mine.

3 Cold mountains and the midnight air
  Witnessed the fervor of Thy prayer;
  The desert Thy temptations knew,
  Thy conflict and Thy victory too.

4 Be Thou my pattern; make me bear
  More of Thy gracious image here;
  Then God, the Judge, shall own my name,
  Amongst the followers of the Lamb.
                    Isaac Watts, 1709.

"He hath done all things well."

342 L. M.

NOW, in a song of grateful praise,
To my dear Lord my voice I'll raise;
With all His saints I'll join to tell
That Jesus hath done all things well.

2 Wisdom, and power, and love divine,
In all His works, unrivaled, shine,
And force the wondering world to tell
That He alone did all things well.

3 Howe'er mysterious are His ways,
Or dark or sorrowful my days;
And though my spirit oft rebel,
I know He still doth all things well.

4 And when I stand before His throne,
And all His ways are fully known,
This note in sweetest strains shall swell,
That Jesus hath done all things well.

Samuel Medley.

THIRTEENTH SUNDAY AFTER TRINITY.

"Blessed are the eyes, which see the things that ye see."

343 S. M.

HOW beauteous are their feet,
  Who stand on Zion's hill!
Who bring salvation on their tongues,
  And words of peace reveal!

2 How charming is their voice!
  How sweet the tidings are!
"Zion! behold thy Saviour King,
  He reigns and triumphs here!"

3 How happy are our ears,
  That hear this joyful sound,
Which kings and prophets waited for,
  And sought, but never found!

4 How blessèd are our eyes,
  That see this heavenly light!
Prophets and kings desired it long,
  But died without the sight.

5 The watchmen join their voice,
   And tuneful notes employ;
Jerusalem breaks forth in songs,
   And deserts learn the joy.

6 The Lord makes bare His arm,
   Through all the earth abroad;
Let every nation now behold
   Their Saviour and their God. *Isaac Watts*, 1707.

" Go and do thou likewise."

344   C. M.

WHEN from the city of our God
   Man wander'd far away,
He fell into the Tempter's hands;
   Was stripp'd, and wounded lay.

2 Christ bound our wounds, and pour'd in oil
   And wine with tender care,
And bore us to an Inn—His Church—
   And safely lodged us there.

3 He gave us to the host in charge,
   And "at that future day
When I shall come again," He said,
   "I will Thy pains repay."

4 What beams of grace and mercy, Lord,
   In Thy example shine!
O may we give Thee thanks and praise,
   By showing love like Thine.

5 So may we, at that future day,
   With joy Thy coming see,
And hear that blessing,—"What ye did
   To mine, ye did to Me." *C. Wordsworth.*

"There is therefore now no condemnation to them which are in Christ Jesus."

345   C. M.

DEAREST of all the names above,
   My Jesus and my God!
Who can resist Thy heavenly love,
   Or trifle with Thy blood?

2 'Tis by the merits of Thy death,
   The Father smiles again;
'Tis by Thine interceding breath,
   The Spirit dwells with men.

3 Till God in human flesh I see,
  My thoughts no comfort find;
 The holy, just, and sacred Three
  Are terrors to my mind.

4 But, if Immanuel's face appear,
  My hope, my joy begins;
 His name forbids my slavish fear,
  His grace removes my sins.

5 While Jews on their own law rely,
  And Greeks of wisdom boast;
 I love th' incarnate mystery,
  And there I fix my trust.
                                Isaac Watts, 1709.

" For if the inheritance be of the law, it is no more of promise."

346   C. M.

VAIN are the hopes, the sons of men
  On their own works have built;
 Their hearts, by nature, all unclean,
  And all their actions guilt.

2 Let Jew and Gentile stop their mouths,
  Without a murm'ring word;
 And the whole race of Adam stand
  Guilty before the Lord.

3 In vain we ask God's righteous law,
  To justify us now,
 Since to convince, and to condemn,
  Is all the law can do.

4 Jesus! how glorious is Thy grace!
  When in Thy name we trust,
 Our faith receives a righteousness,
  That makes the sinner just.
                                Isaac Watts, 1709.

"And walk in love, as Christ also hath loved us, and hath given Himself for us."

347   C. M.

BEHOLD, where in a mortal form
  Appears each grace divine!
 The virtues, all in Jesus met,
  With mildest radiance shine.

2 To spread the rays of heavenly light,
  To give the mourner joy,
 To preach glad tidings to the poor,
  Was His divine employ.

3 Lowly in heart, to all His friends
  A friend and servant found;
 He washed their feet, He wiped their tears
  And healed each bleeding wound.

4 'Midst keen reproach and cruel scorn,
  Patient and meek He stood,
 His foes, ungrateful, sought His life;
  He labored for their good.

5 Be Christ our Pattern and our Guide!
  His image may we bear!
 O may we tread His holy steps,
  His joys and glory share!
  William Enfield, 1772.

FOURTEENTH SUNDAY AFTER TRINITY.

"And it came to pass, that, as they went, they were cleansed."

348 C. M.

LORD, once afar removed from Thee,
  The race of Adam stood,
 Tainted by sin's foul leprosy,
  A wretched brotherhood.

2 Thou hast come down in love from heaven
  To us, O gracious Lord;
 And by Thy sanctifying blood
  We are to health restored.

3 Thy mercies on our weary souls
  Fall like refreshing dews,
 And every day and every hour
  Thy gifts of grace renews.
  C. Wordsworth.

"The communion of the Holy Ghost be with you all."

349 8s & 7s, 8 *lines.*

HOLY Ghost! dispel our sadness,
  Pierce the clouds of sinful night;
 Come, Thou Source of sweetest gladness!
  Breathe Thy life, and spread Thy light:

Come, Thou best of all donations
  God can give, or we implore!
Having Thy sweet consolations,
  We need wish for nothing more.

2 From that height which knows no measure,
    As a gracious shower descend,
  Bringing down the richest treasure
    Man can wish or God can send:
  Author of the new creation!
    Come, with unction and with power;
  Make our hearts Thy habitation;
    On our souls Thy graces shower.

3 Manifest Thy love forever;
    Fence us in on every side;
  In distress be our Reliever;
    Guard and teach, support and guide:
  Hear, Oh! hear our supplication,
    Loving Spirit, God of peace!
  Rest upon this congregation,
    With the fullness of Thy grace.

Paul Gerhard, 1653.
Trans. A. M. Toplady, 1776.

"*Walk in the Spirit.*"

350 L. M.

O THOU who makest souls to shine
    With light from lighter worlds above,
  And droppest glistening dew divine
    On all who seek a Saviour's love:

2 Do Thou Thy benediction give
    On all who teach, on all who learn,
  That so Thy Church may holier live,
    And every lamp more brightly burn.

3 Give those who teach pure hearts and wise,
    Faith, hope, and love, all warmed by prayer;
  Themselves first training for the skies,
    They best will raise their people there.

4 Give those who learn the willing ear,
    The spirit meek, the guileless mind:
  Such gifts will make the lowliest here
    Far better than a kingdom find.

5 O bless the shepherd; bless the sheep;
    That guide and guided both be one,
  One in the faithful watch they keep,
    Until this hurrying life be done.

6 If thus, Good Lord, Thy grace be given,
  In Thee to live, in Thee to die,
Before we upward pass to heaven
  We taste our immortality. *John M. Neale.*

"*I will put my Spirit within you.*"

351 S. M.

COME, Holy Spirit! come
  With energy divine,
And on this poor benighted soul,
  With beams of mercy shine.

2 From the celestial hills,
  Light, life, and joy dispense;
And may I daily, hourly feel
  Thy quickening influence.

3 Oh! melt this frozen heart,
  This stubborn will subdue;
Each evil passion overcome,
  And form me all anew.

4 The profit will be mine,
  But Thine shall be the praise;
Cheerful to Thee will I devote
  The remnant of my days.
              Benj. Beddome, 1770.

FIFTEENTH SUNDAY AFTER TRINITY.

"*Take no thought for your life, what ye shall eat, or what ye shall drink.*"

352 S. M.

COMMIT thou all thy griefs
  And ways into His hands,
To His sure truth and tender care
  Who earth and heaven commands;

2 Who points the clouds their course,
  Whom winds and seas obey:
He shall direct thy wandering feet,
  He shall prepare thy way.

3 Thou on the Lord rely,
  So safe thou shalt go on:
Fix on His word thy steadfast eye,
  So shall thy work be done.

4 No profit canst thou gain
   By self-consuming care:
 To Him commend thy cause: His ear
   Attends the softest prayer.

5 Thy everlasting truth,
   Father, Thy ceaseless love,
 Sees all Thy children's wants, and knows
   What best for each will prove.   *Paul Gerhardt.*
                              Trans. Jno. Wesley, 1739.

"*Your heavenly Father knoweth that ye have need of all these things.*"

353   C. M.

FATHER, 'tis Thine each day to yield
   Our wants a fresh supply;
 Thou cloth'st the lilies of the field,
   And hear'st the ravens cry:

2 Thy love in all Thy works we see;
   Thy promise, Lord, we plead;
 And humbly cast our care on Thee,
   Who knowest all our need.

3 Let not the world engage our love,
   Nor cares our bosoms fill;
 But fix our heart on things above,
   That we may do Thy will:

4 The comfort of Thy light bestow;
   Our faith and hope increase;
 And let us in Thy presence know
   Contentment, joy, and peace.   *Edward Osler.*

"*Glorious things are spoken of thee, O city of God.*"

354   8s & 7s, 8 lines.

GLORIOUS things of thee are spoken,
   Zion, city of our God;
 He, whose word cannot be broken,
   Formed thee for His own abode;
 On the Rock of Ages founded,
   What can shake thy sure repose?
 With salvation's walls surrounded,
   Thou mayest smile at all thy foes.

2 Thine the streams of living waters
   Springing from the throne above;
 Thither speed thy sons and daughters,
   There all thirst they slake in love;

    Who can faint while such a river
        Ever will their thirst assuage;
    Grace, which, like the Lord, the Giver,
        Never fails from age to age?
3 On their way, around them hovering,
        Pillared cloud or fire appear,
    For a glory and a covering;
        Showing that the Lord is near.
    From their banner thus deriving
        Light by night, and shade by day,
    Bread from heaven, all heart-reviving,
        For their daily food have they.
4 Saviour, we of Zion's city
        Members through Thy grace became;
    Though the world deride or pity,
        We will glory in Thy Name.
    Fading is the worldling's pleasure,
        All his boasted pomp and show;
    Solid joys and lasting treasure
        None but Zion's children know.
                      John Newton, 1779.

"The things which are seen are temporal, but the things which are not seen are eternal."

355   C. M. 8 *lines*.

THE roseate hues of early dawn,
    The brightness of the day,
The crimson of the sunset sky,
    How fast they fade away!
Oh, for the pearly gates of heaven,
    Oh, for the golden floor,
Oh, for the Sun of Righteousness,
    That setteth nevermore.

2 The highest hopes we cherish here,
      How fast they tire and faint;
   How many a spot defiles the robe
      That wraps an earthly saint!
   Oh, for a heart that never sins,
      Oh, for a soul washed white,
   Oh, for a voice to praise our King,
      Nor weary day nor night.

3 Here faith is ours, and heavenly hope,
      And grace to lead us higher;
   But there are perfectness, and peace
      Beyond our best desire.

Oh, by Thy love, and anguish, Lord!
    And by Thy life laid down,
Grant that we fall not from Thy grace,
    Nor cast away our crown.
            Cecil Frances Alexander, 1853.

" Mercifully fix our hearts on things above."
            8s & 7s, 6 *lines.*

356

LIGHT'S abode, celestial Salem,
    Vision whence true peace doth spring,
Brighter than the heart can fancy,
    Mansion of the Highest King;
O how glorious are the praises,
    Which of thee the prophets sing!

2 There for ever and for ever
    Alleluia is outpoured;
For unending, for unbroken,
    Is the feast-day of the Lord;
All is pure, and all is holy
    That within thy walls is stored.

3 There no cloud nor passing vapor
    Dims the brightness of the air;
Endless noon-day, glorious noon-day,
    From the Sun of suns is there;
There no night brings rest from labor:
    There unknown are toil and care.

4 O how glorious and resplendent,
    Fragile body, shalt thou be,
When endued with so much beauty,
    Full of health, and strong, and free,
Full of vigor, full of pleasure
    That shall last eternally!

5 Now with gladness, now with courage,
    Bear the burden on thee laid,
That hereafter these thy labors
    May with endless gifts be paid,
And in everlasting glory
    Thou with brightness be arrayed

6 Laud and honor to the Father,
    Laud and honor to the Son,
Laud and honor to the Spirit,
    Ever Three and ever One,
Consubstantial, co-eternal,
    While unending ages run.   *Hymnal Noted.*

SIXTEENTH SUNDAY AFTER TRINITY.

"Now when He came nigh to the gate of the city."

357 C. M.

O SAVIOUR, who at Nain's gate
   Didst dry a widow's tears,
And raise her only son, the prop
   Of her declining years;

2 What holy raptures, Lord, through Thee
   Thy suffering saints await,
When raised from death by Thee they stand
   At Thy own City's gate!

3 What ecstasies will then be theirs
   In that blest city, Lord,
When sons to parents will by Thee
   For ever be restored!

4 O grant us so together, Lord,
   To live in holy love,
That we together may be join'd
   In holy bliss above.

5 Members of Christ our bodies are,
   The Holy Spirit's shrine;
Then grant us so to use them now,
   That they may be like Thine.
                Christopher Wordsworth.

"Of whom the whole family in heaven and earth is named."

358 C. M.

LET saints below in concert sing
   With those to glory gone;
For all the servants of our King
   In earth and heaven are one.

2 One family—we dwell in Him—
   One Church, above, beneath,
Though now divided by the stream,
   The narrow stream of death;

3 One army of the living God,
   To His command we bow;
Part of the host have crossed the flood,
   And part are crossing now.

4 Some to their everlasting home
　This solemn moment fly;
And we are to the margin come,
　And soon expect to die.

5 E'en now, by faith, we join our hands
　With those that went before,
And greet the ransomed blessèd bands
　Upon th' eternal shore.

6 Lord Jesus! be our constant Guide:
　And, when the word is given,
Bid death's cold flood its waves divide,
　And land us safe in heaven.
　　　　　　　　　　Charles Wesley.

"Keep us who are still in the body, in everlasting fellowship with all that wait for Thee on earth, and with all that are around Thee in heaven."

359　　　　C. M.

JESUS, we sing Thy matchless grace
　That calls us as Thine own;
Give us among Thy saints a place
　To make Thy glories known!

2 Allied to Thee, our vital Head,
　We live, and grow, and thrive;
From Thee divided, each is dead,
　When most he seems alive.

3 Thy saints on earth, and those above,
　Here join in one accord;
One body all in mutual love,
　And Thou the common Lord.

4 O may our faith each moment gain
　More of Thy Spirit's grace;
Till Thou present us all complete
　Before Thy Father's face.

"They sing the song of Moses, the servant of God, and the song of the Lamb."

360　　　　S. M.

AWAKE, and sing the song
　Of Moses and the Lamb;
Wake every heart, and every tongue,
　To praise the Saviour's name.

2 Sing of His dying love;
　　Sing of His rising power;
　Sing how He intercedes above
　　For those whose sins He bore.

3 Sing, till we feel our hearts
　　Ascending with our tongues;
　Sing, till the love of sin departs,
　　And grace inspires our songs.

4 Sing, on your heavenly way,
　　Ye ransomed sinners, sing;
　Sing on, rejoicing every day
　　In Christ, th' eternal King.

5 Soon shall ye hear Him say,
　　"Ye blessèd children, come."
　Soon will He call you hence away
　　And take His wanderers home.

6 There shall our raptured tongue
　　His endless praise proclaim,
　And sweeter voices tune the song
　　Of Moses and the Lamb.

William Hammond, 1745.
Altered by M. Madan, 1760.

"Unto Him be glory in the Church by Christ Jesus, throughout all ages, world without end, Amen."

361
6s & 10s.

YE angel-hosts above,
　　Ye righteous souls at rest in Paradise,
Ye faithful still on earth,
Let all your songs to God in concert rise.

2 Yea, their one Maker's praise
The countless orders of creation sing:
　　Innumerable worlds
Pay homage to the Universal King.

3 Before th' eternal throne
The Elders, seated round the crystal sea,
　　Cast down their golden crowns
In worship of the Triune Majesty.

4 Responsive rolls the chant
From side to side in heav'n's own liturgy:
　　"Thrice Holy, Lord of Hosts,
Which was, and is, and evermore shall be."

5 Nor are those spirits mute,
Who to the Church Expectant now belong;
   They to the Saving Name
In adoration pour their thankful song.

6 With these the Church on earth
In ceaseless worship bears its equal part:
   In every land and tongue
Go up glad hymns of praise from voice and heart.

7 O when shall discords cease?
When shall Christ's family on earth be one?
   When shall His will supreme
As with one mind by all His saints be done?

8 Blest Spirit, may Thy grace
Our hymns of earth with those of angels blend,
   Until their notes be changed
For that "new song" of heaven that ne'er shall end!

9 To Thee, O Trinity;
To Thee, O Father; Thee, Eternal Son;
   O Holy Ghost, to Thee
Be glory while th' unending ages run!

Benjamin Webb.

"And to know the love of Christ, which passeth knowledge."

362 C. M.

THE Saviour! O what endless charms
   Dwell in the blissful sound!
Its influence every fear disarms,
   And spreads sweet comfort round.

2 Here pardon, life, and joys divine,
   In rich effusion flow,
For guilty rebels lost in sin,
   And doomed to endless woe.

3 The Almighty Former of the skies,
   Stooped to our vile abode:
While angels viewed with wondering eyes,
   And hailed th' incarnate God.

4 O the rich depths of love divine,
   Of bliss a boundless store!
Dear Saviour, let me call Thee mine;
   I cannot wish for more.

  5 On Thee alone my hope relies,
    Beneath Thy cross I fall;
   My Lord, my life, my sacrifice,
    My Saviour, and my All!
Anne Steele.

SEVENTEENTH SUNDAY AFTER TRINITY.

"Dispose and assist us by Thy grace to follow the example of His great humility and heavenly-minded love.

363   C. M.

JESUS, exalted far on high,
 To whom a name is given,
A name surpassing every name
 That's known in earth or heaven;

2 Before whose throne shall every knee
 Bow down with one accord;
Before whose throne shall every tongue
 Confess that Thou art Lord;

3 Jesus, who, in the form of God,
 Didst equal honor claim;
Yet, to redeem our guilty souls,
 Didst stoop to death and shame:

4 O may that mind in us be formed,
 Which shone so bright in Thee!
A humble, meek, and lowly mind,
 From pride and envy free.

5 May we to others stoop, and learn
 To emulate Thy love;
So shall we bear Thine image here
 And share Thy throne above.
Thomas Cotterill, 1812.

"One Lord, one faith, one baptism."

364   H. M.

ONE sole baptismal sign,
 One Lord, below, above,
Zion, one faith is thine:
 One only watchword, Love.
From different temples though it rise,
One song ascendeth to the skies.

2 Our Sacrifice is one ;
  One Priest before the throne,
The slain, the risen Son,
  Redeemer, Lord alone.
Thou who didst raise Him from the dead,
Unite Thy people in their Head!

3 O may that holy prayer,
  His tenderest and His last,
His constant, latest care,
  Ere to His throne He passed,
No longer unfulfilled remain,
The world's offence, His people's stain!

4 Head of Thy Church beneath,
  The catholic, the true,
On all her members breathe,
  Her broken frame renew!
Then shall Thy perfect will be done,
When Christians love and live as one.
George Robinson, 1843, *altered.*

"One God and Father of all, who is above all, and through all, and in you all."

365 7s, 8 *lines.*

FATHER, Son, and Spirit, hear
  Faith's effectual fervent prayer;
Hear, and our petitions seal,
Let us now the answer feel.
Still our fellowship increase ;
Knit us in the bond of peace ;
Join our new-born spirits, join
Each to each, and all to Thine.

2 Build us in one body up,
  Called in one high calling's hope ;
One the Spirit, whom we claim ;
One the pure baptismal flame ;
One the faith, and common Lord ;
One the Father lives adored,
Over, through, and in us all,
God incomprehensible.

3 One with God, the Source of bliss,
  Ground of our communion this :
Life of all that live below,
Let Thine emanations flow!

Rise eternal in our heart:
Thou our long-sought Eden art;
Father, Son, and Holy Ghost,
Be to us what Adam lost!

Charles Wesley.

" For I have given you an example, that ye should do as I have done to you."

366   L. M. 8 *lines.*

OH! who like Thee, so calm, so bright,
   Lord Jesus Christ, Thou Light of Light;
Oh! who like Thee did ever go
So patient through a world of woe?
Oh! who like Thee so humbly bore
The scorn, the scoffs of men, before;
So meek, so lowly, yet so high,
So glorious in humility?

2 Through all Thy life-long weary years,
A Man of sorrows and of tears,
The cross, where all our sins were laid,
Upon Thy bending shoulders weighed;
And death, that sets the prisoner free,
Was pang, and scoff, and scorn to Thee;
Yet love through all Thy torture glowed,
And mercy with Thy life-blood flowed.

3 O wondrous Lord, our souls would be
Still more and more conformed to Thee;
Would lose the pride, the taint of sin,
That burns these fevered veins within;
And learn of Thee, the lowly One,
And, like Thee, all our journey run,
Above the world, and all its mirth,
Yet weeping still with weeping earth.

4 Be with us as we onward go;
Illumine all our way of woe;
And grant us ever on the road
To trace the footsteps of our God:
That when Thou shalt appear, arrayed
In light, to judge the quick and dead,
We may to life immortal soar
Through Thee, who livest evermore.

Arthur C. Coxe.

"The desire of our souls is to Thy name, and to the remembrance of Thee."

367 C. M.

JESUS, the very thought of Thee
  With sweetness fills my breast;
But sweeter far Thy face to see,
  And in Thy presence rest.

2 Nor voice can sing, nor heart can frame,
  Nor can the memory find,
A sweeter sound than Thy blest name,
  O Saviour of mankind!

3 O hope of every contrite heart,
  O joy of all the meek,
To those who fall, how kind Thou art!
  How good to those who seek!

4 But what to those who find? ah! this
  Nor tongue, nor pen can show:
The love of Jesus, what it is,
  None but His loved ones know.

5 Jesus, our only joy be Thou,
  As Thou our prize wilt be;
Jesus be Thou our glory now,
  And through eternity.

Bernard of Clairvaux.
Trans. E. Caswall.

EIGHTEENTH SUNDAY AFTER TRINITY.

"My song shall be always of the loving-kindness of the Lord."

368 C. M.

THOU lovely Source of true delight,
  Whom I unseen adore!
Unveil Thy beauties to my sight,
  That I may love Thee more.

2 Thy glory o'er creation shines;
  But in Thy sacred word,
I read in fairer, brighter lines,
  My bleeding, dying Lord.

3 'Tis here, whene'er my comforts droop,
  And sins and sorrows rise,
Thy love, with cheerful beams of hope,
  My fainting heart supplies.

    4 Jesus, my Lord, my Life, my Light,
       Oh! come with blissful ray;
    Break radiant through the shades of night
    And chase my fears away.

    5 Then shall my soul with rapture trace
       The wonders of Thy love;
    But the full glories of Thy face
    Are only known above.
                          Anne Steele, 1760.

"What think ye of Christ? whose Son is He?"

369
L. M.

O CHRIST, Thou glorious King, we own
   Thee to be God's eternal Son;
The Father's fulness, life divine,
Mysteriously are also Thine.

2 When rolling years brought on the day,
Foretold and fix'd for this display,
Our great deliv'rance to obtain,
Thou didst our nature not disdain.

3 At God's right hand, now, Lord, Thou'rt placed,
And with Thy Father's glory graced,
True God and Man, in person One;
A Judge to pass our final doom.

4 From day to day, O Lord, do we
   On high exalt and honor Thee;
Thy name we worship and adore,
World without end, for evermore.

"And blessed be His glorious name forever and ever."

370
H. M.

JOIN all the glorious names
   Of wisdom, love and power,
That ever mortals knew,
   That angels ever bore:
All are too mean to speak His worth,
To mean to set my Saviour forth.

2 Great Prophet of my God,
   My tongue would bless Thy name;
By Thee the joyful news
   Of our salvation came:
The joyful news of sins forgiven,
Of hell subdued, and peace with heaven.

3 Jesus, my great High Priest,
  Offered His blood and died;
 My guilty conscience needs
  No sacrifice beside:
 His powerful blood did once atone,
 And now it pleads before the throne.

4 My dear and mighty Lord,
  My Conqueror and my King:
 Thy sceptre and Thy sword,
  Thy reigning grace I sing:
 Thine is the power; behold! I sit
 In willing bonds beneath Thy feet.
                          Isaac Watts.

" Ye are enriched by Him in all utterance."

371   S. M.

COME we that love the Lord,
  And let our joys be known;
 Join in a song with sweet accord,
  And thus surround the throne.

2 Let those refuse to sing
   That never knew our God;
  But favorites of the heavenly King
   May speak their joys abroad.

3 The men of grace have found
   Glory begun below:
  Celestial fruits on earthly ground
   From faith and hope may grow.

4 The hill of Zion yields
   A thousand sacred sweets,
  Before we reach the heavenly fields
   Or walk the golden streets.

5 Then let our songs abound,
   And every tear be dry;
  We're marching through Immanuel's ground,
   To fairer worlds on high.
                       Isaac Watts, 1707.

" Waiting for the coming of our Lord Jesus Christ."

372   L. M.

JESUS! my Lord, my God, my all!
  How can I love Thee as I ought?
 And how revere this wondrous gift
  So far surpassing hope or thought?

2 O earth! grow flowers beneath His feet,
   And thou, O sun, shine bright this day!
 He comes! He comes! O heaven on earth,
   Our Jesus comes upon His way!

3 He comes! He comes! the Lord of hosts,
   Borne on His throne triumphantly;
 We see Thee, and we know Thee, Lord,
   And yearn to shed our blood for Thee!

4 Our hearts leap up; our trembling song
   Grows fainter still; we can no more;
 Silence! and let us weep—and die
   Of very love, while we adore.
                        Frederick W. Faber.

"God is faithful, by whom ye were called unto the fellowship of His Son, Jesus Christ our Lord."

373   L. M.

LORD! let my heart still turn to Thee,
   In all my hours of waking thought;
 Nor let this heart e'er wish to flee,
   Or think, or feel, where Thou art not.

2 In every hour of pain and woe,
   When nought on earth this heart can cheer,
 When sighs will burst and tears will flow,
   Lord, hush the sigh and chase the tear.

3 In every dream of earthly bliss,
   Do Thou, dear Jesus, present be;
 Nor let a thought of happiness
   On earth intrude apart from Thee!

4 To my last ling'ring thought at night,
   Do Thou, Lord Jesus, still be near;
 And ere the dawn of opening light,
   In still small accents wake mine ear.

5 And when before the throne I kneel,
   Hear from that throne of grace my prayer,
 And let each hope of heaven I feel
   Burn with the thought to meet Thee there.

6 Thus teach me, Lord, to look to Thee
   In every hour of waking thought;
 Nor ever let me wish to be,
   Or think, or feel, where Thou art not!
                        Lady Powerscourt (?) 1833.

NINETEENTH SUNDAY AFTER TRINITY.

"Son, be of good cheer; thy sins be forgiven thee."

374 C. M.

WHEN, wounded sore, the stricken soul
  Lies bleeding and unbound,
One only hand, a piercèd hand,
  Can heal the sinner's wound.

2 When sorrow swells the laden breast,
  And tears of anguish flow,
One only heart, a broken heart,
  Can feel the sinner's woe.

3 When penitence has wept in vain
  Over some foul dark spot,
One only stream, a stream of blood,
  Can wash away the blot.

4 'Tis Jesus' blood that washes white,
  His hand that brings relief,
His heart, that's touched with all our joys,
  And feels for all our grief,

5 Lift up Thy bleeding hand, O Lord,
  Unseal that cleansing tide;
We have no shelter from our sin
  But in Thy wounded side.
            Cecil Frances Alexander, 1858.

"I will praise Thee forever, because Thou hast done it."

375 L. M.

REDEEM'D from guilt, redeem'd from fears,
  My soul enlarged and dried my tears,
What can I do, O Love divine,
What, to repay such gifts as Thine?

2 What can I do, so poor, so weak,
  But from Thy hands new blessings seek,
  A heart to feel Thy mercies more,
  A soul to know Thee, and adore?

3 O teach me at Thy feet to fall,
  And yield Thee up myself, my all!
  Before Thy saints my debts to own,
  And live and die to Thee alone!

    4 Thy Spirit, Lord, at large impart,
      Expand and raise and fill my heart!
    So may I hope my life shall be
      Some faint return, O Lord, to Thee.
                    Henry Francis Lyte, 1834.

"For Thou hast been a shelter for me, and a strong tower from the enemy."

376   C. M.

O JESUS, Saviour of the lost,
    My Rock and Hiding-place,
By storms of sin and sorrow tost,
    I seek Thy sheltering grace.

    2 Guilty, forgive me, Lord! I cry;
      Pursued by foes I come;
    A sinner, save me, or I die;
      An outcast, take me home.

    3 Once safe in Thine almighty arms,
      Let storms come on amain;
    There danger never, never harms;
      There death itself is gain.

    4 And when I stand before Thy throne
      And all Thy glory see,
    Still be my righteousness alone
      To hide myself in Thee.
                    Edward H. Bickersteth, 1858.

"In whom we have redemption through His blood, the forgiveness of sins."

377   C. M.

JESUS, Thou art my Righteousness,
    For all my sins were Thine;
Thy death hath bought of God my peace,
    Thy life hath made Him mine.

    2 Spotless and just in Thee I am;
      I feel my sins forgiven;
    I taste salvation in Thy Name,
      And antedate my heaven.

    3 For ever here my rest shall be,
      Close to Thy bleeding side;
    This all my hope, and all my plea,
      For me the Saviour died!

4 My dying Saviour and my God,
　　Fountain for guilt and sin,
　Sprinkle me ever with Thy blood,
　　And cleanse and keep me clean!

5 Wash me, and make me thus Thine own;
　　Wash me, and mine Thou art!
　Wash me, but not my feet alone;
　　My hands, my head, my heart!

6 Th' atonement of Thy blood apply,
　　Till faith to sight improve;
　Till hope in full fruition'die,
　　And all my soul be love.
　　　　　　　　　Charles Wesley, 1740.

"Him hath God exalted to be a Prince and a Saviour, for to give repentance to Israel and forgiveness of sins."

378　　　　　　C. M.

MAJESTIC sweetness sits enthroned
　　Upon the Saviour's brow;
His head with radiant glories crowned,
　　His lips with grace o'erflow.

2 No mortal can with Him compare
　　Among the sons of men;
　Fairer is He, than all the fair
　　That fill the heavenly train.

3 He saw me plunged in deep distress;
　　He flew to my relief;
　For me He bore the shameful cross
　　And carried all my grief.

4 To Him I owe my life and breath,
　　And all the joys I have;
　He makes me triumph over death,
　　And saves me from the grave.

5 To heaven, the place of His abode,
　　He brings my weary feet;
　Shows me the glories of my God,
　　And makes my joys complete.

6 Since from His bounty I receive
　　Such proofs of love divine,
　Had I a thousand hearts to give,
　　Lord! they should all be Thine!
　　　　　　　　　Samuel Stennett, 1787.

TWENTIETH SUNDAY AFTER TRINITY.

"The kingdom of heaven is like unto a certain king, which made a marriage for His Son."

379 C. M.

THOU, who hast call'd us by Thy word
  The marriage feast to share
Of Thy dear Son, our only Lord,
  Thy bidden guests prepare!

2 No vain excuse we dare to make,
  Thy call we do not slight;
We come unworthy; for His sake
  Help us to come aright!

3 Thy marriage-garment we require,
  Thyself to us impart,
And with Thy precious gifts inspire
  A pure and thankful heart.

4 And Thou, to whom the Father's love
  The wedding guests has brought,
Who ever helpest from above
  Those whom Thy blood has bought,

5 Lord of the feast! our coming bless,
  And round our souls entwine
The garment of Thy righteousness,
  In which Thy saints shall shine.
                        John Ernest Bode, 1860.

"That we might be made the righteousness of God in Him."

380 10s.

HERE, O my Lord, I see Thee face to face;
  Here would I touch and handle things unseen;
Here grasp with firmer hand th' eternal grace,
  And all my weariness upon Thee lean.

2 Here would I feed upon the Bread of God;
  Here drink with Thee the royal Wine of Heaven;
Here would I lay aside each earthly load,
  Here taste afresh the calm of sin forgiven.

3 I have no help but Thine; nor do I need
  Another arm save Thine to lean upon:
It is enough my Lord; enough, indeed;
  My strength is in Thy might, Thy might alone.

4 I have no wisdom, save in Him who is
    My Wisdom and my Teacher, both in one;
  No wisdom can I lack while Thou art wise,
    No teaching do I crave, save Thine alone.

5 Mine is the sin, but Thine the righteousness;
    Mine is the guilt, but Thine the cleansing blood,
  Here is my robe, my refuge, and my peace,
    Thy blood, Thy righteousness, O Lord my God!

6 Feast after feast thus comes, and passes by;
    Yet, passing, points to the glad Feast above,
  Giving sweet foretaste of the festal joy,
    The Lamb's great bridal Feast of bliss and love.
                                    Horatius Bonar, 1856.

"Search me, O God, and know my heart."

381   L. M.

O THOU, to whose all-searching sight,
    The darkness shineth as the light,
  Search, prove my heart, it pants for Thee;
  Oh, burst these bonds and set it free!

2 Wash out its stains, refine its dross,
    Nail my affections to the cross:
  Hallow each thought, let all within
  Be clean, as Thou, my Lord, art clean.

3 If in this darksome wild I stray
    Be Thou my light, be Thou my Way;
  No foes, no violence I fear,
  No fraud, while Thou, my God, art near.

4 When rising floods my soul o'erflow,
    When sinks my heart in waves of woe,
  Jesus, Thy timely aid impart,
  And raise my head and cheer my heart.

5 Saviour, where'er Thy steps I see,
    Dauntless, untried, I follow Thee;
  Oh, let Thy hand support me still,
  And lead me to Thy holy hill!

6 If rough and thorny be the way,
    My strength proportion to my day;
  Till toil and grief and pain shall cease,
  Where all is calm and joy and peace.
                            Gerhard Tersteegen, 1731.
                            Trans. John Wesley, 1739.

"That the name of our Lord Jesus Christ may be glorified in you, and ye in Him."

382 7s.

SON of God, eternal Word,
Glorious Day-spring, Christ the Lord,
Shine upon us with Thy rays,
While we celebrate Thy praise.

2 When Thou madest heaven and earth,
Angels shouted at their birth;
Morning stars in chorus sang,
When the world from darkness sprang.

3 When in sin and death we lay,
Thou didst wake us into day;
Thou, in human nature born,
Wast to us a glorious morn.

4 When Thou didst arise from death,
We were quicken'd by Thy breath;
We arose with Thee our Head,
First begotten from the dead.

5 Keep us safe from harm and sin,
Foes around us and within;
May we know Thee ever nigh,
Ever walk as in Thine eye.

6 Lead us onward, Lord, we pray,
To the pure and perfect day,
Where we may the glory see
Of the blessed Trinity. *Christopher Wordsworth.*

"Singing and making melody in your hearts to the Lord."

383 7s.

CHILDREN of the heav'nly King,
As ye journey, sweetly sing;
Sing your Saviour's worthy praise,
Glorious in His works and ways.

2 Lift your eyes, ye sons of Light!
Zion's city is in sight:
There our endless home shall be,
There our Lord we soon shall see.

3 Fear not, brethren; joyful stand
On the borders of your land:
Jesus Christ, your Father's Son,
Bids you undismayed go on.

4 Lord! obediently we go,
 Gladly leaving all below;
 Only Thou our Leader be,
 And we still will follow Thee!

5 Seal our love, our labors end;
 Let us to Thy bliss ascend;
 Let us to Thy kingdom come;
 Lord! we long to be at home.

John Cennick, 1742.

TWENTY-FIRST SUNDAY AFTER TRINITY.

"Lord, Thou hast been our refuge from one generation to another."

384 C. M.

O GOD, our help in ages past,
  Our hope for years to come,
Our shelter from the stormy blast,
  And our eternal home.

2 Beneath the shadow of Thy throne
   Thy saints have dwelt secure;
 Sufficient is Thine arm alone,
   And our defence is sure.

3 Before the hills in order stood,
   Or earth received her frame,
 From everlasting Thou art God,
   To endless years the same.

4 A thousand ages in Thy sight
   Are like an evening gone;
 Short as the watch that ends the night
   Before the rising sun.

5 Time, like an ever-rolling stream,
   Bears all its sons away;
 They fly forgotten, as a dream
   Dies at the opening day.

6 O God, our help in ages past,
   Our hope for years to come;
 Be Thou our guard while troubles last,
   And our eternal home.

Isaac Watts, 1719.

"Behold, O God our Shield, and look upon the face of Thine anointed."

385 8s & 7s, 8 *lines.*

HERE on earth, where foes surround us,
   While our trembling souls within
Feel the fetters which have bound us,
   Feel the burden of our sin;
Lord, on Thee alone relying,
   Strength we crave to burst our chain,
Ever pleading, ever crying,
   "Lord, for us the Lamb was slain."

2 In those high and holy regions
   Where the blest Thy praise prolong,
Cherubs and seraphic legions
   Know no theme of nobler song;
White-robed saints, who there adore Thee
   Throned above the glassy main,
Sing, and cast their crowns before Thee,
   "Lord, for us the Lamb was slain."

3 Thus, Thy Church, whate'er her dwelling,
   Heaven above or earth below,
One harmonious chorus swelling,
   Loves her Saviour's praise to show:
Here in trial, there in glory,
   Changeless rings th' immortal strain,
Changeless sounds the wondrous story,
   "Lord, for us the Lamb was slain."

"I will lift up mine eyes to the hills, from whence cometh my help."

386 C. M.

THROUGH all the changing scenes of life,
   In trouble and in joy,
The praises of my God shall still
   My heart and tongue employ.

2 O magnify the Lord with me,
   With me exalt His name;
When in distress to Him I called,
   He to my rescue came.

3 The hosts of God encamp around
   The dwellings of the just;
Deliv'rance He affords to all
   Who on His succor trust.

 4 O make but trial of His love,
  Experience will decide
  How blessed are they, and only they,
  Who in His truth confide.

 5 Fear Him, ye saints, and you will then
  Have nothing else to fear;
  Make you His service your delight,
  Your wants shall be His care.
Nahum Tate, 1696.

"Be strong in the Lord, and in the power of His might."

387   S. M.

SOLDIERS of Christ! arise
 And put your armor on,
Strong, in the strength which God supplies,
 Through His eternal Son:

2 Strong, in the Lord of hosts,
 And in His mighty power;
Who in the strength of Jesus trusts,
 Is more than conqueror.

3 Stand, then, in His great might,
 With all His strength endued;
And take, to arm you for the fight,
 The panoply of God:

4 That, having all things done,
 And all your conflicts past,
You may o'ercome through Christ alone
 And stand entire at last.

5 From strength to strength go on;
 Wrestle, and fight, and pray;
Tread all the powers of darkness down,
 And win the well-fought day.

6 Still let the Spirit cry,
 In all His soldiers, "Come,"
Till Christ, the Lord, descends from high,
 And takes the conquerors home.
Charles Wesley, 1745.

"That we may be able to fight manfully the good fight of faith, and so finish our course with joy."

388   7s, 6s.

BRIEF life is here our portion;
 Brief sorrow, short-lived care;
The life that knows no ending,
 The tearless life, is *there*.

2 O happy retribution!
   Short toil, eternal rest;
For mortals and for sinners
   A mansion with the blest.

3 And now we fight the battle,
   But then shall wear the crown
Of full and everlasting
   And passionless renown;

4 And now we watch and struggle,
   And now we live in hope,
And Zion in her anguish
   With Babylon must cope;

5 But He, whom now we trust in,
   Shall then be seen and known;
And they that know and see Him
   Shall have Him for their own.

6 The morning shall awaken,
   The shadows shall decay,
And each true-hearted servant
   Shall shine as doth the day;

7 There God, our King and Portion,
   In fulness of His grace,
Shall we behold for ever
   And worship face to face.

Bernard of Morlaix, 1150.
Trans. Jno. M. Neale, altered.

"O Lord my God, Thou art become exceeding glorious; Thou art clothed with majesty and honor."

389
10s & 11s.

O WORSHIP the King, all-glorious above;
   O gratefully sing His power and His love;
Our Shield and Defender, the Ancient of days,
Pavilioned in splendor, and girded with praise.

2 O tell of His might, O sing of His grace,
Whose robe is the light, whose canopy space;
His chariots of wrath the deep thunder-clouds form,
And dark is His path on the wings of the storm.

3 Frail children of dust, and feeble as frail,
In Thee do we trust, nor find Thee to fail;
Thy mercies how tender, how firm to the end,
Our Maker, Defender, Redeemer, and Friend.

4 O measureless Might! ineffable Love!
  While angels delight to hymn Thee above,
  The humbler creation, though feeble their lays,
  With true adoration shall sing to Thy praise.
                              Robert Grant, 1839, *altered*.

"The angel of the Lord encampeth round about them that fear Him, and delivereth them."

390   C. M.

TO Zion's hill I lift mine eyes,
     From thence expecting aid;
  From Zion's hill, and Zion's God,
     Who heaven and earth has made.

2 Thou, then, my soul in safety rest,
     Thy Guardian will not sleep;
  His watchful care that Israel guards,
     Will Thee in safety keep.

3 Sheltered beneath th' Almighty's wings,
     Thou shalt securely rest;
  Where neither sun nor moon shall thee
     By day or night molest.

4 At home, abroad, in peace, in war,
     Thy God shall thee defend;
  Conduct thee through life's pilgrimage,
     Safe to thy journey's end.
                              Isaac Watts, 1719.

TWENTY-SECOND SUNDAY AFTER TRINITY.

"There remaineth therefore a rest for the people of God."

391   C. P. M.

THERE is a dwelling-place above;
     Thither to meet the God of love,
       The poor in spirit go;
  There is a paradise of rest;
  For contrite hearts and souls distrest
       Its streams of comfort flow.

2 There is a voice to mercy true;
  To them who mercy's path pursue
       That voice shall bliss impart;
  There is a sight from man concealed;
  That sight, the face of God revealed,
       Shall bless the pure in heart.

3 There is a name in heaven bestowed ;
    That name, which hails them sons of God,
        The friends of peace shall know ;
        There is a kingdom in the sky,
    Where they shall reign with God on high,
        Who serve Him here below.
                                Richard Mant.

"That we may not seek our rest in this mortal state, but inwardly long after that which is far better, to be with Christ in heaven."

392   C. M.

O JESUS, Thou the Beauty art
    Of angel-worlds above ;
Thy name is music to the heart,
    Inflaming it with love.

2 Celestial sweetness unalloyed !
    Who eat Thee, hunger still ;
  Who drink of Thee still feel a void,
    Which nought but Thou can fill.

3 O most sweet Jesus, hear the sighs
    Which unto Thee we send ;
  To Thee our inmost spirit cries,
    To Thee our prayers ascend.

4 Abide with us, and let Thy light
    Shine, Lord, on every heart ;
  Dispel the darkness of our night,
    And joy to all impart.

5 Jesus, our Love and Joy, to Thee
    The Virgin's holy Son
  All might and praise and glory be
    While endless ages run.
                        Bernard of Clairvaux, 1140.
                        Trans. E. Caswall, altered.

"I forgave thee all that debt : shouldst not thou also have had compassion on thy fellow-servant ?"

393   8s & 7s, 8 lines.

LORD of glory ! Thou hast bought us,
    With Thy life-blood as the price,
Never grudging, for the lost ones,
    That tremendous sacrifice ;
And, with that, hast freely given
    Blessings, countless as the sand,
To th' unthankful and the evil
    With Thine own unsparing hand.

2 Grant us hearts, dear Lord! to yield Thee
 Gladly, freely, of Thine own;
With the sunshine of Thy goodness,
 Melt our thankless hearts of stone;
Till our cold and selfish natures,
 Warmed by Thee, at length believe,
That more happy, and more blessed,
 'Tis to give than to receive.

3 Wondrous honor hast Thou given
 To our humblest charity,
In Thine own mysterious sentence,—
 " Ye have done it unto Me:"
Give us faith, to trust Thee boldly,
 Hope, to stay our souls on Thee:
But, Oh!— best of all Thy graces—
 Give us Thine own charity.
Alderson, 1868.

"And this I pray, that your love may abound yet more and more."

394 L. M.

JESUS, most merciful and kind,
 Beloved and loving, both combined;
Jesus, Thou good and gracious One!
Of Mary and of God, the Son.

2 Who can conceive, or who record,
What bliss it is to love Thee, Lord!
To dwell in humble faith with Thee,
Is boundless, full felicity.

3 Let saints below and saints above,
Show forth Thy faithful, endless love;
And know the joy Thy people see,
Who suffer and who weep with Thee.

4 Infinite Majesty above!
Our Hope, our Life, our Joy and Love;
Thy fulness, Jesus, let us see,
And evermore abide in Thee.

5 Thus, seeing and enjoying Thee,
In earth and heaven our joy shall be;
And grateful praise to Thee be given,
Through all the blissful life of heaven!

TWENTY-SECOND SUNDAY AFTER TRINITY.

"The Lord our Righteousness."

395   C. M.

WE, in ourselves, unrighteous are ;
    With sorrow we confess
Our great and grievous sins to Thee,
    The Lord our Righteousness.

2 Not to Thine angels, nor to saints
    Do we our prayer address;
We fly to Thee, and only Thee,
    The Lord our Righteousness.

3 Thou, Christ, the great Jehovah art,
    The Fount of holiness;
And, God with us, Thou art become
    The Lord our Righteousness.

4 O wash us with Thy blood, and clothe
    With Thy pure spotless dress;
O hide us in Thyself, and be
    The Lord our Righteousness.

5 Make us by grace to be in deed
    What we in word profess;
O make us like unto Thyself,
    The Lord our Righteousness.

6 Pour on us plenteous showers of grace,
    Increase our fruitfulness,
That we may yield Thine own to Thee,
    The Lord our Righteousness,

7 So, in Thy glorious image rais'd,
    May we Thy mercy bless;
And sing for ever praise to Thee,
    The Lord our Righteousness.
Christopher Wordsworth.

"In all these things we are more than conquerors through Him that loved us."

396   C. M.

MY God, the Spring of all my joys,
    The Life of my delights,
The Glory of my brightest days,
    And Comfort of my nights!

2 In darkest shades, if He appear,
   My dawning is begun ;
   He is my soul's sweet Morning Star,
   And He my rising Sun.

3 The opening heavens around me shine,
   With beams of sacred bliss,
   While Jesus shows His heart is mine,
   And whispers—I am His.

4 My soul would leave this heavy clay,
   At that transporting word ;
   Run up with joy the shining way,
   T'embrace my dearest Lord.

5 Fearless of hell and ghastly death,
   I'd break through every foe ;
   The wings of love, and arms of faith
   Should bear me conqueror through.
                                Isaac Watts, 1707.

TWENTY-THIRD SUNDAY AFTER TRINITY.

"Render unto God, the things that are God's."

397 L. M.

BEFORE Jehovah's awful throne,
   Ye nations, bow with sacred joy ;
Know that the Lord is God alone ;
   He can create, and He destroy.

2 His sov'reign power, without our aid,
   Made us of clay, and form'd us men ;
   And when, like wand'ring sheep we strayed,
   He brought us to His fold again.

3 We are His people, we His care,
   Our souls, and all our mortal frame :
   What lasting honors shall we rear,
   Almighty Maker ! to Thy name?

4 We'll crowd Thy gates with thankful songs,
   High as the heav'ns our voices raise ;
   And earth, with her ten thousand tongues,
   Shall fill Thy courts with sounding praise.

5 Wide as the world is Thy command,
   Vast as eternity Thy love ;
   Firm as a rock Thy truth shall stand,
   When rolling years shall cease to move.
                      Isaac Watts, 1719, *altered*.

"Heaven and earth are full of the majesty of Thy glory."

398 8s & 7s.

ROUND the Lord in glory seated,
   Cherubim and Seraphim
Filled His temple, and repeated
   Each to each th' alternate hymn.

2 "Lord, Thy glory fills the heaven,
   Earth is with its fulness stored:
Unto Thee be glory given,
   Holy, Holy, Holy, Lord!"

3 Heaven is still with glory ringing,
   Earth takes up the angels' cry,
"Holy, Holy, Holy," singing,
   "Lord of Hosts, the Lord most high!"

4 With His seraph-train before Him,
   With His holy church below,
Thus conspire we to adore Him,
   Bid we thus our anthem flow:

5 "Lord, Thy glory fills the heaven,
   Earth is with its fulness stored:
Unto Thee be glory given,
   Holy, Holy, Holy, Lord!"

Richard Mant.

"For our conversation is in heaven."

399 C. M.

O MOTHER dear, Jerusalem!
   When shall I come to thee?
When shall my sorrows have an end,
   Thy joys when shall I see?

2 Jerusalem the city is
   Of God our King alone;
The Lamb of God, its light and bliss,
   Sits on His glorious throne.

3 O happy harbor of God's saints!
   O sweet and pleasant soil!
In thee no sorrow may be found,
   No grief, no care, no toil.

4 No dimming clouds o'ershadow thee,
   No dull nor darksome night!
But every soul shines as the sun,
   For God Himself gives light.

5 Jerusalem! God's dwelling-place!
   I love and long to see;
 O that my sorrows had an end,
   That I might dwell in thee.

6 Thy walls are made of precious stones,
   Thy bulwarks diamond-square;
 Thy gates are made of orient pearl,
   O God! if I were there!

7 With cherubim and seraphim,
   And holy souls of men,
 To sing Thy praise, O God of hosts,
   For ever, and amen!

Francis Baker, 1616.
Altered by *David Dickson*, 1649.

"*They desire a better country, that is, an heavenly.*"

400 *7s & 6s.*

FOR thee, O dear, dear country!
   Mine eyes their vigils keep;
 For very love, beholding
   Thy happy name, they weep.

2 The mention of thy glory
   Is unction to the breast,
 And medicine in sickness,
   And love, and life, and rest.

3 O one, O only mansion!
   O Paradise of joy!
 Where tears are ever banished,
   And smiles have no alloy;

4 The Lamb is all thy splendor;
   The Crucified thy praise;
 His laud and benediction
   Thy ransomed people raise.

5 With jasper glow thy bulwarks,
   Thy streets with emeralds blaze;
 The sardius and the topaz
   Unite in thee their rays;

6 Thine ageless walls are bonded
   With amethyst unpriced;
 The saints build up its fabric,
   The corner-stone is Christ.

    7 Thou hast no shore, fair ocean!
       Thou hast no time, bright day!
      Dear fountain of refreshment
       To pilgrims far away!

    8 Upon the Rock of Ages
       They raise thy holy tower;
      Thine is the victor's laurel,
       And thine the golden dower.
              Bernard of Morlaix, 1150.
                Trans. Jno. M. Neale, altered.

"*From whence also we look for the Saviour, the Lord Jesus Christ.*"

401
C. M.

FAIR vision! how thy distant gleam
   Brightens time's saddest hue:
Far fairer than the fairest dream,
   And yet how strangely true;

2 With thee in view, how poor appear
   The world's most winning smiles:
Vain is the Tempter's subtlest snare,
   And vain hell's varied wiles.

3 Then welcome toil and care and pain,
   And welcome sorrow too:
All toil is rest, all grief is gain,
   With such a prize in view.

4 Come crown and throne, come robe and palm,
   Burst forth, glad stream of peace:
Come, holy city of the Lamb!
   Rise, Sun of Righteousness!

5 When shall the clouds that veil thy rays
   For ever be withdrawn?
Why dost thou tarry, day of days?
   When shall thy gladness dawn?
                Horatius Bonar.

"*That we may pass through the world as pilgrims and strangers, looking for and hastening unto the Second Advent of the Lord Jesus.*"

402
L. M.

'TIS gone—the sacred day is o'er,
   And we must leave its rest awhile;
Oh! may our waiting hearts once more
   Be gladden'd with the Master's smile.

2 So shall this love our spirits raise,
    While at the cross we kneel in prayer;
Dear Saviour, Thine be all the praise
    If we have left our burdens there.

3 Spirit of holiness and power!
    Spirit of truth and love divine!
Thy presence cheers this closing hour;
    Still dwell with us for we are Thine.

4 For the pure manna of Thy word,
    And streams of life so richly given;
As pilgrims here, we bless Thee, Lord!
    But wait the perfect rest of heaven.

5 Sweet hope! a few more changing days
    And weary cares our faith shall try;
Then for the songs of nobler praise,
    The ceaseless Sabbath of the sky.

Alfred Rooker.

FOURTH SUNDAY BEFORE ADVENT.

"Bless the Lord, O my soul, and forget not all His benefits."

403 S. M.

MY soul, repeat His praise
    Whose mercies are so great,
Whose anger is so slow to rise,
    So ready to abate.

2 High as the heavens are rais'd
    Above the ground we tread,
So far the riches of His grace
    Our highest thoughts exceed.

3 His power subdues our sins;
    And His forgiving love,
Far as the east is from the west,
    Doth all our guilt remove.

4 The pity of the Lord
    To those that fear His name,
Is such as tender parents feel;
    He knows our feeble frame.

5 Our days are as the grass,
    Or like the morning flower;
If one sharp blast sweep o'er the field,
    It withers in an hour.

6 But Thy compassions, Lord,
   To endless years endure,
 And children's children ever find
   Thy words of promise sure.

Isaac Watts, 1719.

"Who hath delivered us from the power of darkness."

404   C. M.

PLUNGED in a gulf of dark despair
   We wretched sinners lay,
 Without one cheerful beam of hope,
   Or spark of glimm'ring day.

2 With pitying eyes, the Prince of Grace
   Beheld our helpless grief;
 He saw, and oh! amazing love!
   He ran to our relief.

3 Down from the shining seats above
   With joyful haste He fled;
 Entered the grave in mortal flesh,
   And dwelt among the dead.

4 Oh! for this love, let rocks and hills
   Their lasting silence break,
 And all harmonious human tongues
   The Saviour's praises speak!

5 Angels, assist our mighty joys;
   Strike all your harps of gold!
 But, when you raise your highest notes,
   His love can ne'er be told.

Isaac Watts, 1709.

"Looking unto Jesus, the Author and Finisher of our faith, who for the joy that was set before Him, endured the cross."

405   8s, 7s, & 4s.

HOLY Saviour, we adore Thee!
   Seated on the throne of God;
 All heaven's hosts bow down before Thee,
   And we sing Thy praise aloud.
     Thou art worthy!
   We were ransomed by Thy blood.

2 Saviour, though the world despised Thee,
   Though Thou here wast crucified,
 Yet the Father's glory raised Thee,
   Lord of all creation wide;
     Thou art worthy!
   We shall live, for Thou hast died.

3 And though here on earth rejected,
   'Tis but fellowship with Thee;
What besides could be expected,
   Than like Thee, our Lord, to be?
     Thou art worthy!
   Thou from earth hast set us free.

4 Haste the day of Thy returning,
   With Thy ransomed Church to reign;
Then shall end our days of mourning;
   We shall sing with rapture then,
     "Thou art worthy!"
   Come, Lord Jesus, come. Amen.
Samuel P. Tregelles.

"Knowing that if our earthly house of this tabernacle be dissolved we have a building of God."

406   8s, 6s, 8s, 6s, 6s, 6s, 6s, 6s.

O PARADISE, O Paradise,
   Who doth not crave for rest?
Who would not seek the happy land,
   Where they that loved are blest?
     Where loyal hearts and true
      Stand ever in the light,
     All rapture through and through,
      In God's most holy sight.

2 O Paradise, O Paradise,
   The world is growing old;
Who would not be at rest and free
   Where love is never cold?
     Where loyal hearts and true, &c.

3 O Paradise, O Paradise,
   'Tis weary waiting here;
I long to be where Jesus is,
   To feel, to see Him near;
     Where loyal hearts and true, &c.

4 O Paradise, O Paradise,
   I want to sin no more;
I want to be as pure on earth,
   As on thy spotless shore;
     Where loyal hearts and true, &c.

5 O Paradise, O Paradise,
   I greatly long to see
The special place my dearest Lord
   Is destining for me;
     Where loyal hearts and true, &c.

 6 O Paradise, O Paradise,
  I feel 'twill not be long;
 Patience! I almost think I hear
  Faint fragments of thy song;
  Where loyal hearts and true
   Stand ever in the light,
 All rapture through and through,
  In God's most holy sight.
Frederick W. Faber, 1849.

"Strengthened with all might, according to His glorious power, unto all patience and long-suffering with joyfulness."

407
S. M.

YOUR harps, ye trembling saints,
 Down from the willows take;
Loud to the praise of Love divine,
 Bid every string awake.

2 Though in a foreign land,
 We are not far from home;
And nearer to our house above,
 We every moment come.

3 His grace will to the end
 Stronger and brighter shine;
Nor present things, nor things to come,
 Shall quench the spark divine.

4 Soon shall our doubts and fears
 Subside at His control;
His loving-kindness shall break through
 The midnight of the soul.

5 Wait, till the shadows flee;
 Wait thine appointed hour;
Wait, till the Bridegroom of thy soul
 Reveal His love with power.

6 The time of love will come,
 When thou shalt clearly see,
Not only that He shed His blood,
 But that it flowed for thee!
Augustus M. Toplady, 1772.

" Give place, for the maid is not dead, but sleepeth."

408
10*s*.

WE need Thee, Saviour! when dear eyes are closing,
 When on the cheek the shadow lieth strong,
When the soft lines are set in that reposing
 That never mother cradled with a song.

2 Then *most* we need the gentle Human Feeling
   That throbs with all our sorrows and our fears,
And that great Love Divine its light revealing
   In short bright flashes through a mist of tears.

3 Then most we need the Voice that while it weepeth
   Yet hath a solemn undertone that saith—
"Weep not, thy darling is not dead, but sleepeth;
   Only believe, for I have conquered death."

4 Then most we need the thoughts of Resurrection,
   Not the life here, 'mid pain, and sin, and woe,
But ever in the fulness of perfection,
   To walk with Him in robes as white as snow.

5 Didst Thou not enter in when that cold sleeper
   Lay still, with pulseless heart and leaden eyes,
Put calmly forth each loud tumultuous weeper,
   And take her by the hand and bid her rise?

6 Come to us, Saviour! in our lone dejection,
   Speak calmly to our wild and helpless grief,
Bring us the hopes and thoughts of Resurrection,
   Bring us the comfort of a true Belief.

7 Come! with that Human Voice that breaks in weeping,
   Come! with that awful Tenderness Divine,
Come! tell us that they are not dead but sleeping,
   But gone before to Thee, for they are Thine.
                        Cecil Frances Alexander.

THIRD SUNDAY BEFORE ADVENT.

"So shall also the coming of the Son of Man be."
409   L. M.

THE Lord will come— the earth shall quake,
   The hills their fixèd seat forsake;
And, withering from the vault of night,
The stars withdraw their feeble light.

2 The Lord will come,—but not the same
   As once in lowly form He came,
A silent Lamb to slaughter led,
The bruised, the suff'ring and the dead.

3 The Lord will come,—a dreadful form,
   With wreath of flame, and robe of storm,
On cherub-wings and wings of wind,
Appointed Judge of humankind.

4 Can this be He, who wont to stray
  A pilgrim on the world's highway,—
  By power oppressed, and mocked by pride?
  O God! is this the Crucified?

5 Go, tyrants! to the rocks complain,
  Go, seek the mountain's cleft in vain;
  But faith, victorious o'er the tomb,
  Shall sing for joy,—" The Lord is come!"
                        Reginald Heber, 1811.

"Even so them also which sleep in Jesus will God bring with Him."

410   L. M.

WE sing His love, who once was slain,
    Who soon o'er death revived again,
That all His saints through Him might have
Eternal conquests o'er the grave

2 The saints who now with Jesus sleep,
  His own almighty power shall keep,
  Till dawns the bright illustrious day,
  When death itself shall die away.

3 How loud shall our glad voices sing,
  When Christ His risen saints shall bring
  From beds of dust, and silent clay,
  To realms of everlasting day!

4 When Jesus we in glory meet,
  Our utmost joys shall be complete;
  When landed on that heavenly shore,
  Death and the curse will be no more.

5 Hasten, dear Lord! the glorious day,
  And this delightful scene display,
  When all Thy saints from death shall rise
  Raptured in bliss beyond the skies.
                        Rowland Hill, 1796.

"Who hast promised to bring up again from the dead the bodies of them which sleep in Jesus."

411   L. M.

ASLEEP in Jesus! blessed sleep,
  From which none ever wakes to weep,
A calm and undisturbed repose,
Unbroken by the last of foes!

2 Asleep in Jesus! Oh! how sweet
　To be for such a slumber meet,
　With holy confidence to sing—
　That death hath lost his venomed sting!

3 Asleep in Jesus! peaceful rest,
　Whose waking is supremely blest;
　No fear, no woe, shall dim that hour
　That manifests the Saviour's power.

4 Asleep in Jesus! Oh! for me
　May such a blissful refuge be!
　Securely shall my ashes lie,
　Waiting the summons from on high.

5 Asleep in Jesus! far from thee
　Thy kindred and their graves may be;
　But thine is still a blessed sleep,
　From which none ever wakes to weep.
　　　　　　　　Margaret Mackay, 1832.

"Make us to be numbered with Thy saints in glory everlasting."

412　　　　　　10s, 5 *lines.*

OUR year of grace is wearing to its close,
　　Its autumn-storms are low'ring from the sky:
Shine on us with Thy light, O God most high:
Abide with us where'er our pathway goes,—
Our Guide in toil, our Guardian in repose.

2 All through the months hath beamed Thy cheering light,
　　From Bethl'hem's Day-star waxing ever on:
　　Through every cloud Thy blessed Sun hath shone:
Earth may be dark to them that walk by sight,
But for Thy Church the day is always bright.

3 Light us in life, that we may see Thy will,
　　The track Thine hand hath ordered for our way:
　　Light us, when shadows gather o'er our day:
Shine on us in that passage lone and chill,
And then our darkness with Thy glory fill.

4 Praise be to God from earth's remotest coast,
　　From lands and seas, and each created race:
　　Praise from the worlds His hand hath launched in space:
Praise from the Church, and from the heavenly host:
Praise to the Father, Son, and Holy Ghost.
　　　　　　　　Henry Alford, 1867.

"And so shall we ever be with the Lord."

413   C. M.

JERUSALEM! my happy home!
   Name ever dear to me!
When shall my labors have an end,
   In joy, and peace, and thee?

2 When shall these eyes thy heaven-built walls
   And pearly gates behold?
Thy bulwarks, with salvation strong,
   And streets of shining gold?

3 O when, thou city of my God,
   Shall I thy courts ascend,
Where congregations ne'er break up,
   And Sabbaths have no end?

4 There happier bowers than Eden's bloom,
   Nor sin, nor sorrow know;
Blest seats! through rude and stormy scenes,
   I onward press to you.

5 Why should I shrink at pain and woe,
   Or feel at death dismay?
I've Canaan's goodly land in view,
   And realms of endless day.

6 Apostles, martyrs, prophets there,
   Around my Saviour stand;
And soon my friends in Christ below
   Will join the glorious band.

7 Jerusalem! my happy home!
   My soul still pants for thee;
Then shall my labors have an end,
   When I thy joys shall see.

Francis Baker, 1616.
Altered by Dickson & others.

SECOND SUNDAY BEFORE ADVENT.

"When the Lord Jesus shall be revealed from heaven with His mighty angels, in flaming fire taking vengeance on them that know not God."

414   8s, 3 *lines.*

DAY of vengeance without morrow!
   Earth shall end in flame and sorrow,
As from saint and seer we borrow.

2 Ah! what terror is impending,
  When the Judge is seen descending,
  And each secret vail is rending.

3 To the throne, the trumpet sounding,
  Through the sepulchres resounding,
  Summons all, with voice astounding.

4 Death and nature, mazed, are quaking,
  When, the grave's long slumber breaking,
  Man to judgment is awaking.

5 On the written Volume's pages,
  Life is shown in all its stages—
  Judgment-record of past ages!

6 Sits the Judge, the raised arraigning,
  Darkest mysteries explaining,
  Nothing unavenged remaining.

7 What shall I then say, unfriended,
  By no advocate attended,
  When the just are scarce defended?

8 King of majesty tremendous,
  By Thy saving grace defend us;
  Fount of pity! safety send us.

9 Holy Jesus, meek, forbearing,
  For my sins the death-cross wearing,
  Save me, in that day, despairing.

10 Worn and weary Thou hast sought me;
   By Thy cross and passion bought me;
   Spare the hope Thy labors brought me.

11 Righteous Judge of retribution,
   Give, O give me absolution
   Ere the day of dissolution.

12 As a guilty culprit groaning,
   Flushed my face, my errors owning,
   Hear, O God, my spirit's moaning.

13 Thou to Mary gav'st remission,
   Heardst the dying thief's petition,
   Bad'st me hope in my contrition.

14 In my prayers no grace discerning,
   Yet on me Thy favor turning,
   Save my soul from endless burning.

15 Give me, when Thy sheep confiding
Thou art from the goats dividing,
On Thy right a place abiding.

16 When the wicked are confounded,
And by bitter flames surrounded,
Be my joyful pardon sounded!

17 Prostrate, all my guilt discerning,
Heart as though to ashes turning,
Save, O save me from the burning.

18 Day of weeping, when from ashes
Man shall rise 'mid lightning flashes,
Guilty, trembling with contrition,
Save him, Father, from perdition!

Thomas of Celano, 1230.
Trans: John A. Dix.

"*When the Son of Man shall come in His glory.*"

415 S. M.

THE Son of Man shall come
With angel hosts around,
'Mid darkening sun and falling stars,
And trumpet's solemn sound.

2 Awake, ye slumbering souls,
It is no time for rest;
He comes, as comes the lightning flash
Shining from east to west.

3 Thy servants, Lord, prepare
For that tremendous day;
Fill every heart with watchful care,
And stir us up to pray.

4 Help us to wait the hour
In toil and holy fear,
When, manifested with Thy saints,
Thou shalt again appear.

5 Then, when the wailing earth
Thy sign in heaven shall see,
Thou shalt send forth Thine angel band
To gather us to Thee. *H. W. Beadon.*

"*Come ye blessed of my Father, inherit the kingdom.*"

416 8s & 7s.

LO, the day of Christ's appearing,
Day of life, and day of light,
Day when death itself shall perish,
Day which ne'er shall set in night.

2 Steadily that day is coming,
　　When the just shall find their rest,
　When the wicked cease from troubling,
　　And the patient reign most blest.

3 Oh, how past all utterance happy,
　　Sweet, and joyful, will it be!
　When they who, unseen, have loved Him,
　　Jesus face to face shall see.

4 Blessèd, then, earth's patient mourners,
　　Who for Him have toiled and died;
　Called to share with Him His glory,
　　With Him ever to abide.

5 What will be the bliss and rapture
　　None can dream and none can tell,
　There to reign among the angels,
　　In that heavenly home to dwell.

6 To those realms, just Judge, Oh, call us;
　　Deign to open that blest gate;
　Thou, whom seeking, looking, longing,
　　We with eager joy await.　　　*Elizabeth Charles.*

"*When He shall come to be glorified in His saints.*"

417　　　　　7s.

CHRIST will come and not delay,
　And His glory will display,
To reward the suffering just,
Who in Him have placed their trust.

2 O how happy! O how sweet!
When those souls shall Jesus meet,
Whom in life they truly loved,
And His faithful servants proved.

3 Happy those who mourned and wept,
And their souls in patience kept;
Those to whom the world gave pain
Now in endless bliss shall reign.

4 There shall dwell no grief, nor fear;
None shall ever shed a tear;
Nor shall want, nor age, nor care,
Nor defeat be ever there.

5 None the rapture can conceive,
Nor the perfect joy believe
In heaven's glory to remain,
And with angels ever reign.

6 To that realm Thy children call,
O Thou righteous Judge of all;
Thee we seek, on Thee rely,
Thee implore with frequent cry.

Trans. F. C. Husenbeth.

"Gather not our souls with sinners, but make us to be numbered with Thy saints."

418　　　　　　　*7s, 3 lines.*

LORD, in this Thy mercy's day,
　Ere from us it pass away,
On our knees we fall and pray.

2 Holy Jesus, grant us tears,
　Fill us with heart-searching fears,
Ere that day of doom appears.

3 Lord, on us Thy Spirit pour,
　Kneeling lowly at the door,
Ere it close for evermore.

4 By Thy night of agony,
　By Thy supplicating cry,
By Thy willingness to die,

5 By Thy tears of bitter woe
　For Jerusalem below,
Let us not Thy love forego.

6 Judge and Saviour of our race,
　Grant us, when we see Thy face,
With Thy ransomed ones a place.

Isaac Williams.

SUNDAY BEFORE ADVENT.

"Behold the Bridegroom cometh; go ye out to meet Him."

419　　　　　*7s & 6s, 8 lines.*

REJOICE, all ye believers!
　And let your lights appear;
The evening is advancing,
　And darker night is near;
The Bridegroom is arising,
　And soon He draweth nigh;
Up! pray, and watch, and wrestle;
　At midnight comes the cry.

2 The watchers on the mountain
    Proclaim the Bridegroom near;
Go meet Him as He cometh,
    With hallelujahs clear;
The marriage-feast is waiting,
    The gates wide open stand;
Up! up! ye heirs of glory!
    The Bridegroom is at hand.

3 Ye saints! who here in patience
    Your cross and sufferings bore,
Shall live and reign forever,
    Where sorrow is no more;
Around the throne of glory,
    The Lamb ye shall behold,
In triumph cast before Him
    Your diadems of gold.

4 Our Hope and Expectation,
    O Jesus! now appear;
Arise, Thou Sun so longed for,
    O'er this benighted sphere:
With hearts and hands uplifted,
    We plead, O Lord! to see
The day of earth's redemption,
    That brings us unto Thee.

Laurentius Laurenti, 1700.
Trans. Jane Borthwick, 1853.

"And He that sat upon the throne said, Behold, I make all things new."

420   7s, 8 *lines.*

HARK!—the song of jubilee,
    Loud as mighty thunders roar,
Or the fulness of the sea,
    When it breaks upon the shore;
"Hallelujah! for the Lord
    God omnipotent shall reign!"
Hallelujah! let the word
    Echo round the earth and main.

2 Hallelujah!—hark!—the sound,
    From the depths unto the skies,
Wakes, above, beneath, around,
    All creation's harmonies:
See Jehovah's banners furled!
    Sheathed His sword! He speaks—tis done,
And the kingdoms of this world
    Are the kingdoms of His Son.

3 He shall reign from pole to pole
    With illimitable sway;
He shall reign, when, like a scroll,
    Yonder heavens have passed away;
Then the end ;—beneath His rod,
    Man's last enemy shall fall ;
Hallelujah !—Christ is God,
    God in Christ, is all in all.   *James Montgomery*, 1819.

"Nevertheless we, according to His promise, look for new heavens and a new earth."

421
7s & 6s.

JERUSALEM the golden !
    With milk and honey blest ;
Beneath Thy contemplation
    Sink heart and voice opprest.

2 I know not, Oh ! I know not
    What joys await us there,
What radiancy of glory,
    What bliss beyond compare.

3 They stand, those halls of Zion,
    All jubilant with song,
And bright with many an angel,
    And all the martyr-throng :

4 The Prince is ever in them,
    The daylight is serene ;
The pastures of the blessed
    Are decked in glorious sheen.

5 There is the throne of David ;
    And there, from care released,
The shout of them that triumph,
    The song of them that feast ;

6 And they, who with their Leader
    Have conquered in the fight,
For ever and for ever
    Are clad in robes of white.

Bernard of Morlaix, 1150.
Trans. Jno. M. Neale, 1851, *altered.*

"Seeing then that all these things shall be dissolved, what manner of persons ought ye to be in all holy conversation aud godliness."

422
7s & 6s, 8 lines.

THE world is very evil,
    The times are waxing late,
Be sober and keep vigil,
    The Judge is at the gate ;

The Judge who comes in mercy,
  The Judge who comes with might,
Who comes to end the evil,
  Who comes to crown the right.

2 Arise, arise, good Christian,
    Let right to wrong succeed;
  Let penitential sorrow
    To heavenly gladness lead;
  To light that has no evening,
    That knows no moon nor sun,
  The light so new and golden,
    The light that is but one.

3 O home of fadeless splendor,
    Of flowers that fear no thorn,
  Where they shall dwell as children
    Who here as exiles mourn;
  'Midst power that knows no limit,
    Where wisdom has no bound,
  The Beatific Vision
    Shall glad the saints around.

4 O happy, holy portion,
    Refection for the blest,
  True vision of true beauty,
    True cure of the distrest:
  Strive, man, to win that glory;
    Toil, man, to gain that light,
  Send hope before to grasp it,
    Till hope be lost in sight.

5 O sweet and blessèd country,
    The home of God's elect!
  O sweet and blessèd country,
    That eager hearts expect!
  Jesus, in mercy bring us
    To that dear land of rest;
  Who art, with God the Father,
    And Spirit, ever blest.

Bernard of Morlaix, 1150.
Trans. Jno. M. Neale, 1851, *altered*.

"*Watch, therefore, for ye know neither the day nor the hour when the Son of Man cometh.*"

423 S. M. 8 *lines.*

THOU Judge of quick and dead,
  Before whose bar severe,

With holy joy, or guilty dread,
  We all shall soon appear;
Oh! teach us to prepare
  For that tremendous day:
And fill us now with watchful care,
  And stir us up to pray.

2 To pray, and wait the hour,
    That awful hour unknown;
  When, robed in majesty and power,
    Thou shalt from heaven come down,
  Th' immortal Son of Man,
    To judge the human race,
  With all Thy Father's dazzling train,
    With all Thy glorious grace.

3 To temper earthly joys,
    To waken duteous fears,
  For ever let the Archangel's voice
    Be sounding in our ears
  The solemn midnight cry,
    "Arise! The Judge is come;
  Ye saints, go meet Him in the sky,
    Ye sinners, wait your doom."

4 Oh! may we thus be found,
    Obedient to His word,
  Still listening for the trumpet's sound,
    And looking for our Lord:
  Oh! may we thus insure
    Our lot among the blest,
  And watch a moment, to secure
    An everlasting rest.
                    Charles Wesley, 1740, altered.

THE HOLY COMMUNION.

"*For My flesh is meat indeed, and My blood is drink indeed.*"

424 7s, 6 lines.

BREAD of heaven! on Thee we feed,
  For Thy flesh is meat indeed;
Ever may our souls be fed
With this true and living Bread:
Day by day with strength supplied
Through the life of Him that died.

2 Vine of heaven! Thy blood supplies
This blest cup of sacrifice:
Lord, Thy wounds our healing give;
To Thy cross we look and live:
Jesus, may we ever be
Grafted, rooted, built in Thee.
Josiah Conder, 1836.

"This is My body which is given for you."
425   *8s & 7s, 8 lines.*

IN the name of God the Father,
    In the name of God the Son,
In the name of God the Spirit,
    One in Three, and Three in One;
In the name which highest angels
    Speak not ere they veil their face,
Crying—Holy! Holy! Holy!
    Come we to this sacred place.

2 Here in figure represented,
    See the Passion once again,
Here behold the Lamb most Holy
    As for our redemption slain;
Here the Saviour's body broken,
    Here the blood which Jesus shed,
Mystic food of life eternal,
    See for our refreshment spread.

3 Here shall highest praise be offered,
    Here shall meekest prayers be poured,
Here with body, soul, and spirit
    God incarnate be adored.
Holy Jesus! for Thy coming
    May Thy love our hearts prepare:
Thine we fain would have them wholly,
    Enter, Lord, and tarry there.
J. W. Hewett, 1867.

"He that eateth My flesh, and drinketh My blood, dwelleth in Me and I in him."
426   *8s, 6s, 8s, 6s, 8s, 8s.*

LORD, when before Thy throne we meet,
    Thy goodness to adore,
From heaven, th' eternal mercy-seat,
    On us Thy blessing pour,
And make our inmost souls to be
A habitation meet for Thee!

2 The Body for our ransom givèn;
   The blood in mercy shed;
With this immortal food from heavèn,
   Lord! let our souls be fed!
And, as we round Thy table kneel,
Help us Thy quickening grace to feel!

3 Be Thou, O Holy Spirit, nigh!
   Accept the humble prayer,
The contrite soul's repentant sigh,
   The sinner's heartfelt tear!
And let our adoration rise,
A fragrant incense, to the skies.

427
"Come, for all things are now ready."
C. M.

O GOD, unseen, yet ever near,
   Thy presence may we feel;
And thus inspired with holy fear,
   Before Thine altar kneel.

2 Here may Thy faithful people know
   The blessings of Thy love;
The streams that through the desert flow;
   The manna from above.

3 We come, obedient to Thy word,
   To feast on heavenly food;
Our meat, the Body of the Lord;
   Our drink, His precious Blood.

4 Thus would we all Thy words obey;
   For we, O God, are Thine;
And go rejoicing on our way,
   Renewed with strength divine.

Edward Osler, 1836.

428
"This is My blood of the New Testament which is shed for many."
L. M.

TO Jesus, our exalted Lord,
   Dear name, by heaven and earth adored!
Fain would our hearts and voices raise
A cheerful song of sacred praise.

2 But all the notes which mortals know
Are weak, and languishing, and low;
Far, far above our mortal songs,
The theme demands immortal tongues.

3 Yet, while around His board we meet,
  And worship at His glorious feet,
  Oh! let our warm affections move,
  In glad returns of grateful love.

4 Let faith our feeble senses aid,
  To see Thy wondrous love displayed,
  Thy broken flesh, Thy bleeding veins,
  Thy dreadful agonizing pains.

5 Let humble, penitential woe,
  With painful, pleasing anguish, flow;
  And Thy forgiving smiles impart
  Life, hope, and joy to every heart.
                                Anne Steele, 1760.

"In this was manifested the love of God toward us, because that God sent His only begotten Son into the world, that we might live through Him."

429 C. M.

HERE at Thy table, Lord! we meet,
    To feed on food divine;
  Thy body is the bread we eat,
    Thy precious blood the wine.

2 He that prepares this rich repast,
    Himself comes down, and dies;
  And then invites us thus to feast
    Upon the sacrifice.

3 Sure, there was never love so free,
    Dear Saviour! so divine;
  Well Thou may'st claim that heart of me,
    Which owes so much to Thine.

4 Yes, Thou shalt surely have my heart,
    My soul, my strength, my all;
  With life itself I'll freely part,
    My Jesus! at Thy call.
                          Samuel Stennett, 1787.

"Whoso eateth My flesh and drinketh My blood hath eternal life."

430 L. M.

BODY of Jesus, oh, sweet food!
  Blood of my Saviour, precious blood!
  On these Thy gifts, Eternal Priest!
  Grant Thou my soul in faith to feast.

2 Weary and faint I thirst and pine
  For Thee, my Bread, for Thee, my Wine,
  Till strengthened, as Elijah trod,
  I journey to the mount of God.

3 There, clad in white, with crown and palm,
  At the great Supper of the Lamb,
  Be mine, with all Thy saints to rest,
  Like him that leaned upon Thy breast.

4 Saviour! till then, I fain would know
  That feast above by this below;
  This bread of life, this wondrous food,
  Thy body and Thy precious blood.

Arthur C. Coxe.

"The bread which we break, is it not the communion of the body of Christ?"

431   S. M.

JESUS invites His saints
  To meet around His board;
Here pardon'd rebels sit, and hold
  Communion with their Lord.

2 For food He gives His flesh;
  He bids us drink His blood:
  Amazing favor, matchless grace,
  Of our descending God!

3 This holy bread and wine
  Maintain our fainting breath,
  By union with our living Lord,
  And int'rest in His death.

4 Our heavenly Father calls
  Christ and His members one;
  We, the young children of His love,
  And He, the first-born Son.

5 We are but several parts
  Of the same broken Bread,
  One body with its several limbs,
  But Jesus is the Head.

6 Let all our powers be joined,
  His glorious name to raise;
  Pleasure and love fill every mind,
  And every voice be praise.

Isaac Watts, 1707.

HOLY BAPTISM.

"According to His mercy He saved us by the washing of regeneration and renewing of the Holy Ghost."

432 7s.

PARDONED through redeeming grace,
  In Thy blessed Son revealed,
Worshiping before Thy face,
  Lord, to Thee ourselves we yield.

2 Thou the sacrifice receive,
    Humbly offered through Thy Son;
  Quicken us in Him to live;
    Lord, in us Thy will be done.

3 By the hallowed outward sign,
    By the cleansing grace within,
  Seal, and make us wholly Thine:
    Wash, and keep us pure from sin.

4 Called to bear the Christian name,
    May our vows and life accord,
  And our every deed proclaim
    "Holiness unto the Lord!"

Edward Osler, 1836.

"He shall gather the lambs in His arms and carry them in His bosom."

433 6s & 4s.

SHEPHERD of tender youth!
  Guiding in love and truth,
    Through devious ways;
Christ, our triumphant King!
We come Thy name to sing,
And here our children bring,
    To shout Thy praise.

2 Thou art our holy Lord!
  The all-subduing Word,
    Healer of strife!
  Thou didst Thyself abase,
  That from sin's deep disgrace
  Thou mightest save our race,
    And give us life!

3 Thou art the great High Priest!
  Thou hast prepared the feast
    Of heavenly love;

While in our mortal pain,
None calls on Thee in vain,
Help Thou dost not disdain,—
  Help from above.

4 Ever be Thou our Guide,
Our Shepherd and our Pride,
  Our Staff and Song!
Jesus! Thou Christ of God!
By Thy perennial Word
Lead us where Thou hast trod,
  Make our faith strong.

5 So now, and till we die,
Sound we Thy praises high,
  And joyful sing!
Let all the holy throng,
Who to Thy Church belong,
Unite and swell the song
  To Christ our King! *Clement of Alexandria*, 200.
  Trans. H. M. Dexter.

"Except a man be born of water and of the Spirit, he cannot enter into the kingdom of God."

434 *German Choral.*

BLESSED Jesus, here we stand,
  Met to do as Thou hast spoken;
And this child, at Thy command,
  Now we bring to Thee, in token
That to Thee it here is given;
For of such shall be Thy heaven.

2 Yes, Thy warning voice is plain,
  And we fain would keep it duly.
"He who is not born again,
  Heart and life renewing truly,
Born of water and the Spirit,
Will My kingdom ne'er inherit."

3 Therefore hasten we to Thee;
  Take the pledge we bring, O take it!
Let us here Thy glory see,
  And in tender pity make it
Now Thy child, and leave it never,—
Thine on earth and Thine for ever.

4 Make it, Lord, Thy member now;
  Shepherd, take Thy lamb, and feed it;
Prince of Peace, its peace be Thou;
  Way of life, to heaven lead it;

Vine, this branch may nothing sever,
  Be it graft in Thee for ever.

5 Now upon Thy heart it lies!
  What our hearts so dearly treasure;
Heavenward lead our burdened sighs,
  Pour Thy blessing without measure;
Write the name we now have given,—
  Write it in the book of heaven.
                    Benjamin Schmolk, 1704.
                 Trans. *Catherine Winkworth*, 1858.

CONFIRMATION.

*"Strengthen them through the Holy Ghost, the Comforter,
and daily increase in them the manifold gifts
of Thy grace."*

435 L. M.

COME, ever-blessed Spirit, come,
  And make Thy servants' hearts Thy home:
Thus consecrated, Lord, to Thee
May each a living temple be!

2 Enrich that temple's holy shrine
With sevenfold gifts of grace divine:
With wisdom, light, and knowledge bless,
Strength, counsel, fear, and godliness!

3 O Trinity in Unity,
One only God in Persons Three,
In whom, through whom, by whom we live,
In Thee we praise and glory give!

4 O grant us so to use Thy grace,
That we may see Thy glorious face,
And ever, with the heavenly host,
Praise Father, Son, and Holy Ghost.
                    Christopher Wordsworth.

MARRIAGE.

*"O Lord, bless them both, and grant them to inherit Thine
everlasting kingdom."*

436 S. M.

HOW welcome was the call,
  And sweet the festal lay,
When Jesus deigned in Cana's hall
  To bless the marriage day.

2 And happy was the Bride,
　　And glad the Bridegroom's heart,
　For He who tarried at their side
　　Bade grief and ill depart.

3 O Lord of life and love,
　　Come Thou again to-day;
　And bring a blessing from above
　　That ne'er shall pass away.

4 O bless, as erst of old,
　　The Bridegroom and the Bride;
　Bless with the holier stream that flowed
　　Forth from Thy pierced side.

5 Before Thine altar-throne
　　This mercy we implore;
　As Thou dost knit them, Lord, in one,
　　So bless them evermore.
　　　　　　　　Henry W. Baker, 1861.

"God the Father, God the Son, God the Holy Ghost,
bless, preserve, and keep you."

437
7s & 6s.

THE voice that breathed o'er Eden,
　　That earliest wedding day,
　The primal marriage blessing,
　　It hath not passed away:

2 Still in the pure espousal
　　Of Christian man and maid
　The holy Three are with us,
　　The threefold grace is said.

3 Be present, awful Father,
　　To give away this Bride,
　As Eve Thou gav'st to Adam
　　Out of his own pierced side!

4 Be present, Son Eternal,
　　To join their loving hands,
　As Thou didst bind two natures
　　In Thine eternal bands;

5 Be present, Holy Spirit,
　　To bless them as they kneel,
　As Thou for Christ, the Bridegroom,
　　His Spouse the Church, doth seal.

6 O spread Thy pure wing o'er them,
  Let no ill power find place,
When onward to Thine altar
  The hallowed path they trace.

7 To cast their crowns before Thee,
  In perfect sacrifice,
Till to the home of gladness
  With Christ's own Bride they rise.

John Keble, 1857.

ORDINATION AND INSTALLATION OF MINISTERS.

"Let Thy priests be clothed with righteousness."

438 L. M.

LORD, pour Thy Spirit from on high,
  And Thine ordainèd servants bless;
Graces and gifts to each supply,
  And clothe Thy priests with righteousness.

2 Within Thy temple when they stand,
    To teach the truth as taught by Thee,
  Saviour, like stars in Thy right hand,
    Let all Thy Church's pastors be.

3 Wisdom, and zeal, and love impart,
    Firmness and meekness from above,
  To bear Thy people in their heart
    And love the souls whom Thou dost love.

4 To love, and pray, and never faint,
    By day and night their guard to keep,
  To warn the sinner, form the saint,
    To feed Thy lambs, and tend Thy sheep.

5 So, when their work is finished here,
    They may in hope their charge resign;
  So, when their Master shall appear,
    They may with crowns of glory shine.

James Montgomery.

"Let your loins be girded about, and your lights burning."

439 S. M.

YE servants of the Lord!
  Each in his office wait,
Observant of His heavenly word,
  And watchful at His gate.

2 Let all your lamps be bright,
    And trim the golden flame;
Gird up your loins as in His sight,
    For awful is His name.

3 Watch! 'tis your Lord's command;
    And, while we speak, He's near:
Mark the first signal of His hand,
    And ready all appear.

4 O happy servant he,
    In such a posture found!
He shall his Lord with rapture see,
    And be with honor crowned.

Philip Doddridge, 1740.

"A watchful guardian over Thy fold and a follower of the true Shepherd who giveth His life for the sheep."

440   C. M.

LORD, Thine appointed servants bless,
    That they may faithful be,
To preach the truth in righteousness,
    And sinners win to Thee.

2 Uphold them by Almighty power,
    Thy strength divine impart,
And, in each dark and trying hour,
    Cheer Thou their fainting heart.

3 In holy watchfulness and prayer,
    O keep them near Thy side;
May they with loving zeal declare
    A Saviour crucified.

4 Great Shepherd of the sheep, draw near,
    Thy Spirit now be given;
That they who preach, and those who hear,
    May sing Thy praise in heaven.

"Send down the Holy Ghost upon Thy servant."

441   6s & 4s.

O HOLY Lord, our God,
    By heavenly hosts adored,
    Hear us, we pray:
To Thee the cherubim,
Angels and Seraphim,
Unceasing praises bring—
    Their homage pay.

2 Here give Thy word success;
And this Thy servant bless;
His labors own;
And while the sinners' Friend
His life and words commend,
Thy Holy Spirit send,
And make Him known.

3 May every passing year
More happy still appear
Than this glad day;
With numbers fill the place,
Adorn Thy saints with grace;
Thy truth may all embrace,
O Lord, we pray.

ORDINATION AND INSTALLATION OF ELDERS AND DEACONS.

"Let every fruit of the Spirit appear and abound in them."

442 C. M.

FATHER of mercies! condescend
To hear our fervent prayer,
While these our brethren we commend
To Thy paternal care.

2 Before them set an open door;
Their various efforts bless;
On them Thy Holy Spirit pour,
And crown them with success.

3 Endow them with a heavenly mind;
Supply their every need;
Make them in spirit meek, resigned,
But bold in word and deed.

4 In every tempting, trying hour,
Uphold them by Thy grace,
And guard them by Thy mighty power,
Till they shall end their race.

Thomas Morell, 1818, *altered.*

THE BURIAL OF THE DEAD.

"Whosoever liveth and believeth in Me shall never die."

443 S. M.

IT is not death to die,—
To leave this weary road,

And, midst the brotherhood on high,
  To be at home with God.

2 It is not death to close
  The eye long dimmed by tears,
And wake, in glorious repose
  To spend eternal years.

3 It is not death to fling
  Aside this sinful dust,
And rise, on strong exulting wing,
  To live among the just.

4 Jesus, Thou Prince of life!
  Thy chosen cannot die;
Like Thee, they conquer in the strife,
  To reign with Thee on high.

George W. Bethune, 1847.

"Behold I show you a mystery: we shall not all sleep, but we shall all be changed."

444 C. M.

AS Jesus died, and rose again
  Victorious from the dead,
So His disciples rise, and reign
  With their triumphant Head.

2 The time draws nigh, when, from the clouds,
  Christ shall with shouts descend;
And the last trumpet's awful voice
  The heavens and earth shall rend.

3 Then they who live shall changèd be,
  And they who sleep shall wake;
The graves shall yield their ancient charge,
  And earth's foundations shake.

4 The saints of God, from death set free,
  With joy shall mount on high;
The heavenly host, with praises loud,
  Shall meet them in the sky.

5 Together to their Father's house,
  With joyful hearts, they go;
And dwell forever with the Lord,
  Beyond the reach of woe.

Michael Bruce, 1768.

"Earth to earth, ashes to ashes, dust to dust."

445　　　　　11s.

THE things of the earth, in the earth let us lay,
　　The ashes with ashes, the dust with the clay:
But lift up the heart, and the eye, and the love,
O lift up the soul to the regions above!

2 Since He, the Immortal, hath entered the gate,
So too shall we mortals, or sooner or late:
Then stand we on Christ; let us mark Him ascend,
For His is the glory and life without end.

3 On earth with His own ones, the Giver of good,
Bestowing His blessing, a little while stood:
Now nothing can part us, nor distance, nor foes,
For lo! He is with us, and who can oppose?

4 So, Lord, we commit this our *brother* to Thee,
Whose body is dead, but whose spirit is free:
We know that thro' grace, when our life here is done,
We live still in Thee, and forever in one.

5 All glory to Thee, Father, Spirit, and Son,
Who Three art in Person, in substance but One,
In whom we have victory over the grave,
Who lovest Thy people to pardon and save.
　　　　　　　　　　From the Greek.
　　　　　　Trans. Jno. M. Neale, 1864, *altered.*

SERVICE AT SEA.

" So He bringeth them unto their desired haven."

446　　　　　L. M.

ALMIGHTY Father, hear our cry,
　　As o'er the trackless deep we roam;
Be Thou our haven always nigh,
　　On homeless waters Thou our home!

2 O Jesus, Saviour, at whose voice
　　The tempest sank to perfect rest,
Bid Thou the mourner's heart rejoice,
　　And cleanse and calm the troubled breast.

3 O Holy Ghost, beneath whose power
　　The ocean woke to life and light,
Command Thy blessing in this hour,
　　Thy fostering warmth, Thy quickening might.

4 Thee, God, the Holy Trinity,
   We love, we worship, we adore;
  Our refuge on time's changeful sea,
   Our joy on heaven's eternal shore.
E. H. Bickersteth.

"He maketh the storm a calm, so that the waves thereof are still."

447   C. M.

O LORD, be with us when we sail
   Upon the lonely deep,
Our guard when on the silent deck
   The midnight watch we keep.

2 We need not fear, though all around
   'Mid rising winds we hear
The multitude of waters surge:
   For Thou, O God, art near.

3 The calm, the breeze, the gale, the storm,
   That pass from land to land,
All, all are Thine, are held within
   The hollow of Thine hand.

4 If duty calls from threatened strife
   To guard our native shore,
And shot and shell are answering
   The booming cannon's roar;

5 Be Thou the mainguard of our host,
   Till war and dangers cease,
Defend the right, put up the sword,
   And through the world make peace.

6 To Thee the Father, Thee the Son,
   Whom earth and sky adore,
And Spirit, moving o'er the deep,
   Be praise for evermore. .

"When thou passest through the waters I will be with thee."

448   7s, 6s, 8 *lines.*

THE ocean hath no danger
   For those whose prayers are made
To Him, who in a manger
   A helpless Babe was laid;
Who, born to tribulation,
   And every human ill,
Yet, Lord of His creation,
   The wildest waves can still.

2 If fierce the tempest round us,
  And white the angry deep;
Yet He, when lost who found us,
  Can still His treasure keep:
Nor wind nor wave can harm us,
  Though hope itself grow dim,
No tempest need alarm us,
  If peace we seek in Him.

3 Though life itself be waning,
  And waves shall o'er us sweep,
The wild winds' sad complaining
  Shall lull us still to sleep:
For as a gentle slumber
  E'en death itself shall prove
To those, whom Christ doth number,
  As worthy of His love.

4 Then, Holy Jesus, hear us,
  And keep us free from harm;
Have pity, Lord, and bear us
  On Thy supporting arm:
Should storm or calm befall us,
  Whate'er our lot may be,
When all is o'er, then call us
  Home, Saviour, home to Thee.

Godfrey Thring.

"*God is our refuge and strength, a very present help in trouble.*"

449 S. M.

O THOU who didst prepare
  The ocean's sounding deep,
And bid the gath'ring waters there
  In mighty concourse sweep:

2 Toss'd in our reeling bark
  On this tumultuous sea,
Thy wondrous ways, O Lord, we mark,
  And lift our hearts to Thee.

3 Borne on the stormy wave,
  In measured sweep we go,
Nor dread th' unfathomable grave
  That ever yawns below.

4 Jesus is nigh who trod
  Of old that foaming spray,
Whose billows own'd th' Incarnate God,
  And died in calm away.

   5 Tho' swells the threat'ning tide
      Mounting to heaven above,
   We know in whom our souls confide
      And fearless trust His love.

   6 Snatch'd from a darker deep,
      And waves of wilder foam,
   Thou, Lord, our trusting souls shalt keep,
      And waft them safely home.

   7 Home where no tempests sound,
      Nor angry waters roar,
   Nor troublous billows heave around
      Th' eternal, peaceful shore.   *Tonna.*

"He bowed the heavens also, and came down, and darkness was under Him."

450   C. M.

THE Lord descended from above,
    And bowed the heavens most high,
And underneath His feet He cast
    The darkness of the sky.

2 On cherub and on cherubim
    Full royally He rode;
And on the wings of mighty winds
    Came flying all abroad.

3 And like a den most dark He made
    His hidden secret place;
With waters black and airy clouds
    Encompassèd He was.

4 He sat serene upon the floods,
    Their fury to restrain;
And He, as sovereign Lord and King,
    For evermore shall reign.
                     Thomas Sternhold, 1549.

THE LAYING OF A CORNER-STONE.

" The glory of Lebanon shall come unto thee, the fir tree, the pine tree, and the box tree together, to beautify the place of My sanctuary."

451   L. M.

O LORD of hosts, whose glory fills
    The bounds of the eternal hills,
And yet vouchsafes, in Christian lands,
To dwell in temples made with hands:

2 Grant that we, who here to-day
  Rejoicing this foundation lay,
  May be in very deed Thine own,
  Built on the precious Corner-stone.

3 Endue the creatures with Thy grace,
  That shall adorn Thy dwelling-place;
  The beauty of the oak and pine,
  The gold and silver, they are Thine.

4 To Thee they all pertain; to Thee
  The treasures of the earth and sea;
  And when we bring them to Thy throne,
  We render, Lord, to Thee Thine own.

5 The architects endue with skill:
  The hands that work preserve from ill;
  May all who build this house to Thee,
  Built in Thy heavenly Temple be.

6 Both now and ever, Lord, protect
  The temple of Thine own elect;
  Be Thou in them, and they in Thee,
  O ever blessed Trinity.

John M. Neale.

"*That Thine eyes may be open towards this house night and day, even toward the place of which Thou hast said, 'My name shall be there.'*"

452 L. M.

THIS stone to Thee in faith we lay,
  We build the temple, Lord, to Thee.
Thine eye be open night and day
  To guard this house and sanctuary.

2 Here, when Thy people seek Thy face,
    And dying sinners pray to live,
  Hear Thou in heaven, Thy dwelling-place,
    And when Thou hearest, O forgive.

3 Here, when Thy messengers proclaim
    The blessed gospel of Thy Son,
  Still by the power of His great name
    Be mighty signs and wonders done.

4 Hosanna! to their heavenly King,
    When children's voices raise that song,
  Hosanna! let their angels sing
    And heaven with earth the strain prolong.

5 But will, indeed, Jehovah deign
   Here to abide, no transient guest?
Here will the world's Redeemer reign?
   And here the Holy Spirit rest?

6 That glory never hence depart?
   Yet choose not, Lord, this house alone:
Thy kingdom come to every heart,
   In every bosom fix Thy throne.

James Montgomery.

THE CONSECRATION OF A CHURCH.

"The Lord loveth the gates of Zion more than all the dwellings of Jacob."

453   C. M.

O GOD, who lovest to abide,
   In Zion's chosen gate,
More than the thousand tents beside,
   Where Israel's faithful wait;

2 Accept our works, and hear our vows,
   Unworthy though we be;
And look in mercy on the House
   We dedicate to Thee.

3 Here answer Thou, as Thou art wont,
   Thy people when they pray;
Here in the waters of Thy font
   Let sin be washed away.

4 Here set Thy Confirmation's seal
   For ghostly strength and good;
Here give Thy people, as they kneel,
   Their Saviour's Flesh and Blood.

5 If after sin they seek Thy face,
   And by Thy precepts live,
Hear Thou in heaven Thy dwelling-place,
   And when Thou hear'st, forgive!

6 If there be famine in the land,
   Or pestilence, or foe,
Stretch out from heaven Thy strong right hand,
   When here Thy flock fall low.

7 Bless those, O Lord, and hear their cry,
   That raised Thy Temple here:
   That in Thy House beyond the sky,
   With joy they may appear!

8 All worship be to God alone;
   Praise to the Father be,
   To Christ, the precious Corner-stone,
   And Holy Ghost, to Thee.

John M. Neale.

"Jesus Christ Himself being the chief Corner-stone."
8s & 7s, 6 lines.

454
CHRIST is made the sure Foundation,
   And the precious Corner-stone,
Who, the two-fold walls surmounting,
   Bind them closely into one:
Holy Zion's help for ever,
   And her confidence alone.

2 All that dedicated City
   Dearly loved by God on high,
In exultant jubilation
   Pours perpetual melody;
God the One, and God the Trinal,
   Singing everlastingly.

3 To this temple, where we call Thee,
   Come, O Lord of Hosts, to-day!
With Thy wonted loving-kindness
   Hear Thy people as they pray;
And Thy fullest benediction
   Shed within its walls for aye.

4 Here vouchsafe to all Thy servants
   What they supplicate to gain:
Here to have and hold for ever
   Those good things their prayers obtain;
And hereafter in Thy glory
   With Thy blessed ones to reign.

5 Laud and honor to the Father;
   Laud and honor to the Son;
Laud and honor to the Spirit;
   Ever Three and ever One:
Consubstantial, Coeternal,
   While unending ages run.

Latin Hymn.
Trans. John. M. Neale, 1851.

"Behold the tabernacle of God is with men."

455 15s.

WHEN the Architect Almighty fashion'd had the heaven and earth,
Temple of the glorious Godhead, angels shouted at their birth;
Morning stars in holy concert sang a joyful Jubilee;
And the whole creation chanted, Hallelujah, Lord to Thee!

2 In a moving Tabernacle, Thou, O Lord, didst deign to dwell,
In the darkness and the stillness of the holy oracle;
In the awful cloud was shrouded, in the fire Thy presence shone,
In the consecrated Temple of the royal Solomon.

3 God in human flesh appearing, shrining man with Deity,
And presented in the Temple did of old vouchsafe to be;
In the Temple holy Jesus as a Child and Teacher sate;
And the Feast of Dedication God with us did celebrate.

4 Look from heaven, and shine upon us with the lustre of Thy face,
Send on us the Pentecostal benedictions of Thy grace;
Ever present and propitious to the eye of faith appear
In the worship of the Temple which to Thee to-day we rear.

5 Here, O Lord, an earthly temple to Thy name we dedicate,
And we pray Thee with Thy Holy Spirit us to consecrate;
Consecrate us to be temples of the Blessed Three in One,
Founded on Apostles, Prophets, Jesus Christ the Corner-stone.

6 So when all our earthly temples are dissolvèd in the dust,
May we at Thy Resurrection rise in glory with the just,
When the heavenly city shining, and adornèd as a Bride
For her Husband, in His glory shall be ever glorified.

7 When that holy City gleaming with its jewels, pearls, and gold,
Shall descend, and in its portals all the risen saints enfold;
May we in its light eternal sing with all the heavenly host
'Glory be to God the Father, to the Son and Holy Ghost.'

Christopher Wordsworth.

THE CONSECRATION OF A BURIAL GROUND.

"For the hour is coming in the which all that are in the graves shall hear His voice, and come forth."

456 C. M.

THE trump shall sound, and in the clouds
  The Lord shall be reveal'd,
And every grave shall open'd be,
  And every tomb unseal'd.

2 Christ will transform His risen saints
    With power and love divine;
  Their bodies will in heavenly light
    Like to His body shine.

3 Call'd forth to meet their coming Lord,
    And caught up in the air,
  They will to heaven be borne, and dwell
    With Him for ever there.

4 O therefore bless the Lord of life,
    Who pluck'd from Death his sting,
  And will His people through the grave
    To joys immortal bring.

5 Lord, give us grace to die to sin,
    And rise to life renewed;
  That we may rise to endless life
    In Thy similitude.

6 Glory to Father, and to Son,
    Who died that we may live,
  And quickening Spirit, ever blest,
    Eternal glory give.

C. Wordsworth.

THANKSGIVING.

"Enter into His gates with thanksgiving, and into His courts with praise."

457 L. M.

ALL people, that on earth do dwell!
  Sing to the Lord with cheerful voice;
Him serve with fear, His praise forth tell;
  Come ye before Him, and rejoice.

2 Know that the Lord is God indeed:
    Without our aid He did us make;
  We are His flock, He doth us feed,
    And for His sheep He doth us take.

3 Oh, enter then His gates with praise,
    Approach with joy His courts unto;
  Praise, laud, and bless His name always,
    For it is seemly so to do.

4 For why? The Lord our God is good,
His mercy is forever sure;
His truth at all times firmly stood,
And shall from age to age endure.
John Hopkins, or Wm. Kethe, about 1562.

"*Make a joyful noise unto the Lord all ye lands.*"

458
SING Alleluia forth in duteous praise,
O citizens of heaven; and sweetly raise
An endless Alleluia.

2 Ye next, who stand before th' Eternal Light,
In hymning choirs re-echo to the height
An endless Alleluia.

3 The Holy City shall take up your strain,
And with glad songs resounding wake again
An endless Alleluia.

4 In blissful antiphons ye thus rejoice
To render to the Lord with thankful voice
An endless Alleluia.

5 Ye who have gained at length your palms in bliss,
Victorious ones, your chant shall still be this,
An endless Alleluia.

6 There, in one grand acclaim, for ever ring
The strains which tell the honor of your king
An endless Alleluia.

7 This is the rest for weary ones brought back,
This is the food and drink which none shall lack,
An endless Alleluia.

8 While Thee, by whom were all things made, we praise
For ever, and tell out in sweetest lays
An endless Alleluia.

9 Almighty Christ, to Thee our voices sing
Glory for evermore; to Thee we bring
An endless Alleluia.
From the Latin.
Trans. Jno. Ellerton.

"*And on His head were many crowns.*"
S. M. 8 *lines.*

459
CROWN Him with many crowns,
The Lamb upon His throne;
Hark how the heavenly anthem drowns
All music but its own;

With His most precious Blood
From sin He set us free;
We hail Him as our matchless King
Through all eternity.

2 Crown Him, the virgin's Son
The God Incarnate born,
Whose arm those crimson trophies won,
Which now His brow adorn:
Fruit of the mystic Rose,
As of that Rose the Stem;
The Root whence mercy ever flows,
The Babe of Bethlehem.

3 Crown Him, the Lord of Love:
Behold His hands and side,
Rich wounds, yet visible above
In beauty glorified;
No angel in the sky
Can fully bear that sight,
But downward bends his burning eye
At mysteries so bright.

4 Crown Him, the Lord of Peace:
Whose power a sceptre sways
From pole to pole, that wars may cease,
And all be prayer and praise:
His reign shall know no end,
And round His piercèd feet
Fair flowers of Paradise extend
Their fragrance ever sweet.

5 Crown Him the Lord of years,
The Potentate of time,
Creator of the rolling spheres,
Ineffably sublime;
Glassed in a sea of light,
Whose everlasting waves
Reflect His form,—the Infinite—
Who lives, and loves, and saves.

6 Crown Him the Lord of heaven,
One with the Father known,
One with the Spirit through Him given
From yonder glorious throne!
To Thee be endless praise,
For Thou for us hast died:
Be Thou, O Lord, through endless days
Adored and magnified. *Matthew Bridges.*

"Bless the Lord, O my soul."
German Choral.

460

NOW thank we all our God,
  With hearts, and hands, and voices,
Who wondrous things hath done,
  In whom His world rejoices ;
    Who from our mother's arms
      Hath blessed us on our way
    With countless gifts of love,
      And still is ours to-day.

2 O may this bounteous God
    Through all our life be near us,
  With ever joyful hearts
    And blessed peace to cheer us ;
      And keep us in His grace,
        And guide us when perplexed,
      And free us from all ills
        In this world and the next.

3 All praise and thanks to God
    The Father now be given,
  The Son, and Him who reigns
    With them in highest heaven,
      The One eternal God,
        Whom heaven and earth adore ;
      For thus it was, is now,
        And shall be evermore.

Martin Rinckart, 1644.
Trans. Catherine Winkworth, 1858.

*"All thy works praise Thee, O Lord ; and Thy saints
give thanks unto Thee."*

461
7s, 6 lines.

PRAISE to God, immortal praise.
    For the love that crowns our days ;
Bounteous Source of every joy,
Let Thy praise our tongues employ :
All to Thee, O God, we owe,
Source whence all our blessings flow.

2 All the blessings of the fields,
  All the stores the garden yields,
  Flocks that whiten all the plain,
  Yellow sheaves of ripened grain :
  Lord, for these our souls shall raise
  Grateful vows and solemn praise.

3 Clouds that drop their fattening dews,
Suns that genial warmth diffuse
All the plenty summer pours,
Autumn's rich, o'erflowing stores:
Lord, for these our souls shall raise
Grateful vows and solemn praise.

4 Peace, prosperity, and health,
Private bliss, and public wealth,
Knowledge with its gladdening streams,
Pure religion's holier beams;
Lord, for these our souls shall raise
Grateful vows and solemn praise.
Anna L. Barbauld, 1772.

"*It is a good thing to give thanks unto the Lord, and to sing praises unto Thy name, O most High.*"

462 *German Choral.*

PRAISE to the Lord! He is King over all the creation!
Praise to the Lord! O my soul, as the God of salvation!
Join in the song—
Psaltery and harp, roll along
Praise in your solemn vibration.

2 Praise to the Lord! Who in glorious majesty reigning,
Beareth Thee upward, on wings like the eagles sustaining—
Thee to uphold,
Arms of His mercy enfold—
Faithful 'mid all Thy complaining.

3 Praise to the Lord! Who with honor and blessing hath crowned thee,
Pouring His gifts out of heaven like showers around thee;
Think of it too,
What the Almighty can do—
How by His love He hath bound thee.

4 Praise to the Lord! and let all that is in me adore Him:
All that hath breath sing, with Abraham's children before Him—
He is our light,
Fountain of glory and might,
Come, let us kneel and adore Him!

Joachim Neander.
Trans. Thomas C. Porter.

NATIONAL THANKSGIVING.

"O let the nations be glad and sing for joy, for Thou shalt judge the people righteously, and govern the nations upon earth."

463　　　　　　　　H. M.

BEFORE the Lord we bow,
　　The God who reigns above,
And rules the world below,
　　Boundless in power and love:
Our thanks we bring in joy and praise,
Our hearts we raise to heaven's high King.

2 The nation Thou hast blessed
　　May well Thy love declare,
From foes and fears at rest,
　　Protected by Thy care;
For this fair land, for this bright day,
Our thanks we pay,—gifts of Thy hand.

3 May every mountain height,
　　Each vale and forest green,
Shine in Thy Word's pure light,
　　And its rich fruits be seen;
May every tongue be tuned to praise,
And join to raise a grateful song.

4 Earth! hear thy Maker's voice,
　　Thy great Redeemer own;
Believe, obey, rejoice,
　　And worship Him alone;
Cast down thy pride, thy sin deplore,
And bow before the Crucified.

5 And when in power He comes,
　　Oh! may our native land,
From all its rending tombs,
　　Send forth a glorious band,
A countless throng, ever to sing,
To heav'n's high King, salvation's song.
　　　　　　Francis Scott Key, 1832, *altered.*

"Blessed is the nation whose God is the Lord."

464　　　　　　　6s & 4s.

GOD bless our native land!
　　Firm may she ever stand,
Through storm and night;

When the wild tempests rave,
Ruler of winds and wave!
Do Thou our country save,
  By Thy great might.

2 For her our prayer shall rise
To God above the skies;
  On Him we wait;
Thou who art ever nigh,
Guardian with watchful eye!
To Thee aloud we cry,—
  God save the State!

John S. Dwight, 1844.

MISSIONS.

"Freely ye have received, freely give."
7s & 6s, 8 *lines.*

465

FROM Greenland's icy mountains,
  From India's coral strand,
Where Afric's sunny fountains
  Roll down their golden sand;
From many an ancient river,
From many a palmy plain,
They call us to deliver
  Their land from error's chain.

2 What though the spicy breezes
  Blow soft o'er Ceylon's isle,
Though every prospect pleases,
  And only man is vile;
In vain with lavish kindness
  The gifts of God are strown,
The heathen in his blindness
  Bows down to wood and stone.

3 Can we whose souls are lighted
  With wisdom from on high,
Can we to men benighted
  The lamp of life deny?
Salvation! oh, salvation!
  The joyful sound proclaim,
Till each remotest nation
  Has learned Messiah's name.

4 Waft, waft, ye winds, His story,
   And you, ye waters, roll,
Till like a sea of glory
   It spreads from pole to pole;
Till o'er our ransomed nature
   The Lamb for sinners slain,
Redeemer, King, Creator,
   In bliss returns to reign.
Reginald Heber, 1819.

"So shall He sprinkle many nations."

466   8s & 7s, 8 *lines.*

SAVIOUR! sprinkle many nations,
   Fruitful let Thy sorrows be;
By Thy pains and consolations,
   Draw the Gentiles unto Thee.
Of Thy cross the wondrous story,
   Be it to the Gentiles told;
Let them see Thee in Thy glory
   And Thy mercy manifold.

2 Far and wide, though all unknowing,
   Pants for Thee each mortal breast;
Human tears for Thee are flowing,
   Human hearts in Thee would rest.
Thirsting as for dews of even,
   As the new-mown grass for rain;
Thee they seek, as God of heaven,
   Thee as Man for sinners slain.

3 Saviour, lo! the isles are waiting,
   Stretched the hand, and strained the sight,
For Thy Spirit, new creating,
   Love's pure flame and wisdom's light:
Give the word, and of the preacher
   Speed the foot and touch the tongue;
Till on earth by every creature
   Glory to the Lamb be sung.
Arthur Cleveland Coxe, 1851.

"And He shall set up an ensign for the nations."

467   L. M.

UPLIFT the banner! Let it float
   Sky-ward and sea-ward, high and wide;
The sun shall light its shining folds,
   The Cross, on which the Saviour died.

2 Uplift the banner! Angels bend
    In anxious silence o'er the sign,
  And vainly seek to comprehend
    The wonder of the love divine.

3 Uplift the banner! Heathen lands
    Shall see from far the glorious sight,
  And nations, gathering at the call,
    Their spirits kindle in its light.

4 Uplift the banner! Let it float
    Sky-ward and sea-ward, high and wide;
  Our glory only in the Cross,
    Our only hope the Crucified.

5 Uplift the banner! Wide and high
    Sea-ward and sky-ward let it shine:
  Nor skill, nor might, nor merit ours;
    We conquer only in that sign.
                    George W. Doane.

"*That Thy way may be known upon earth; Thy saving health among all nations.*"

468
7s.

HASTEN, Lord the glorious time,
    When, beneath Messiah's sway,
  Every nation, every clime,
    Shall the gospel call obey.

2 Mightiest kings His power shall own,
    Heathen tribes His name adore;
  Satan and his host, o'erthrown,
    Bound in chains shall hurt no more.

3 Then shall war and tumults cease,
    Then be banished grief and pain;
  Righteousness and joy and peace
    Undisturbed shall ever reign.

4 Bless we, then, our gracious Lord,
    Ever praise His glorious name;
  All His mighty acts record,
    All His wondrous love proclaim.
                    Harriet Auber, 1829.

MORNING.

"*My mouth shall daily speak of Thy righteousness and salvation.*"

469
C. M.

AGAIN the Lord of life and light
    Awakes the kindling ray,

  Unseals the eyelids of the morn,
   And pours increasing day.

2 Oh! what a night was that, which wrapt
   The heathen world in gloom!
  Oh! what a Sun, which broke this day
   Triumphant from the tomb!

3 Ten thousand mortal lips shall join
   To hail this welcome morn,
  Which scatters blessings from its wings
   To nations yet unborn.

4 The powers of darkness leagued in vain
   To bind His soul in death;
  He shook their kingdom, when He fell,
   With His expiring breath.

5 Exalted high at God's right hand,
   The Lord of all below,
  Through Him is pardoning love dispensed,
   And boundless blessings flow.

6 And still for erring, guilty, man
   A Brother's pity flows;
  And still His bleeding heart is touched
   With memory of our woes.

7 To Thee, our Saviour, and our King,
   Glad homage we will give,
  And stand prepared like Thee to die,
   That we with Thee may live!

Anna L. Barbauld, 1772.

"The sun shall be no more thy light by day; but the Lord shall be unto thee an everlasting light."

470
    8s & 7s, 8 *lines.*

BRIGHTNESS of the Father's glory:
  Of His light essential ray;
Light of life, all light enshrining;
  Day, illumining the day:
Jesus, Sun divine, upon us
  With perpetual brilliance gleam;
Fill our hearts, each sense enlighten,
  With the Spirit's hallowing beam.

2 Thee we pray, too, Holy Father,
  Fount of life, and Source of grace,
By the cleansing of Thy Spirit
  Taint of sin from us efface:

In each strong resolve be with us,
  And the Tempter's rage subdue;
Turn to good each sad misfortune;
  Be our guide in all we do.

3 Rule our inmost thought and action;
  Grant us heavenly purity,
Faith that glows with holy fervor,
  Incorrupt simplicity.
Feed us with the Bread from heaven,
  And that drink that cannot cloy;
Comfort us in all our weakness
  With the Spirit's holy joy.

4 Thus shall speed the day in gladness,
  Modesty like dawn shall glow,
Faith shall shine as light at noon-day,
  And the soul no night shall know.
Praise and glory to the Father,
  Praise and glory to the Son,
Praise and glory to the Spirit,
  Ever Three and ever One.

Ambrose, 340-397.
Trans. W. S. Copeland, altered.

"Awake, thou that sleepest, and arise from the dead."

471 L. M.

AWAKE, my soul, and with the sun
  Thy daily stage of duty run;
Shake off dull sloth, and early rise
To pay thy morning sacrifice.

2 Redeem thy misspent moments past,
  And live this day as if thy last;
Thy talents to improve take care,
For the great day thyself prepare.

3 Let all thy converse be sincere,
  Thy conscience like the noon-day clear:
Think how all-seeing God thy ways,
And all thy secret thoughts surveys.

4 Awake, lift up thyself, my heart,
  And with the angels bear thy part,
Who all night long unwearied sing
High glory to th' eternal King.

5 All praise to Thee, who safe hast kept
  And hast refreshed me whilst I slept;
  Grant, Lord, when I from death shall wake,
  I may of endless life partake.

6 Lord, I my vows to Thee renew;
  Disperse my sins as morning dew:
  Guard my first springs of thought and will,
  And with Thyself my spirit fill.

7 Direct, control, suggest this day
  All I design, or do, or say;
  That all my powers with all their might
  In Thy sole glory may unite.
              Thomas Ken, 1697.

472

"*Gott des Himmels und der Erden.*"
       German Choral.

GOD who madest earth and heavèn,
    Father, Son, and Holy Ghost,
Who the day and night hast given;
    Sun and moon and starry host,
All things wake at Thy command,
Held in being by Thy hand.

2 God, I thank Thee! in Thy keeping
    Safely have I slumber'd here;
  Thou hast guarded me while sleeping,
    From all danger, pain, and fear:
  And the cunning of my foe
  Hath not wrought my overthrow.

3 Let the night of sin, that shrouded
    All my life, with this depart;
  Shine on me with beams unclouded.
    Jesus! In Thy loving heart
  Is my help and hope alone,
  For the evil I have done.

4 Help me as the morn is breaking,
    In the spirit to arise,
  So from careless sloth awaking
    That when o'er the aged skies
  Shall the morn of Doom appear,
  I may see it free from fear.

5 Lead me and forsake me never,
    Guide my wand'rings by Thy Word;

As Thou hast been, be Thou ever
  My Defence, my Refuge, Lord.
Never safe except with Thee,
  Thou my faithful Guardian be!

6 O my God, I now commend me
  Wholly to Thy mighty hand;
All the powers that Thou dost lend me
  Let me use at Thy command;
Thou my boast, my strength divine,
Keep me with Thee, I am Thine.

7 Thus afresh with each new morning
  Save me from the power of sin,
Hourly let me feel Thy warning,
  Ruling, prompting me within,
Till my final rest be come,
And Thine angel bear me home.

Henry Albert, 1644.
Trans. Catherine Winkworth.

"For a day in Thy courts is better than a thousand."

473   *7s, 6 lines.*

SAFELY through another week,
  God has brought us on our way;
Let us now a blessing seek,
  Waiting in His courts to-day:
Day of all the week the best,
Emblem of eternal rest.

2 While we pray for pard'ning grace,
  Through the dear Redeemer's name,
Show Thy reconcilèd face,
  Take away our sin and shame;
From our worldly cares set free,
May we rest, this day, in Thee.

3 Here we come Thy name to praise;
  May we feel Thy presence near:
May Thy glory meet our eyes,
  While we in Thy house appear:
Here afford us, Lord! a taste
Of our everlasting feast.

4 May Thy Gospel's joyful sound
  Conquer sinners, comfort saints;

Make the fruits of grace abound,
　　Bring relief for all complaints:
　Thus may all our Sabbaths prove,
　Till we join the Church above.
John Newton, 1779, *altered.*

"To show forth Thy loving-kindness in the morning, and Thy faithfulness every night."

474　　　　　L. M.

1 MY God! how endless is Thy love!
　　Thy gifts are every evening new;
　And morning mercies from above
　　Gently distill, like early dew.

2　Thou spread'st the curtains of the night,
　　Great Guardian of my sleeping hours!
　Thy sovereign word restores the light,
　　And quickens all my drowsy powers.

3　I yield my powers to Thy command;
　　To Thee I consecrate my days;
　Perpetual blessings, from Thy hand,
　　Demand perpetual songs of praise.
Isaac Watts, 1709.

"In all thy ways acknowledge Him, and He shall direct thy paths."

475　　　　　7s.

1 AS the sun doth daily rise
　　Bright'ning all the morning skies,
　So to Thee with one accord
　Lift we up our hearts, O Lord!

2　Day by day provide us food,
　For from Thee come all things good;
　Strength unto our souls afford
　From Thy living Bread, O Lord!

3　Be our Guard in sin and strife;
　Be the Leader of our life;
　Lest like sheep we stray abroad,
　Stay our wayward feet, O Lord!

4　Quickened by the Spirit's grace,
　All Thy holy will to trace,
　While we daily search Thy Word,
　Wisdom true impart, O Lord!

5　When the sun withdraws his light;
　When we seek our beds at night,
　Thou, by sleepless hosts adored,
　Hear the prayer of faith, O Lord!

6 When the hours are dark and drear,
  When the Tempter lurketh near,
  By Thy strength'ning grace outpoured,
  Save the tempted ones, O Lord!

7 Praise we with the heavenly host,
  Father, Son, and Holy Ghost;
  Thee would we with one accord
  Praise and magnify, O Lord!

King Alfred, 900.
Trans. Earl Nelson, 1864.

" But let us who are of the day, be sober, putting on the breastplate of faith and love."

476
L. M.

NOW with the rising, golden dawn,
  Let us, the children of the day,
Cast off the darkness which so long
  Has led our guilty souls astray.

2 O may the morn so pure, so clear,
  Its own sweet calm in us instill;
A guileless mind, a heart sincere,
  Simplicity of word and will.

3 And ever, as the day glides by,
  May we the busy senses rein;
Keep guard upon the hand and eye,
  Nor let the body suffer stain.

4 Grant us a body pure within;
  A wakeful heart, a ready will;
That no dark deed nor cherished sin,
  The fervor of the soul may chill.

5 Fill Thou our souls, Redeemer true!
  With Thy most pure, celestial ray;
So may we walk in safety through
  All the temptations of this day.

6 Upon our fainting souls distill
  The grace of Thy celestial dew;
Let no fresh snare to sin beguile,
  No former sin revive anew.

7 Grant us the grace, for love of Thee,
  To scorn all vanities below;
Faith to detect each falsity;
  And knowledge Thee alone to know.

Latin Hymn.
Trans. E. Caswall.

EVENING.

"Bow down Thine ear to me, and deliver me speedily."

477 : C. M.

O GOD, bow down Thine ear on earth,
  And hear Thy children's cry,
And fill our weak and throbbing hearts
  With blessings from on high.

2 Forsake us not, O loving Lord,
  But hear us while we pray;
And, Jesus, when at last we die,
  Wipe all our tears away.

3 O Jesus, there is naught to fear,
  If Thou the blessing give;
Keep us from every danger free,
  And guard us, while we live.

4 Give us a heart to love Thee, Lord;
  And Thine Almighty Son,
And may we love the Holy Ghost
  While this short life we run.

F. H. (aetat. X.)

EVENING.

"He will not suffer thy foot to be moved: He that keepeth thee will not slumber."

478 L. M.

O LIGHT of life, O Saviour dear,
  Before we sleep, bow down Thine ear;
Through day and dark, o'er land and sea,
We have no other hope but Thee.

2 Oft from Thy royal road we part,
  Lost in the mazes of the heart;
Our lamps put out, our course forgot,
We seek for God, and find Him not.

3 What sudden sunbeams cheer our sight!
  What dawning risen upon the night!
Thou giv'st Thyself to us, and we
Find Guide and Path and all in Thee.

4 Through day and darkness, Saviour dear,
  Abide with us more nearly near;
Till on Thy face we lift our eyes,
The Sun of God's own Paradise.

5 Praise God, our Maker and our Friend!
  Praise Him through time, till time shall end!
  Till psalm and song His Name adore
  Through Heaven's great day of Evermore.
  Francis T. Palgrave.

"There is sprung up a light for the righteous."

479   L. M.

O BLEST Creator, God most High,
  Great Ruler of the starry sky,
Who, robing day with beauteous light,
Hast clothed in soft repose the night.

2 That sleep may wearied limbs restore,
  And fit for toil and use once more;
  May gently soothe the careworn breast,
  And lull our anxious griefs to rest;

3 We thank Thee for the day that's gone;
  We pray Thee, now the night comes on:
  O help us sinners as we raise
  To Thee our votive hymn of praise.

4 To Thee our hearts their music bring,
  To Thee our lips in concord sing;
  To Thee our rapt affections soar,
  And Thee our chastened souls adore.

5 Lord, when the parting beams of day
  In evening's shadows fade away,
  Let faith no wildering darkness know,
  But night with faith's own splendor grow.
  J. D. Chambers.

"Under His wings shalt thou trust."

480   L. M.

ALL praise to Thee, my God this night,
  For all the blessings of the light;
Keep me, O keep me, King of kings,
Beneath Thine own almighty wings.

2 Forgive me, Lord, for Thy dear Son,
  The ill that I this day have done;
  That with the world, myself, and Thee,
  I, ere I sleep, at peace may be.

3 Teach me to live, that I may dread
  The grave as little as my bed;
  To die, that this vile body may
  Rise glorious at the awful day.

4 O may my soul on Thee repose,
  And may sweet sleep mine eyelids close:
  Sleep that shall me more vigorous make
  To serve my God when I awake.

5 When in the night I sleepless lie,
  My soul with heavenly thoughts supply;
  Let no ill dreams disturb my rest,
  No power of darkness me molest.

6 O when shall I in endless day
  For ever chase dark sleep away,
  And praise with the angelic choir
  Incessant sing, and never tire.

Thomas Ken, 1697.

"And at even, when the sun did set, they brought unto Him all that were diseased."

481　　　　L. M.

AT even ere the sun was set,
   The sick, O Lord, around Thee lay:
Oh! in what divers pains they met!
Oh! with what joy they went away!

2 Once more 'tis eventide, and we
  Oppressed with various ills, draw near:
  What if Thy form we cannot see?
  We know and feel that Thou art here.

3 O Saviour Christ, our woes dispel:
  For some are sick, and some are sad,
  And some have never loved Thee well,
  And some have lost the love they had.

4 And some have found the world is vain,
  Yet from the world they break not free;
  And some have friends who give them pain,
  Yet have not sought a friend in Thee.

5 And none, O Lord, have perfect rest,
  For none are wholly free from sin;
  And they, who fain would love Thee best,
  Are conscious most of wrong within.

6 O Saviour Christ, Thou too art Man,
  Thou hast been troubled, tempted, tried;
  Thy kind but searching glance can scan
  The very wounds that shame would hide.

EVENING.

7 Thy touch has still its ancient power;
   No word from Thee can fruitless fall;
   Hear in this solemn evening hour,
   And in Thy mercy heal us all.
                                    H. Twells.

"Even the night shall be light about me."

482 L. M.

SUN of my soul, Thou Saviour dear,
  It is not night if Thou be near;
O may no earth-born cloud arise
To hide Thee from Thy servant's eyes!

2 When the soft dews of kindly sleep
  My wearied eyelids gently steep,
  Be my last thought, how sweet to rest,
  For ever on my Saviour's breast.

3 Abide with me from morn to eve,
  For without Thee I cannot live;
  Abide with me when night is nigh,
  For without Thee I dare not die.

4 If some poor wandering child of Thine
  Have spurned to-day the voice divine,
  Now, Lord, the gracious work begin;
  Let him no more lie down in sin.

5 Watch by the sick; enrich the poor
  With blessings from Thy boundless store;
  Be every mourner's sleep to-night,
  Like infant's slumbers, pure and light.

6 Come near and bless us when we wake,
  Ere through the world our way we take;
  Till in the ocean of Thy love
  We lose ourselves in heaven above.
                                John Keble, 1827.

"The darkness and light to Thee are both alike."

483 10s, 6 *lines.*

THE day is gently sinking to a close,
  Fainter and yet more faint the sunlight glows;
O Brightness of Thy Father's glory, Thou,
Eternal Light of Light, be with us now;
Where Thou art present, darkness cannot be:
Midnight is glorious noon, O Lord, with Thee.

27*

2 Our changeful lives are ebbing to an end,
　Onward to darkness and to death we tend;
　O Conqueror of the grave, be Thou our Guide,
　Be Thou our Light in death's dark eventide;
　Then in our mortal hour will be no gloom,
　No sting in death, no terror in the tomb.

3 Thou, who in darkness walking didst appear
　Upon the waves, and Thy disciples cheer,
　Come, Lord, in lonesome days, when storms assail,
　And earthly hopes and human succors fail:
　When all is dark, may we behold Thee nigh,
　And hear Thy voice, "Fear not, for it is I."

4 The weary world is mouldering to decay,
　Its glories wane, its pageants fade away;
　In that last sunset, when the stars shall fall,
　May we arise, awakened by Thy call,
　With Thee, O Lord, forever to abide
　In that blest day which has no eventide.
　　　　　　　　　　Christopher Wordsworth.

484　"*Thou shalt not be afraid for the terror by night.*"
　　　　　　　　　8s & 7s.

AND now the day is past and gone,
　　Holy God, we bow to Thee!
Again, as nightly shades come on,
　　To Thy sheltering side we flee.

2 For all the ills this day hath done
　　Let our bitter sorrow plead;
　And keep us from the wicked One,
　　When ourselves we cannot heed.

3 Rav'ning, he prowls Thy fold around,
　　In his watchful circuitings;
　Father! this night let us be found
　　Under the shadow of Thy wings.

4 O! when shall that Thy day have come,
　　Day ne'er sinking to the West;
　That country and that holy home
　　Where no foe shall break our rest!

5 Now to the Father and the Son,
　　We our feeble voice would raise,
　With Holy Spirit, joined in One,
　　And, from age to age would praise! *Latin Hymn.*
　　　　　　　　　　　　　　　　　　　　　Trans!

"I will lay me down in peace and sleep, for Thou Lord, only makest me dwell in safety."

German Choral.

485

QUIETLY rest the woods and dales,
  Silence round the earth prevails,
    The world is all asleep;
Thou, my soul in thought arise,
Seek thy Father in the skies,
    And holy vigils with Him keep.

2 Sun, where hidest thou thy light?
Art thou driven hence by night,
    Thy dark and ancient foe?
Go! another Sun is mine,
Jesus comes with light divine
    To cheer my pilgrimage below.

3 Now that the day has passed away,
Golden stars in bright array
    Bespangle the blue sky;
Bright and clear, so would I stand,
When I hear my Lord's command
    To leave this earth and upward fly.

4 Now this body seeks for rest,
From its vestments all-undrest,
    Types of mortality.
Christ shall give me soon to wear,
Garments beautiful and fair,—
    White robes of glorious majesty.

5 Head, and feet, and hands once more,
Joy to think of labor o'er,
    And night with gladness see.
Oh, my heart, thou too shalt know
Rest from all thy toil below,
    And from earth's turmoil soon be free.

6 Weary limbs, now rest ye here,
Safe from danger and from fear,
    Seek slumber on this bed;
Deeper rest ere long to share,
Other hands shall soon prepare
    My narrow couch among the dead.

7 While mine eyes I gently close,
Stealing o'er me soft repose,

      Who shall my Guardian be?
      Soul and body now I leave—
      And Thou wilt the trust receive,
        O Israel's Watchman! unto Thee.

8 O my friends, from you this day
  May all ill have fled away,
    No danger near have come;
  Now, my God, these dear ones keep,
  Give to Thy beloved sleep,
    And angels send to guard their home.
Paul Gerhardt.
Trans. Jane Borthwick.

" The Lord shall give His people the blessing of peace."

486
               10s.

SAVIOUR, again to Thy dear Name we raise
  With one accord our parting hymn of praise;
Once more we bless Thee ere our worship cease,
Then, lowly kneeling, wait Thy word of peace.

2 Grant us Thy peace upon our homeward way;
With Thee begun, with Thee shall end the day;
Guard Thou the lips from sin, the hearts from shame,
That in this house have called upon Thy name.

3 Grant us Thy peace, Lord, thro' the coming night,
Turn Thou for us its darkness into light;
From harm and danger keep Thy children free,
For dark and light are both alike to Thee.

4 Grant us Thy peace throughout our earthly life,
Our Balm in sorrow, and our Peace in strife;
Then, when Thy voice shall bid our conflict cease,
Call us, O Lord, to Thine eternal peace.
John Ellerton.

DOXOLOGIES.

1 L. M.
PRAISE God from Whom all blessings flow;
  Praise Him all creatures here below;
Praise Him above, ye heavenly host:
Praise Father, Son, and Holy Ghost.

2 L. M.
TO God the Father, God the Son,
  And God the Spirit, Three in One,
Be honor, praise, and glory given,
By all on earth and all in heaven;
As was through ages heretofore,
Is now, and shall be evermore.

3 L. M.
TO Father, Son and Holy Ghost,
  The God whom heaven and earth adore,
Be glory, as it was of old,
Is now, and shall be evermore.

4 C. M.
LET God the Father, and the Son,
  And Spirit be adored,
Where there are works to make Him known,
  Or saints to love the Lord.

5 C. M.
TO Father, Son, and Holy Ghost,
  The God whom we adore
Be glory, as it was, is now,
  And shall be evermore.

6 S. M.
TO the eternal Three,
  In will and essence one;
To Father, Son, and Spirit be
  Coequal honors done.

7 S. M.
JESUS, our risen Lord,
  We praise Thee, and adore,
Who art with God the Father one,
  And Spirit evermore.

8   7s.

SING we to our God above,
   Praise eternal as His love;
Praise Him, all ye heavenly host,
Father, Son, and Holy Ghost.

9   7s.

PRAISE the name of God most high,
   Praise Him all below the sky,
Praise Him all ye heavenly host,
Father, Son, and Holy Ghost;
As through countless ages past,
Evermore His praise shall last.

10   8s & 7s.

HONOR, glory, might, dominion,
   To the Father and the Son,
With the everlasting Spirit,
   While eternal ages run.

11   8s & 7s.

LORD, Thy glory fills the heaven,
   Earth is with its fulness stored:
Unto Thee be glory given,
   Holy, Holy, Holy Lord!

12   8s & 7s, 6 *lines.*

GLORY to our God, and honor;
   Highest He above all height;
Father, Son, and Holy Spirit,
   One in praise, and one in might;
Might and praise enduring ever,
   In the changeless realms of light.

13   8s & 7s, 6 *lines.*

TO the everlasting Father,
   To the everlasting Son,
To the coeternal Spirit,
   Undivided Three in One,
Honor, praise, dominion, blessing,
   Now and evermore be done.

14   8s, 7s & 4s.

GLORY be to God the Father,
   Glory to th' eternal Son;
Sound aloud the Spirit's praises;
   Join the elders round the throne.
      Hallelujah,
Hail the glorious Three in One.

DOXOLOGIES.

15   H. M.

TO God, the only wise,
    The one immortal King,
Let Alleluias rise
    From ev'ry living thing;
Let earth and heaven, with all their host,
Praise Father, Son, and Holy Ghost.

16   L. P. M.

NOW to the great and sacred Three,
    The Father, Son, and Spirit, be
Eternal power and glory giv'n,
Through all the worlds where God is known
By all the angels near the throne,
And all the saints in earth and heav'n.

17   C. P. M.

TO Father, Son, and Holy Ghost,
    The God, whom heaven's triumphant host,
And saints on earth adore;
Be glory as in ages past,
And now it is, and so shall last,
When time shall be no more.

18   7s & 6s. *Iambic.*

PRAISE be to God the Father;
    Praise be to God the Son;
And praise to God the Spirit,
    The glorious Three in One;
With all the hosts of heaven,
    We worship and adore,
Thy Triune name most holy,
    Now and forevermore.

19   7s & 6s. *Trochaic.*

FATHER, Son, and Holy Ghost,
    One God whom we adore,
Join we with the heav'nly host,
    To praise Thee evermore;
Live, by heaven and earth adored,
    Three in One, One in Three,
Holy, holy, holy Lord,
    All glory be to Thee.

20   6s & 4s.

TO God, the Father, Son
    And Spirit, Three in One,

All praise be given !
Crown Him in every song;
To Him our hearts belong;
Let all His praise prolong,
On earth, in heaven !

21 10*s*.

Loud raise the hymn of glory to the Lord,
By Cherubim and Seraphim adored ;
Join the glad strain of heav'n's triumphant host
Praising the Father, Son, and Holy Ghost.

CONTENTS.

	HYMNS.
SUNDAYS IN ADVENT	1– 23
CHRISTMAS	24– 33
ST. STEPHEN'S DAY	34– 36
ST. JOHN'S "	37– 40
INNOCENTS' "	41
SUNDAYS AFTER CHRISTMAS	42– 50
THE CIRCUMCISION	51– 56
EPIPHANY	57– 67
SUNDAYS AFTER EPIPHANY	68– 99
SEPTUAGESIMA	100–105
SEXAGESIMA	106–112
QUINQUAGESIMA	113–118
ASH WEDNESDAY	119–123
SUNDAYS IN LENT	124–165
PASSION WEEK	166–184
EASTER EVEN	185–189
EASTER SUNDAY	190–201
EASTER MONDAY	202–205
SUNDAYS AFTER EASTER	206–234
ASCENSION DAY	235–243
SUNDAY AFTER ASCENSION	244–252
WHITSUNDAY	253–261
WHITMONDAY	262–265
TRINITY	266–271
SUNDAYS AFTER TRINITY	272–402
SUNDAYS BEFORE ADVENT	403–423
HOLY COMMUNION	424–431

	HYMNS.
HOLY BAPTISM	432–434
CONFIRMATION	435
MARRIAGE	436–437
ORDINATION AND INSTALLATION OF MINISTERS	438–441
ORDINATION AND INSTALLATION OF ELDERS AND DEACONS	442
BURIAL OF THE DEAD	443–445
SERVICE AT SEA	446–450
LAYING OF A CORNER STONE	451–452
CONSECRATION OF A CHURCH	453–455
CONSECRATION OF A BURIAL GROUND	456
THANKSGIVING	457–462
NATIONAL THANKSGIVING	463–464
MISSIONS	465–468
MORNING	469–477
EVENING	478–486

A.

	HYMN.
Abide among us with Thy grace	76
Abide with me; fast falls the eventide	203
"Abide with us;" the shades of eve	204
Again the Lord of life and light	469
Alas! and did my Saviour bleed	104
Alas, dear Lord, what law then hast Thou broken,	170
Alleluia, sing to Jesus	200
Alleluia, song of sweetness	99
All hail the power of Jesus' name	205
All people that on earth do dwell	457
All praise to Thee, my God, this night	480
All praise to Thee, O Lord	73
All that I was—my sin, my guilt	334
Almighty Father, hear our cry	446
Almighty God, Thy word is cast	107
Always with us, always with us	222
Amidst a world of hopes and fears	283
And now the day is past and gone	484
An exile for the faith	37
As Jesus died, and rose again	444
Asleep in Jesus! blessed sleep	411
As the sun doth daily rise	475
A strong tower is the Lord our God	137
As with gladness men of old	62
At even ere the sun was set	481
At the Lamb's high feast we sing	194
Awake and sing the song	360
Awake, glad soul! awake! awake!	191
Awake my soul and with the sun	471
Awake my soul, stretch every nerve	101

B.

Before Jehovah's awful throne	397
Before the Lord we bow	463
Behold me here, in grief draw near	135
Behold the glories of the Lamb	242
Behold! the grace appears	44
Behold the sin-atoning Lamb	164
Behold what wondrous grace	98
Behold where in a mortal form	347
Beyond the glittering, starry skies	252
Blessed are the sons of God	317
Blessed Jesus, here we stand	434
Blest are the pure in heart	47
Blest be the tie that binds	279
Body of Jesus, Oh sweet food	430
Bread of heaven, on Thee we feed	424
Brief life is here our portion	388
Brightest and best of the sons of the morning	59
Brightness of the Father's glory	470
Brought to the font with holy care	306
By the angel's word of love	67
By the blood that flowed from Thee	184
By the first bright Easter-Day	261

C.

Calm they sit with closèd door	207
Captain of Israel's host, and Guide	320
Children of the heavenly King	383
Christ above all glory seated	243
Christ is made the sure Foundation	454
Christ the Lord is risen to-day	193
Christ, whose glory fills the sky	66
Christ will come and not delay	417
Cleft are the rocks, the earth doth quake	172
Come, ever-blessed Spirit, come	435

	HYMN.
Come, gracious Spirit, heavenly Dove	265
Come, Holy Spirit, come Let	254
Come, Holy Spirit, come With	351
Come, Holy Spirit, from above	255
Come, Holy Spirit, heavenly Dove!	264
Come, kingdom of our God	15
Come let us join our cheerful songs	165
Come, O Creator, Spirit blest	322
Come, quickly come, dread Judge of all	19
Come sound His praise abroad	337
Come, Thou Redeemer of the Earth	22
Come we that love the Lord	371
Come ye disconsolate, where'er ye languish	149
Commit thou all thy griefs	352
Crown Him with many crowns	459

D.

Day of vengeance without morrow	414
Dearest of all the names above	345
Dear Father, to Thy mercy-seat	136
Dear Lord! I give my heart to Thee	331
Dear Refuge of my weary soul	138
Dear Saviour, we are Thine	301
Did Christ o'er sinners weep?	326
Down from the mountain, Jesus came	78
Draw nigh, all ye faithful	29

E.

Eternal Beam of light divine	134
Eternal Word! God's true and only Son	55

F.

Fair vision! how thy distant gleam	401
Faith is the brightest evidence	148
Far beyond all comprehension	118
Father, blessing every seed-time	230
Father of eternal grace	288
Father of lights! to Thee we pray	224
Father of mercies! condescend	442
Father of mercies, send Thy grace	276
Father! our hearts we lift	45
Father, Son, and Spirit hear	365
Father, 'tis Thine each day to yield	353
Father, whate'er of earthly bliss	312
Fierce raged the storm of wind	84
Fierce raged the tempest o'er the deep	85
Forever here my rest shall be	183
Forever with the Lord	221
For thee, O dear, dear country	400
Forth from the dark and stormy sky	82
Forth to the land of promise bound	321
For Thy mercy and Thy grace	56
For Thy true servants, Lord	35
Forty days and forty nights	125
From all Thy saints in warfare	34
From Greenland's icy mountains	465

G.

Give us, O Lord, the eye of faith	289
Glorious things of thee are spoken	354
Glory and laud and honor	159
Glory be to Jesus	179
Glory, glory to our King	244
Glory to Thee, O Lord	41
God bless our native land	464
God bless the calm and holy cheer	6

	HYMN.
God in His earthly temples lays	70
God moves in a mysterious way	16
God, my Supporter and my Hope	146
God of all power, and truth, and grace	307
God of mercy, God of grace	90
God, who madest earth and heaven	472
Gracious Spirit! Love divine	257
Granted is the Saviour's prayer	259
Great God, what do I see and hear	11
Great Prophet of my God	213
Guide me, O Thou great Jehovah	109

H.

Hail, Jesus! Israel's Hope and Light!	1
Hail the day that sees Him rise	235
Hail! Thou long-expected Jesus	43
Hail! Thou Source of every blessing	10
Hail to the Lord's anointed	61
Hallelujah! Hallelujah!	197
Hark! a thrilling voice proclaiming	17
Hark the glad sound! the Saviour comes!	13
Hark! the herald angels sing	24
Hark! the song of jubilee	420
Hark, the voice of love and mercy	171
Hark, through the courts of heaven	285
Hark! what mean those holy voices	26
Hasten, Lord, the glorious time	468
Health of the weak to make them strong	290
He lives, the great Redeemer lives	212
Here at Thy table, Lord! we meet	429
Here, O my Lord, I see Thee face to face	380
Here on earth, where foes surround us	385
High let us swell our tuneful notes	31
Holy and reverend is the name	335
Holy Ghost! dispel our sadness	349
Holy, Holy, Holy, Lord	269
Holy, Holy, Holy, Lord God Almighty	267
Holy Saviour, we adore Thee	405
Hosanna, raise the pealing hymn	158
Hosanna to the living Lord!	2
Hosanna to the Prince of light	209
Hosanna to the royal Son	69
How beauteous are their feet	343
How oft, alas! this wretched heart	103
How sweet the name of Jesus sounds	53
How welcome was the call	436

I.

If Christ is mine, then all is mine	231
I love Thee, O most gracious Lord	145
I love Thy kingdom, Lord	302
In all our wanderings here below	323
In His temple now behold Him	46
In the name of God the Father	425
I thirst, Thou wounded Lamb of God	110
It is not death to die	443
I will love Thee—all my treasure	147

J.

Jerusalem, my happy home	413
Jerusalem, the golden	421
Jesus! and shall it ever be?	112
Jesus, exalted far on high	363
Jesus, I live to Thee	304
Jesus, I love Thy charming name	50
Jesus, I my cross have taken	291
Jesus invites His saints	431
Jesus lives and so shall I	192

	HYMN.
Jesus lives, no longer now	198
Jesus, Lord, we kneel before Thee	141
Jesus, Lord, we look to Thee	299
Jesus, Lover of my soul	155
Jesus, Master of the feast	280
Jesus, most merciful and kind	394
Jesus, my eternal Trust	208
Jesus, my Lord, how rich Thy grace	233
Jesus, my Lord, my God, my All	372
Jesus, my Lord, 'tis sweet to rest	228
Jesus, my Shepherd, let me share	215
Jesus, o'er the grave victorious	234
Jesus, our Lord, who tempted wast	124
Jesus, Refuge of the weary	117
Jesus shall reign where'er the sun	65
Jesus, the Author of our life	186
Jesus, the Shepherd of the sheep	211
Jesus, the very thought of Thee	367
Jesus, Thou art my righteousness	377
Jesus, Thou joy of loving hearts	313
Jesus, Thy blood and righteousness	163
Jesus, Thy boundless love to me	114
Jesus, Thy Church with longing eyes	23
Jesus, to Thy cross I hasten	142
Jesus, we sing Thy matchless grace	359
Jesus, who hath gone before us	227
Jesus, with all Thy saints above	154
Join all the glorious names	370
Joy to the world,—the Lord is come	14
Just as I am—without one plea	139

L.

Lead kindly light, amid the encircling gloom	324
Let me be with Thee where Thou art	217
Let saints below in concert sing	358
Let us adore th' eternal Word	281
Lift up your heads, ye mighty gates	329
Light of the lonely pilgrim's heart	295
Light of those whose dreary dwelling	9
Light's abode, celestial Salem	356
Lo! from the desert home	18
Lo! He comes, with clouds descending	8
Lo, the 'day of Christ's appearing	416
Look, ye saints! the sight is glorious	241
Lord, as to Thy dear cross we flee	300
Lord, I am vile, conceiv'd in sin	133
Lord, in this Thy mercy's day	418
Lord, in Thy kingdom there shall be	278
Lord! in Thy name Thy servants plead	229
Lord! let my heart still turn to Thee	373
Lord, like the publican I stand	333
Lord of glory! Thou hast bought us	393
Lord of life, whose words have taught us	115
Lord of the hearts of men	116
Lord of the worlds above	49
Lord, once afar removed from Thee	348
Lord, pour Thy Spirit from on high	438
Lord, Thine appointed servants bless	440
Lord, when before Thy throne we meet	426
Lord, with glowing heart I'd praise Thee	336
Love divine, all loves excelling	97

M.

Majestic sweetness sits enthroned	378
Master, Lord, to Thee we cry	247
May we Thy precepts, Lord, fulfil	286
Mighty Saviour, gracious King	250
Moses from Sinai brings the law	339

	HYMN.		HYMN.
My dear Redeemer and my Lord	341	O loving Jesus, for us crucified	305
My faith looks up to Thee	292	O Master it is good to be	95
My God, how endless is Thy love	474	O Mother dear, Jerusalem	399
My God, how wonderful Thou art	282	Once more, O Lord, Thy sign shall be..	7
My God! permit my tongue	319	One sole bapti mal sign	364
My God, the Spring of all my joys	396	On Jordan's bank the Baptist's cry	12
My Hope, my All, my Saviour Thou	287	On the fount of life eternal	293
My Saviour, my Almighty Friend	315	O Paradise, O Paradise	406
My sins, my sins, my Saviour	122	O sacred Head now wounded	173
My soul repeat His praise	403	O Saviour, who at Nain's gate	357
My spirit on Thy care	303	O Saviour, who for man hast trod	238
		O Spirit of the living God	263
N.		O Thou, at whose divine command	106
Nearer, my God, to Thee	128	O Thou, descended from above	274
No more, my God! I boast no more	308	O Thou eternal Victim slain	156
No more sadness now, nor fasting	32	O Thou from whom all goodness flows..	127
Not all the blood of beasts	153	O Thou Majesty divine	177
Not by the martyr's death alone	40	O Thou, pure Light of souls in need	162
Not by Thy mighty hand	89	O Thou, the Lord and Life of those	310
Not in anything we do	108	O Thou, to whose all-searching sight	381
Not to the terrors of the Lord	338	O Thou, who didst prepare	449
Now, in a song of grateful praise	342	O Thou, who gav'st Thy servant grace..	38
Now may He, who, from the dead	214	O Thou, who makest souls to shine	350
Now, my soul, thy voice uprising	175	O Thou, who once on Tabor's hill	94
Now thank we all our God	460	O Thou, who through this holy week	160
Now the Church's song of gladness	102	Our blest Redeemer, ere He breathed	223
Now with the rising golden dawn	476	Our God is love; and all His saints	272
		Our heavenly Father calls	277
O.		Our Lord is risen from the dead	236
O blessed Lord! the earth is Thine	143	Our year of grace is wearing to its close	412
O blest Creator, God most high	479	O very God of very God	20
O Bread to pilgrims given	314	O worship the King	389
O Christ, Redeemer of our race	30		
O Christ, Thou glorious King, we own..	369	**P.**	
O come, O come Emmanuel	3	Pardon'd through redeeming grace	432
O come, loud anthems let us sing	42	Past is her day of grace	327
O'er the distant mountains breaking	4	Plunged in a gulf of dark despair	404
O for a heart to praise my God	332	Praise to God, immortal praise	461
O for a sweet inspiring ray	251	Praise to Thee, O Lord most holy	36
O for a thousand tongues to sing	80	Praise to the Lord! He is king over all.	462
O Fount of good, to own Thy love	275		
O God, bow down Thine ear on earth	477	**Q.**	
O God unseen, yet ever near	427	Quietly rest the woods and dales	485
O God, our help in ages past	384		
O God, who lovest to abide	453	**R.**	
O Guardian of the Church divine	297	Redeem'd from guilt, redeem'd from fears	375
Oh! could I speak the matchless worth.	340	Rejoice all ye believers	419
O help us Lord, each hour of need	130	Rejoice! the Lord is King	219
O Holy Ghost, Thy heavenly dew	258	Resting from His work to-day	185
O holy, holy, holy Lord	266	Rest of the weary! Thou	188
O Holy Lord, our God	441	Rest, weary Son of God; and I with Thee	187
O Holy Spirit, come	328	Rock of ages, cleft for me	132
Oh, what, if we are Christ's	294	Ride on, ride on in majesty	157
Oh! who like Thee, so calm, so bright..	366	Round the Lord in glory seated	398
O Jesus, God and Man	71		
O Jesus, in Thy torture	178	**S.**	
O Jesus, King most wonderful	75	Safely through another week	473
O Jesus! Lord of heavenly grace	246	Salvation! O the joyful sound	83
O Jesus, our salvation	140	Saved by Thy blood, the Red Sea pass'd	218
O Jesus, Saviour of the lost	376	Saviour, again to Thy dear Name we raise	486
O Jesus, Thou the Beauty art	392	Saviour! sprinkle many nations	462
O Jesus, who art gone before	248	Saviour, when in dust to Thee	119
O Lamb of God, who bleeding	174	See now fulfilled what God decreed	65
O Light of life, O Saviour dear	478	See the Conqueror mounts in triumph	237
O Lord, be with us when we sail	447	See what unbounded zeal and love	161
O Lord, how joyful 'tis to see	92	Send us Thy showers of grace, that we..	271
O Lord of health and life, what tongue can tell	79	Shepherd of tender youth	433
O Lord of hosts whose glory fills	451		
O Lord refresh Thy flock	325		
O Lord, the wilderness to me	169		
O Love divine, how sweet Thou art	39		

	HYMN.		HYMN.
Shine on our land, Jehovah, shine	87	Thou, who hast called us by Thy Word	379
Shout, for the blessed Jesus reigns	91	Thou, who on that wondrous journey	113
Show pity, Lord, O Lord forgive	126	Through all the changing scenes of life	386
Silence in the h use of prayer	189	Through Israel's coasts, in times of old	77
Since we kept the Saviour's birth	273	Thy blood, O Christ, hath made our peace	51
Sing Alleluia forth in duteous praise	458	Thy glory Thou didst manifest	74
Sing my tongue, the glorious battle	150	'Tis by the faith of joys to come	88
Soldiers of Christ! arise	387	'Tis gone—the sacred day is o'er	402
Songs of thankfulness and praise	58	'Tis midnight, and on Olive's brow	168
Son of God, eternal Word	382	To Christ, the Prince of peace	111
Sovereign of all the worlds on high	316	To Christ, whose cross repaired our loss	181
Spirit of mercy, truth, and love	256	To God, the only wise	311
Sun of my soul, Thou Saviour dear	482	To Jesus our exalted Lord	428
Sweet the moments, rich in blessing	180	To the Name of our salvation	54
		To the throne He left, victorious	240
T.		To Zion's hill I lift mine eyes	390
Teach me, my God and King	93	'Twas on that dark, that doleful night	166
That Easter-tide with joy was rife	206		
The ancient law departs	52	**U.**	
The burden of my sins, O Lord	131	Uplift the banner! Let it float	467
The Church has waited long	105	Upon the solitary mountain's height	96
The day is gently sinking to a close	483		
Thee, O God, we humbly praise	268	**V.**	
The God of mercy warns us all	100	Vain are the hopes, the sons of men	349
The golden gates are lifted up	249		
The Head, that once was crowned with thorns	232	**W.**	
The Lamb's high banquet called to share	190	Watchman! tell us of the night	5
The Lord descended from above	450	We bless Thee for Thy Church, O Lord	262
The Lord is risen indeed	196	We, in ourselves, unrighteous are	395
The Lord my Shepherd is	210	We love the place, O God	298
The Lord of glory is my light	220	Welcome! that star in Judah's sky	63
The Lord of life is risen	195	We need Thee, Saviour, when dear eyes are closing	408
The Lord of might from Sinai's brow	216	We sing His love, who once was slain	410
The Lord will come—the earth shall quake	409	We sing the praise of Him who died	152
The ocean hath no danger	448	What grace, O Lord, and beauty shone	296
There is a blessèd home	226	What star is this with beams so bright	57
There is a dwelling-place above	391	When from the city of our God	344
There is a fountain filled with blood	144	When God of old came down from heaven	253
The roseate hues of early dawn	355	When I survey the wondrous cross	176
The royal banners forward go	151	When Jordan hushed his waters still	27
The Saviour! O what endless charms	362	When marshalled on the nightly plain	33
The solemn season calls us now	120	When scorn'd by Zion, David's Son	330
The Son of Man shall come	415	When shades of night around us close	21
The strain upraise of joy and praise	199	When the Architect Almighty fashion'd	455
The things of the earth in the earth let us lay	445	When this goodly world to frame	284
The trump shall sound and in the clouds	456	When the faithful were assembled	260
The voice that breathed o'er Eden	437	When two friends on Easter-Day	202
The whole creation groans and waits	318	When wounded sore, the stricken soul	374
The world is very evil	422	Where high the heavenly temple stands	239
Thine forever! God of love	309	While shepherds watched their flocks by night	25
This is My Body, which is given for you	167	While Thou, O my God, art my Help and Defender	86
This stone to Thee in faith we lay	452	Who is this that comes from Edom?	182
Thou art gone up on high	245	Within the Father's house	68
Thou art the Way; to Thee alone	72		
Thou hidden source of calm repose	81	**Y.**	
Thou Judge of quick and dead	423	Ye angel hosts above	361
Thou knowest, Lord, the weariness and sorrow	123	Ye saints proclaim abroad	48
Thou, Lord, baptiz'd in Thine own blood	270	Ye servants of the Lord	439
Thou Lord of all above	129	Yes, the Redeemer rose	201
Thou lovely Source of true delight	368	Your hearts, ye trembling saints	407
Thou loving Saviour of mankind	121		
Thou that art the Father's word	64	**Z.**	
Thou, who dost build for us on high	225	Zion, the marvellous story be telling	28

www.ingramcontent.com/pod-product-compliance
Lightning Source LLC
Chambersburg PA
CBHW021206230426
43667CB00006B/584